The Last Epic Naval Battle

THE LAST EPIC NAVAL BATTLE

Voices from Leyte Gulf

⚓

David Sears

Foreword by Thomas J. Cutler

PRAEGER

Westport, Connecticut
London

Library of Congress Cataloging-in-Publication Data

Sears, David, 1947–
  The last epic naval battle : voices from Leyte Gulf / David Sears ; foreword by Thomas J. Cutler.
      p. cm.
  Includes bibliographical references and index.
  ISBN 0-275-98520-2 (alk. paper)
  1. Leyte Gulf, Battle of, Philippines, 1944. I. Title.
  D774.P5S33 2005
  940.54'25995—dc22   2004028151

British Library Cataloguing in Publication Data is available.

Library of Congress Catalog Card Number: 2004028151
ISBN: 0-275-98520-2

First published in 2005

Praeger Publishers, 88 Post Road West, Westport, CT 06881
An imprint of Greenwood Publishing Group, Inc.
www.praeger.com

Printed in the United States of America

The paper used in this book complies with the Permanent Paper Standard issued by the National Information Standards Organization (Z39.48-1984).

10 9 8 7 6 5 4 3 2 1

For Mary and Jennie

Contents

*Photo essays appear after
chapters 3 and 4.*

FOREWORD

The story of the Battle of Leyte Gulf has been told many times—and well it should be. Often described by such superlatives as "the greatest sea battle of all time" and "the end of the Japanese navy," it is indeed a battle of epic proportions and great importance. Yet it is a battle that, although ending in a "must have" victory for the United States Navy, is tarnished by the near miss that David Sears so effectively describes in this book.

Despite its weakened condition by this point in the war, the Imperial Japanese Navy nearly pulled off its desperate plan to disrupt the landings in the Philippines. Had it done so, it might have had profound effects on the war and possibly on the coming elections back in the United States. At the very least, it would have been a major setback to the Allied march across the Pacific that by then had great momentum and was on the fast track to ending the war.

The reasons that the Japanese nearly succeeded at this critical moment in the war are, of course, complicated—war always is. But chief among the reasons were some critical decisions made at the high command level. Among these was the unwieldy command structure that had two fleet commanders operating independently in the area with no common superior until their respective chains of command reached Washington, D.C. And of course there is the famous decision by Admiral Halsey to take all of his very powerful fleet northward on what turned out to be a decoy chase.

The tarnish that these things put on this battle is polished away, however, at the deck plate and cockpit level. The actions of thousands of sailors—from destroyer captains to seaman gunners—offset the mistakes that had been made, and turned a near certain defeat into the needed victory, and in so doing, wrote one the most heroic chapters in American history.

And that is what makes this most recent telling so worthwhile. David Sears has told this awe-inspiring story through the recollections of those sailors who made it happen. In meticulous but spell-binding detail, he has served as catalyst, letting these men who lived the history tell what happened: what they saw, what they did, what they felt. This is history at its finest: when it captures the human dimension, when it makes it clear that the extraordinary was accomplished by the ordinary. Readers can see something of themselves in these men, and in so doing, can appreciate even more the significance of what they accomplished.

In the World War II Navy signal book, there is a coded signal—TARE VICTOR GEORGE—whose meaning is most fitting for this book: Well Done.

Thomas J. Cutler
Author of *The Battle of Leyte Gulf: 23–26 October 1944*

PREFACE
SHIPS IN THE SEAS
OF THE SOUTH

THE JAPANESE

Just after midnight—hours later than originally planned, hours the loss of which threatened to rob them of the advantages of surprise and the cover of darkness—the formation of twenty-two Japanese warships cleared San Bernardino Strait, the narrow passage separating the islands of Luzon and Samar. Although it was three months into the monsoon season and the night was oppressively hot, the sky was also remarkably clear under a lantern moon.

The ships' crews braced for the worst. Although they had little information about what was ahead of them—other than what they could get from the dim and so far empty screens of their primitive surface search radars—every man on every ship anticipated a confrontation. Much to their surprise and wary relief, they seemed to pass through unnoticed, almost as if they'd been forgotten, as if the war had somehow gone away.

The men on these ships, like all sailors, attended to omens, and two promising ones had marked this journey. At its beginning, a hawk had landed in the top hamper of one of the force's two massive battleships. Captured and caged, the raptor had been placed on the ship's bridge as a symbol of the victory to come. And then, at sunset on one evening as the imposing procession of ships neared Brunei, Borneo, the halfway point of the voyage, their thickly armored wide-beamed hulls and tall skeletal superstructures had been bathed in a sea of spectacular phosphorescence.

During the second half of the voyage, however, favorable omens had given way to horrific reality. Just hours before, crossing east through the island-dotted Sibuyan Sea, the force had been battered by relentless air attacks; two ships and nearly a thousand souls had been lost. Their commander Vice Admiral Takeo Kurita already showed the strains of even worse losses on the day before and the frustration of fighting without covering air power of his own. Kurita had tasted the indignity of having to swim for his own life when his flagship was torpedoed from under him during a submarine attack. That attack had taken the first three of Kurita's big ships. A total of five were gone now along with most of their crews; he fully expected to lose many more before his mission was complete. Perhaps as many as half his ships would be destroyed; without much doubt he would sacrifice his own life.

Commanding from a different bridge, with most of his trusted staff dead or scattered to other ships, Kurita had feared still more air attacks in the remaining hours of daylight. At one point he ordered his ships to reverse course to take them outside the scouting and striking distance of enemy planes, at least until the relative safety of darkness covered them. But then he received a radio-transmitted message from his central command. The message breathed both encouragement and chastisement: "All forces will dash to the attack, trusting in divine guidance." The ships turned back to the east to get on with a plan that was dangerously off schedule.

There were no more air attacks before nightfall—but no sign either of protection from their own air forces, despite Kurita's repeated pleas that they fill the sky to be his eyes, to shield him and avenge his losses. The ships had then entered the Strait. To more safely navigate a narrow channel with a treacherous eight-knot current, the ships realigned from a circular air defense formation to a narrow column. Kurita wanted to move fast, keeping as much ahead of daylight as possible as they entered the Philippine Sea. When Kurita's ships finally cleared the Strait and reached open water they were still mysteriously unopposed. The ships continued east, skirting the rugged jungle mountains of Samar's northern coast until they could turn south.

⚓

In 1515, nearly half a millennium before this night, Samar's coast had been landfall for a less formidable, westward-pointed trio of two-masted carracks commanded by Captain General Ferdinand Magellan—Portuguese explorer in service to Spain. Magellan had navigated his tiny fleet just windward of Samar's reefs, eventually anchoring south of Samar near the mouth of a vast, green water bay. To mark his arrival on the Feast Day of Saint Lazarus, Magellan named his discovery San Lazaro.

With time and more exploration San Lazaro would reveal itself to be a sprawling archipelago of thousands of islands, stretching nearly twelve hundred miles from north to south. According to local legend, the islands had all been part of single mass of land toted on a giant's shoulders. Wearied by the constant quarrels he heard from its inhabitants, the giant angrily tossed his burden into the sea, where it shattered and scattered into many pieces.

THE AMERICANS

On this steamy monsoon night, other ships milled about in operating sectors east of Samar and just north of the bay that had been Magellan's first anchorage. Unaware of what approached them from the north, sailors on these ships went about their routines. The day ahead promised little more than the normal enterprise of war—support of another invasion of another remote Pacific island. There would merciless heat, endless tedium, and the occasional interruption of danger. It was an enterprise that had become as predictable and repetitive as the tide washing against the islands' shores. So on this night, while some men tried to sleep, others stood watch—in pilot houses; on open bridges; in chart rooms; in ready rooms; in radio, radar, signal, and sonar shacks; in boiler rooms and engine rooms; in after steering; in gun turrets—in all of the confining spaces that keep warships alert and afloat.

They were all far from home. One pilot house watch stander, a young Navy officer ten thousand miles from his home in the Central Oregon Cascades, remembered a clear quiet night later punctuated by occasional squalls and by the brief intrusion of a "Black Cat"—a night flying reconnaissance aircraft skimming low across the water and over his ship on its way north, prowling for something. Another young officer fought back the call of sleep until the end of his watch. If his luck held he'd slip back to his rack for two precious hours of sleep before dawn's routine call to battle stations. If it didn't, he might run into the ship's skipper—a lawyer in civilian life—who had a dreaded reputation for corralling sleep-bound junior officers and dragging them off to the wardroom to play all-night games of Monopoly.

Sailors not on watch took sleep where they could find it. Often this meant homesteading small, unclaimed patches of deck topside where there was a chance for a breeze under open sky. Below decks temperatures hovered well into the nineties no matter the time of day. On most nights the decks were littered with forms asleep on mounds of kapok life jackets. To save time and wasted effort, many slept only a step or two away from watch and workstations—under a gun mount, on a catwalk, in an empty passageway or alongside a depth charge rack. One sailor snooped out a particularly good, particularly remote spot—high in his ship's superstructure and so close to the outboard rail that he found himself and his crude canvas hammock swinging trapeze-like over open water as the ship rolled in even the lightest sea.

Impromptu sleeping space was most abundant on the timbered flight decks of the handful of aircraft carriers riding as the center jewels in this formation of ships. It was like sleeping on a crowded but inactive, ever rolling parking lot. The fuselages and folded wings of the chocked-down aircraft sheltered the sleepers when it rained. And, because none of these planes were night creatures, sleep could pass undisturbed, at least until first light and the preparation for morning launch.

Sleep perhaps came easiest for the young pilots of these planes. They performed their long but exhilarating days' work in skies now mostly clear of opposing aircraft. They searched for submarines that rarely threatened the carriers or the screening ships. And they got to play avenging angel: swooping down on request with bombs, rockets, and machine gun fire to clear the way for advancing assault troops.

⚓

Many years after Magellan's Pacific exploration, historians determined that one of Magellan's crew had, earlier in his life, been taken as a slave to San Lazaro. Traveling since then ever west, first to Europe and then outbound to the Pacific with Magellan, this crewman had, in fact, circumnavigated the globe. So it was that Magellan's arrival (more accurately, the arrival of Magellan's crewman) off Samar marked man's actual first global circumnavigation, the symbolic joining of global East and global West. On this night, as one fleet advanced menacingly but blindly, and one fleet waited unsuspecting in waters near Magellan's historic landfall, that connection—both symbolic and actual—had been sundered. For three years the globe and these islands had been lashed by war. Midnight turned the calendar to October 25, 1944. On this night now opening into morning, in what the Japanese called the Seas of the South, a day of decision began to unfold.

Half a world away, the lead story in the October 25th morning edition of the *New York Times* announced events that were already history. In prose that seemed at once detached and portentous, the newspaper's reporters and editors described what was happening in the Southwest Pacific: "It will be the most important test of naval strength since the beginning of the war.... Never before has the enemy fleet appeared so obviously bent on meeting with our Pacific navy.... It is difficult to see how a major engagement can now be avoided."

OCTOBER 25, 1944

On this day, in the hours between midnight and noon, on and above the tropical waters that bound the southernmost islands of the sprawling Philippine archipelago, warships, aircraft, sailors, and airmen fought an epic battle. The battle's outcome once and for all decided the fate of a Japanese navy that, nearly three years before, had devastated the U.S. Pacific Fleet. In retrospect, the events of those twelve hours also first established the U.S. Navy's clear global preeminence. The U.S. Navy became—and remains—the master of any sea in which its ships appear.

The Battle of Leyte Gulf—historical shorthand for a series of four overlapping engagements spread across four days and 100,000 square miles of ocean—shaped the destinies of 280 ships and nearly 200,000 men. Historians have called it the greatest sea battle in history (in company with Trafalgar and Jutland). Virtually every type of surface warship joined the fight: battleships and cruisers; "tin can" destroyers and destroyer escorts; even small mahogany-hulled torpedo boats. Remarkably, for a mode of war that was already becoming long distance (in four of the Pacific war's biggest sea battles, no ship had fired at another ship; the battles had pitted planes against aircraft carriers and against each other), ships and their crews fought, died, and sank well within sight of each other—ships lurched and clashed close in, like ghosts from ancient battles under sail.

Leyte Gulf was a turning point, though not in the way that battles at Midway and Quadalcanal had been earlier in the war. A swift victory at sea and in the air at Midway, followed by a long and agonizing one on land at Quadalcanal, had shown an anxious American public, its political leadership, and its military that the United States could hold its own against the rampaging Japanese war machine—at least until precious war resources could be freed and sent that way.

By October 1944, the duration of the war against Japan remained uncertain, but its outcome didn't. Battles increasingly pitted fighting spirit— what the Japanese understood as *Bushido*—against American technology and logistic might. The Japanese saw *Bushido* as their mystical advantage against the overmatching material resources of the Americans. For the Japanese it was turning out to be a futile competition.

Allied forces in the Southwest Pacific under General Douglas MacArthur had advanced a breathtaking thousand miles in less than four months. They had climbed ladder-like through a series of amphibious assaults along the northern coast of New Guinea to its northwestern tip. MacArthur was poised to step his forces to the next rung—a triumphant return to the Philippines he had barely managed to escape three years before. To the north and nearly as far west, in the Central Pacific's Marianas island chain, U.S. Marines had taken the key islands of the Marianas chain. To Japan, the capture of Saipan, Tinian, and Guam was the bitter loss of home ground. Most of islands defenders had fought to the death; many of its civilian inhabitants had hurled themselves and their children from coastal cliffs in dread of the approaching Marines. Back in Japan, Saipan's fall was cause for the shamed capitulation of her supreme commander, General Hideki Tojo.

As an historic event, the images of MacArthur's return to the Philippines— the General's knee-deep wade to the beach when his landing craft hit bottom, a stirring but also preening radio address once ashore—will likely always overshadow Leyte Gulf. MacArthur's performance was one for the ages, though it also masked the bloody slogging going on in the jungles ahead of him, and ignored the real danger gliding into the waters at his back. The shadow probably lengthened when the U.S. Navy's centerpiece admiral,

William F. "Bull" Halsey, drawn by the all-too-alluring prospect of taking out a Japanese carrier force, charged north with his fleet carriers and away from the real showdown. The Battle of Leyte Gulf, in its ordinary majesty, lacked a spokesman, lacked a Caesar.

⚓

Despite these shadows and distractions, the Battle of Leyte Gulf became a defining moment. It was a showdown, a monumental stopping point fashioned by temporary crews in temporary ships. Leyte Gulf could have been the Pacific's Battle of the Bulge. Japan, a beaten, cornered enemy, was still able to devise and execute a strategy that very nearly stabbed the heart of America's own rampaging war machine. The strategy worked and its planned outcome almost did, coming together in a space of twelve breath-taking hours that threatened (or, for the Japanese, promised) to reverse the fortunes of war. The real margin of victory during these hours came from surprising quarters: from aging ships risen from the graveyard of the Pacific war's infamous first day; from small, hastily constructed ships with largely untested reserve crews; from fragile support ships never intended to be any-where near battles of this scale; from combat aircraft piloted by teenagers.

One desperate footnote to the Japanese plan introduced a new sacri-ficial pawn to the brutal board game of war—a weapon that unraveled assumptions about how young men would fight, how much they would sacrifice, and how this war (and others in the future) might turn out. It was the kamikaze, the suicidal "body crasher," a battle tactic so gruesome and unnerving that America's military and political leaders would not reveal it to the American public until the war was nearly over.

These pages are an account of the events of those twelve hours told from the perspective of sixty seamen and airmen who were boys then and are now aging, proud, and vital men. The memories that cradle these stories are occasionally indistinct, stretched, or (more often) understated. They are recollections—and subject to the fog and sometimes unyielding misrepre-sentations of recollection. Most are not singularly heroic (though some certainly are), but instead are parts of a collective heroism that defined this day's—and the war's—outcome. These many small but vivid pieces com-bine to a heroic mosaic.

Most important, they are lights that still burn fiercely at the source. They are both the living experience of history and the living history of experience. We try here to recapture these lights across a gulf of sixty years. We seek memories at the source. The actions in those memories are im-portant. They are stirring and instructive in only the way that extraordinary events lived and shaped collectively by ordinary individuals can be.

ROLL CALL

From its beginning this has been a book running out of time. Creating an account based substantially on survivor reminiscences meant reaching out to men who, at their youngest, are in their very late seventies—and most often in their eighties. Participants in the October 1944 naval battles in and around Leyte Gulf are a select population diminished during the twelve hours of battle remembered here—lost to gunfire, fire explosion, and exposure at sea. The roll of survivors who escaped sinking ships or downed aircraft dwindled further in the hours and days that followed: from combinations of wounds, exposure to the elements, and shark attacks in the waters off Samar. (In the case of one ship, the USS *Hoel*, only 82 of a crew of 340 men escaped their ship's sinking, and only 40 of those survived the 50 or so hours until they were rescued.) In the remaining ten months of the war in the Pacific still more surviving men and ships were lost to the ravages of the kamikaze attacks. And, of course, in the sixty years since, time, illness, and accident have taken the usual toll.

The still-living survivors were little more than boys (at least in age) during the hours of the actions in Surigao and off Samar. Each mile further from their homes and closer to the events of the day was a mile further than most had ever been, to places they could hardly imagine. What they witnessed was memorable and often horrifying.

I wondered (and worried) what it would be like to retrieve such recollections across this span of nearly sixty years. As it turned out most of these men's memories were sharp and resonant—at least for the important things: what it felt like, what scared or didn't scare them, what lessons they took with them into the rest of their lives. Their memories seldom tasted of bravado, self-importance, or self-conscious heroism. They knew they were boys. Because they were boys they took things in stride—with an unpretentious sense of invincibility. They brought energy, acceptance, and optimism to their lives at sea and in the air. (Few of the men interviewed recalled bouts of seasickness—or anticipatory fear. Few of the survivors thrown into the waters of the Philippine Sea lost faith in the possibility of their ultimate recovery; in general, it was the very youngest of these who best survived the ordeal.)

Because this book is flavored with personal accounts, and because these are the stories of very young men from a long time ago, it is important to distinguish between the accuracy of events and the accuracy of experience. Sometimes, when there were very big differences, I used more traditional sources or my own best judgment to reconcile the two. But I tried never to underestimate the accuracy of experience—even across all these years.

The glue for this book—its network and connections—flows from the voluntary associations supporting the interests of the crews and veterans of U.S. Navy ships. There are literally hundreds of these organizations with amazing permutations and combinations. The most durable of these networks are the ones bound by harsh, singular experience—the shared losses of ships and shipmates. As the years accumulate—and the memberships dwindle—the networks have increased in importance: Those who survived once now find themselves again in the doubly blessed, double anguished roles of survivors. Among the organizations contacted when researching and writing this book, the following were particularly helpful in identifying and reaching out to survivors:

- Escort Carrier Sailors and Airmen Association, Inc. (ECSAA)
- Pearl Harbor Survivors Association
- Peter Tare, Inc.
- PT Boats, Inc., particularly its membership coordinator Allyson Bethune. Samuel Goddess, an Association member and a crewman of Squadron 12's 194 Boat (and the squadron's unofficial historian), who arrived in Leyte following the battle, also provided valuable assistance.
- Tin Can Sailors
- USS *Johnston-Hoel* Association, particularly Larry Morris, one of its members and one of the Voices in this book.
- USS *Samuel B. Roberts* (DE 413) Survivors' Association, particularly its historian Dick Rohde, one of the Voices in this book.
- USS *Gambier Bay* (CVE-73) and VC-10 Association, particularly Tony Potochniak, who serves as ship's historian and maintains *Gambier Bay's* resource-rich Internet site. Tony is also one of the Voices in this book.
- USS *St. Lo* (formerly *Midway*) CVE 63/VC 65 Association Inc.

The substance of the book flows from the memories, reflections, and words of its Voices. I am unceasingly grateful for the time and patience afforded by each of these veteran heroes. Without exception, they responded to my questions, clarified my assumptions, and provided connections to others who would do the same. If there are errors of time, place, terminology, or event, they are mine, not theirs.

The lives of nearly all this book's living Voices are, to this day, sharp and vibrant. Our conversations dealt with the past, but there was no absence of present and future in their thoughts. Although I wish it always to be so, it will not be—nor for any of us. Sadly, during the research and writing of this book, four of its compelling Voices—Robert Barth, Bill Brown, Verner Carlsen, and Bill Mercer—were silenced. I do hope that these words—their words—leave an indelible record of their magnificent accomplishments: for each other, for their families, for this country, and for the cause of peace and freedom.

Voices of Leyte Gulf and Glossaries

VOICES

Barry K. Atkins CO USS *Melvin*, Commander (later Rear Admiral), USN

Robert (Red) Barth USS *Melvin*, Signalman First Class, USN

H. B. (Burt) Bassett USS *Gambier Bay*, XO, VC-10, Lieutenant, USNR (later Captain, USN), TBM Pilot

William Brown CO PT 493, Lieutenant (junior grade) (later Lieutenant Commander), USNR

Albert Brunelle PT 493, Motor Machinist Mate Third Class, USNR

Donald Bujold PT 127, Motor Machinist Mate Second Class, USNR

William R. Campbell Jr. USS *Melvin*, Ensign, USN (later Commander, USN)

George Carbon USS *Samuel B. Roberts*, Seaman First Class, USNR

Verner Carlsen Chaplain, USS *Gambier Bay*, Lieutenant, Chaplain Corps, USNR (later Captain, USNR)

Terry Chambers XO PT 491, Lieutenant (junior grade), USNR (later Lieutenant, USN)

Robert (Bobby) Chastain USS *Johnston*, Seaman First Class, USNR

Marvin T. Childress USS *West Virginia*, Seaman First Class, USNR

Robert Clarkin PT 152, Torpedoman Third Class, USNR

Lawrence R. Collins USS *Midway/St. Lo*, Ensign, USNR

Evan H. (Holly) Crawforth USS *Midway/St. Lo*, Radio Technician Third Class, USNR (later Radio Technician Second Class, USNR)

Emmett R. Crump USS *Albert W. Grant*, Coxswain First Class, USNR

Raymond Dupler USS *Melvin*, Chief Yeoman, USN

Robert Durand USS *Richard P. Leary*, Quartermaster Third Class, USNR (later Quartermaster Second Class, USNR)

Larry Epping USS *Gambier Bay*, Ensign, USNR (later Lieutenant, USNR)

Andrew Gavel PT 194, Torpedoman Second Class, USNR (later Torpedoman First Class, USNR)

Samuel Goddess PT 194, Radioman Second Class, USNR

Vincent N. (Vince) Goodrich USS *Samuel B. Roberts*, Sonar Man Third Class, USNR (later Commander, USNR)

Louis (Lou) Gould USS *Samuel B. Roberts*, Sonar Man Third Class, USNR

Theodore Gurzynski PT 493, Motor Machinist Mate Second Class, USNR

Richard Hamilton PT 493, Third Boat Officer, Lieutenant (junior grade), USNR (later Lieutenant, USNR)

John (Jake) Hanley PT 127, Radioman Second Class, USNR

Mel Harden USS *Samuel B. Roberts*, Seaman Second Class, USN

Dr. Edgar A. (Ed) Hawk USS *Melvin*, Lieutenant, Medical Corps, USNR, Medical Officer

Charles G. Heinl USS *Gambier Bay*, Seaman First Class, USNR

Robert Hollenbaugh USS *Johnston*, Boatswains Mate, First Class, USNR

Walter Kundis PT 524, Gunner's Mate Second Class, USNR (later Chief Master Sergeant, USAF)

James Lischer USS *Gambier Bay*, VC-10 FM-2 Pilot, Lieutenant (junior grade), USNR (later Lieutenant, USNR)

Sam Lucas USS *Hoel*, Seaman First Class, USNR (later Gunner's Mate Third Class, USNR)

Fred Mallgrave USS *Gambier Bay*, Ensign, USNR

Bill McClendon USS *Gambier Bay*, Landing Signal Officer, Lieutenant, USNR (later Rear Admiral, USN)

Joe McGraw USS *Gambier Bay*, VC-10 FM-2 Pilot, Ensign, USNR (later Captain, NSNR[TAR])

Virgil (Mel) Melvin USS *Monssen*, Gunner's Mate Second Class, USNR (later Commander, USN)

William Mercer USS *Johnston*, Seaman First Class, USNR

John Montgomery USS *California*, Seaman First Class, USNR

Larry Morris USS *Hoel*, Seaman First Class, USNR

J. Dudley Moylan USS *Samuel B. Roberts*, Ensign, USNR

Ralph E. Natali USS *Albert W. Grant*, Gunner's Mate Second Class, USNR

Glenn Parkin USS *Hoel*, Seaman First Class, USN

Edward Pfeifer USS *Albert W. Grant*, Torpedo Officer, Lieutenant (junior grade), USNR

Tony Potochniak USS *Gambier Bay*, Aircraft Machinist Mate Third Class (later Aircraft Machinist Mate Second Class, USNR)

Richard Ralstin USS *McDermut*, Motor Machinist Mate Second Class, USNR

Robert Read USS *Richard P. Leary*, Quartermaster Third Class, USNR

Lou Rice USS *Gambier Bay*, Radarman Third Class, USN

William Robie USS *Melvin*, Gunnery Officer, Lieutenant, USN (later Captain, USN)

Richard Roby USS *Gambier Bay*, VC-10 FM-2 Pilot, Lieutenant, USNR

Richard Rohde USS *Samuel B. Roberts*, Radio Man Third Class, USNR

John Ruddick USS *Melvin*, Fireman First Class, USNR

Gene Seitz USS *Gambier Bay*, VC-10 FM-2 Pilot, Lieutenant, USNR (later Captain, USN)

Tom Stevenson USS *Samuel B. Roberts*, Lieutenant (junior grade), USNR

Thomas Tenner PT 127, Quartermaster Second Class, USNR (later Quartermaster First Class, USNR)

Harley Thronson PT 491, Lieutenant (junior grade) (later Lieutenant, USNR)

Brinton E. Turner USS *Melvin*, Lieutenant (junior grade), USNR

Tom Van Brunt USS *Midway/St. Lo*, VC-65 TBM Pilot, Lieutenant, USNR

Bill Wilson USS *Samuel B. Roberts*, Seaman First Class, USNR

Leon Wolper USS *Richard P. Leary*, Ship Fitter Third Class, USNR (later Shipfitter Second Class, USNR)

GLOSSARIES

Abbreviations, Acronyms, and Nicknames

AA antiaircraft gunfire

A-day designated invasion day (October 20, 1944) for the Allied invasion of the Philippines

AH hospital ship ('A' stands for auxiliary)

AMS motor minesweeper

AO fleet tanker

AOG gasoline tanker

AP armor piercing

APA attack transport ship

ASP antisubmarine patrol

B-29 U.S. long-range strategic bomber

BB battleship

basket gunfire director mount

Betty Japanese twin-engine bomber

Black Cat U.S. patrol bomber/float plane equipped for night operations

CA heavy cruiser

callfire Naval gunfire requested and spotted by troops ashore

CAP combat air patrol

CarQuals carrier landing qualifications

CBI China-Burma-India

CIC combat information center

CL light cruiser

CO ship or squadron commanding officer

CPTP Civilian Pilot Training Program

CV fleet aircraft carrier

CVE escort carrier

CVL light aircraft carrier

dazzle camouflage paint design

DD destroyer

DE destroyer escort

DesRon destroyer squadron

e-base elimination base (pre-flight and flight training)

Elco PT boat built by Elco

FCR fire control radar

Fletcher a class of destroyer named for the lead ship in the class

FM-2 U.S. Navy fighter aircraft (also known as the Wildcat)

four-stacker World War I–vintage destroyer equipped with four boiler smoke stacks

Fran Japanese twin-engine bomber

GQ General Quarters, or battle stations

HC high capacity

IFF identification friend or foe—an electronic transmitter/receiver device pulsing encoded signals to detect the "friend or foe" identity of approaching contacts

Indian Country enemy territory

LCI landing craft, infantry

lighter-than-air lighter-than-air military aircraft such as blimps

Lily Japanese bomber aircraft

long lance Japanese torpedo

LSM landing ship, medium

LSO landing signal officer

LST landing ship, tank

MacArthur's Navy informal name for the Seventh Fleet

Mark 15 U.S. Navy surface torpedo

Oscar Japanese fighter aircraft

Polliwog sailor who has not crossed the Equator

PT patrol torpedo boat

Ron PT squadron

SG radar surface search radar installed on U.S. Navy ships

Shellback sailor who has crossed the Equator

SK radar air search radar installed on U.S. Navy ships

snipes ships' personnel working in the below decks engineering and machinery spaces

SNJ U.S. Navy training aircraft

SS submarine

TBM U.S. Navy torpedo bomber

TF task force

TG task group (smaller than a task force, larger than a task unit)

Tin can nickname used to designate destroyers and destroyer escorts

Trade School U.S. Naval Academy

TU task unit (smaller than a task group)

Val Japanese twin-engine bomber

VC Naval air squadron designation (V meaning fixed wing, C meaning composite)

Wildcat U.S. Navy fighter aircraft (also known as the FM-2)

XO ship or squadron executive officer or second in command

YMS auxiliary motor minesweeper

Zero Japanese fighter aircraft

Names

American and Allied

Admiral William F. "Bull" Halsey Commander, U.S. Third Fleet

General Douglas MacArthur Supreme Commander, Allied Forces, Southwest Pacific

Vice Admiral J. S. McCain Third Fleet task group commander

Admiral Chester W. Nimitz Commander of U.S. Central Pacific Forces

Rear Admiral J. B. Oldendorf Commander, Fire Support Unit South, which included the USS *California* (and other invasion battleships) and DesRon 56

Rear Admiral Thomas L. Sprague Seventh Fleet task group commander (no relation to Rear Admiral Clifton Sprague, Taffy 2 commander

Japanese

Vice Admiral Takeo Kurita Commander of First Striking Force and leader of the northern segment of First Striking Force

Vice Admiral Teiji Nishimura Commander of the southern segment of First Striking Force

Vice Admiral Takijiro Onishi Air Fleet Commander

Vice Admiral Jisaburo Ozawa Commander of Mobile Striking Force

Vice Admiral Kiyohide Shima Commander Second Striking Force

General Hideki Tojo Japan's supreme commander until the fall of Saipan

Organizations, Ships, and Squadrons

American and Allied

DesRon 24 Destroyer Squadron, whose assigned ships included HMAS *Arunta*, USS *Bache*, USS *Beale*, USS *Daly*, USS *Hutchins*, USS *Killen*

DesRon 56 Destroyer Squadron, whose assigned ships included USS *Bennion*, USS *Bryant*, USS *Heywood L. Edwards*, USS *Albert W. Grant*, *Halford*, USS *Richard P. Leary*, USS *Leutze*, USS *Newcomb*, USS *Robinson*

HMAS *Arunta* Australian Tribal class destroyer assigned to DesRon 24

HMAS *Shropshire* Australian County Class Heavy Cruiser assigned to TG 77.2

PT 127 PT Boat assigned to PT Squadron 7

PT 152 PT Boat assigned to PT Squadron 12

PT 194 PT Boat assigned to PT Squadron 12

PT 491 PT Boat assigned to PT Squadron 33

PT 493 PT Boat assigned to PT Squadron 33

PT 524 PT Boat assigned to PT Squadron 36

PT Squadron 7 PT Squadron that included PT Boat 127

PT Squadron 12 PT Squadron that included PT Boats 152 and 194

PT Squadron 33 PT Squadron that included PT Boats 491 and 493

PT Squadron 36 PT Squadron that included PT Boat PT 524

King II Code name for the American invasion of the Philippines

Seventh Fleet U.S. Navy Fleet assigned to Southwest Pacific Area; nicknamed MacArthur's Navy

Sixth Army U.S. Army divisions assigned to Southwest Pacific Area; Sixth Army troops comprised the major U.S. invasion forces at Leyte

Taffy 3 Informal name for TU 77.4.3, part of Seventh Fleet

USS *Abner Read* *Fletcher* class destroyer (DD-526) assigned to TG 77.1

USS *Admiral E. W. Eberle* *Admiral W. S. Benson* class troop transport (AP-123) manned by the U.S. Coast Guard

USS *Alabama* *South Dakota* class battleship (BB-60)

USS *Albert W. Grant* *Fletcher* class destroyer (DD-649) assigned to DesRon 56

USS *Alden* *Clemson* class destroyer (DD-211)

USS *Altamaha* *Bogue* class escort carrier (CVE-18)

USS *Bache* *Fletcher* class destroyer (DD-470) assigned to DesRon 24

USS *Beale* *Fletcher* class destroyer (DD-471) assigned to DesRon 24

USS *Belknap* *Dent* class high-speed transport (APD-34)

USS *Belleau Wood* *Independence* class small aircraft carrier (CVL-24)

USS *Bennion* *Fletcher* class destroyer (DD-662) assigned to DesRon 56

USS *Boggs* *Wickes* class destroyer (DMS-3, earlier DD-136)

USS *Boise* *Brooklyn* class light cruiser (CL-47)

USS *Bryant* *Fletcher* class destroyer (DD-665) assigned to DesRon 56

USS *Cabot* *Independence* class small aircraft carrier (CVL-28)

USS *California* *Tennessee* class battleship (BB-44)

USS *Casablanca* Lead ship of *Casablanca* class escort carriers (CVE-55)

USS *Cassin* *Mahan* class destroyer (DD-372)

USS *Colorado* Lead ship of *Colorado* battleship class (BB-45)

USS *Columbia* *Cleveland* class light cruiser (CL-56)

USS *Comfort (II)* Lead ship of *Comfort* class hospital ships (AH-6)

USS *Dace* *Gato* class submarine (SS-247)

USS *Daly* *Fletcher* class destroyer (DD-519) assigned to DesRon 24

USS *Darter* *Gato* class submarine (SS 227)

USS *Dennis* *Butler* class destroyer escort (DE-406) assigned to TU 77.4.3
(Taffy 3)

USS *Denver* *Cleveland* class light cruiser (CL-58)

USS *Downes* *Mahan* class destroyer (DD-375)

USS *England* *Buckley* class destroyer escort (DE 635, later APD-41)

USS *Enterprise* *Yorktown* class aircraft carrier (CV-6)

USS *Essex* Lead ship of *Essex* class aircraft carriers (CV-9, later CVA-9
and CVS-9)

USS *Franklin* *Essex* class aircraft carrier (CV 13)

USS *Gambier Bay* *Casablanca* class escort carrier (CVE-73) assigned to
TU 77.4.3 (Taffy 3)

USS *Halford* *Fletcher* class destroyer (DD-480) assigned to DesRon 56

USS *Hazelwood* *Fletcher* class destroyer (DD-531)

USS *Heermann* *Fletcher* class destroyer (DD-532) assigned to TU 77.4.3
(Taffy 3)

USS *Heywood L. Edwards* *Fletcher* class destroyer (DD 663) assigned to
DesRon 56

USS *Hoel* *Fletcher* class destroyer (DD-533) assigned to TU 77.4.3
(Taffy 3)

USS *Honolulu* *Brooklyn* class light cruiser (CL-48)

USS *Hornet* Lead ship of *Hornet* class aircraft carriers (CV-8)

USS *Hutchins* *Fletcher* class destroyer (DD-476) assigned to DesRon 24

USS *Indianapolis* *Portland* class heavy cruiser (CA-35)

USS *Intrepid* *Essex* class aircraft carrier (CV-11)

USS *John C. Butler* Lead ship of *Butler* class destroyer escorts (DE 339)
assigned to TU 77.4.3 (Taffy 3)

USS *Johnston* *Fletcher* class destroyer (DD-557) assigned to TU 77.4.3 (Taffy 3)

USS *Kane* *Clemson* class destroyer (DD-235, later APD-18)

USS *Killen* *Fletcher* class destroyer (DD-593) assigned to DesRon 24

USS *Kitkun Bay* *Casablanca* class escort carrier (CVE 71) assigned to TU 77.4.3 (Taffy 3)

USS *Leutze* *Fletcher* class destroyer (DD-481) assigned to DesRon 56

USS *Lexington* Aircraft carrier (CV-2)

USS *Lexington* *Essex* class aircraft carrier (CV-16)

USS *Liscome Bay* *Casablanca* class escort carrier (CVE-56)

USS *Louisville* *Northampton* class light cruiser (CA-28, originally CL-28)

USS *Marcus Island* *Casablanca* class escort carrier (CVE-77) assigned to TU 77.4.2 (Taffy 2)

USS *Maryland* *Colorado* class battleship (BB-46)

USS *McDermut* *Fletcher* class destroyer (DD-677) assigned to DesRon 54

USS *Melvin* *Fletcher* class destroyer (DD-680) assigned to DesRon 54

USS *Midway/St. Lo* *Casablanca* class escort carrier (CVE 63) assigned to TU 77.4.3 (Taffy 3)

USS *Milwaukee* *Omaha* class light cruiser (CL-5)

USS *Minneapolis* *New Orleans* class heavy cruiser (CA-36)

USS *Mississippi* *New Mexico* class battleship (BB-41)

USS *Monssen* *Fletcher* class destroyer (DD-798) assigned to DesRon 54

USS *Nashville* *Brooklyn* class light cruiser (CL-43)

USS *Newcomb* *Fletcher* class destroyer (DD 586) assigned to DesRon 56

USS *Norman Scott* *Fletcher* class destroyer (DD-690)

USS *Oyster Bay* Motor torpedo boat (PT) tender (AGP-6)

USS *Parrott* *Clemson* class destroyer (DD 218)

USS *Pennsylvania* Lead ship of *Pennsylvania* class of battleships (BB-38)

USS *Petrof Bay* *Casablanca* class escort aircraft carrier (CVE-80) assigned to TU 77.4.1 (Taffy 1)

USS *Phoenix* *Brooklyn* class light cruiser (CL-46)

USS *Portland* Lead ship of *Portland* class heavy cruisers (CA-33)

USS *Raymond* *Butler* class destroyer escort (DE-341) assigned to TU 7 7.4.3 (Taffy 3)

USS *Richard P. Leary* *Fletcher* class destroyer (DD-664) assigned to DesRon 56

USS *Robinson* *Fletcher* class destroyer (DD 562) assigned to DesRon 56

USS *Samuel B. Roberts* *Butler* class destroyer escort (DE-413) assigned to TU 77.4.3 (Taffy 3)

USS *Sangamon* Lead ship of *Sangamon* class escort aircraft carrier (CVE-26) assigned to TU 77.4.1 (Taffy 1)

USS *Santee* *Sangamon* class escort aircraft carrier (CVE-29) assigned to TU 77.4.1 (Taffy 1)

USS *Saratoga* Aircraft carrier (CV-3)

USS *Shaw* *Mahan* class destroyer (DD-373)

USS *Suwannee* *Sangamon*-class escort aircraft carrier (CVE-27) assigned to TU 77.4.1 (Taffy 1)

USS *Tennessee* Lead ship of *Tennessee* battleship class (BB 44)

USS *Texas* *New York* class battleship (BB-35)

USS *Wadleigh* *Fletcher* class destroyer (DD-689)

USS *West Virginia* *Colorado* class battleship (BB-48)

USS *Yorktown* Lead ship of *Yorktown* class aircraft carriers (CV-5)

VC-10 Composite Squadron 10, assigned to USS *Gambier Bay*

VC-65 Composite Squadron 65, assigned to USS *St. Lo*

Japanese

First Striking Force Japanese fleet section under the command of Vice Admiral Takeo Kuritz

IJN *Abukuma* *Nagara* class light cruiser assigned to Second Striking Force

IJN *Asagumo* *Asasio* class destroyer assigned to southern segment of First Striking Force

IJN *Ashigara* *Myoko* class cruiser assigned to Second Striking Force

IJN *Atago* Lead ship of *Atago* class heavy cruisers assigned to northern segment of First Striking Force

IJN *Chikuma* *Tone* class heavy cruiser assigned to northern segment of First Striking Force

IJN *Chokai* *Takao* class heavy cruiser assigned to northern segment of First Striking Force

IJN *Fuso* Lead ship of *Fuso* battleship class assigned to southern segment of First Striking Force

IJN *Haguro* *Myoko* class heavy cruiser assigned to northern segment of First Striking Force

IJN *Haruna* *Kongo* class battlecruiser assigned to northern segment of First Striking Force

IJN *Kishinami* *Kayero* class destroyer assigned to northern segment of First Striking Force

IJN *Kongo* Lead ship of *Kongo* class battle cruisers assigned to northern segment of First Striking Force

IJN *Kumano* *Mogami* class heavy cruiser assigned to northern segment of First Striking Force

IJN *Michishio* *Asasio* class destroyer assigned to southern segment of First Striking Force

IJN *Mogami* Lead ship of *Mogami* cruiser class assigned to southern segment of First Striking Force

IJN *Musashi* *Yamato* class battleship assigned to southern segment of First Striking Force

IJN *Myoko* Lead ship of *Myoko* heavy cruiser class, assigned to northern segment of First Striking Force

IJN *Nachi* *Myoko* class heavy cruiser, assigned to Second Striking Force, Shima's flagship

IJN *Nagato* Lead ship of *Nagato* battleship class assigned to northern segment of First Striking Force

IJN *Shigure* *Shiratsuyu* class destroyer assigned to southern segment of First Striking Force

IJN *Suzuya* *Mogami* class heavy cruiser assigned to northern segment of First Striking Force

IJN *Takao* Lead ship of *Takao* heavy cruiser class, assigned to northern segment of First Striking Force

IJN *Tone* Lead ship of *Tone* heavy cruiser class assigned to northern segment of First Striking Force

IJN *Yamagumo* *Fubuki* class destroyer assigned to southern segment of First Striking Force

IJN *Yamashiro* *Fuso* class battleship assigned to southern segment of First Striking Force

IJN *Yamato* Lead ship of *Yamato* battleship class assigned to northern segment of First Striking Force

Imperial Fleet Japanese Navy

Mobile Striking Force Japanese fleet contingent under the command of Vice Admiral Jisaburo Ozawa

Second Striking Force Japanese fleet contingent under the command of Vice Admiral Kiyohide Shima

Sho Go Victory Operation plan

Sho 1 Victory Operation plan for the Philippines

Places

Admiralty Islands Island chain in the Southwest Pacific north of New Guinea

Amagusan Point Point of land on the eastern shore of Leyte fronting Surigao Strait

Bias Island near the western entrance to the San Bernardino Strait

Bohol Island in the Mindanao Sea

Borneo Large island, southwest of the Philippine Islands, separated by the Sulu Sea

Brunei Port on the northwest coast of Borneo

Bungo Suido Strait separating Japan's home islands of Kyushu and Shikoku

Calicoan Island in Leyte Gulf

Camiguin Island in the Mindanao Sea

Carolines Island chain in the Central Pacific, south of the Marianas

Catmon Hill Hill near the landing beaches on Leyte

Cebu Island, part of the Philippines

Central Pacific Portion of the Pacific Ocean north of the Equator

Dinagat Island bordering Surigao Strait across from Leyte

Dulag Port town on Leyte

Eniwetok Islands at the western limit of the Marshalls, north of the Gilberts and west of the Marianas

Formosa Island east of China's mainland (Taiwan)

Gilberts Island chain in the Central Pacific, south of the Marshalls and northwest of the Solomons

Guam Island, part of the Marianas

Halmahera Island east of the Celebes Islands

Hibuson Island in Surigao Strait between Leyte and Dinagat Islands

Hingatungan Point Point of land on the eastern shore of Leyte, above Surigao Strait

Hollandia Port on Humboldt Bay

Homonhon Island in Leyte Gulf

Humboldt Bay Bay on the northern coast of New Guinea (Indonesia)

Leyte Island, part of the Philippine Islands

Leyte Gulf Gulf surrounded by Samar, Leyte, and Mindanao Islands

Limasawa Island in the Mindanao Sea

Lingga Roads Island, just south of Singapore

Luzon Island, part of the Philippine Islands

Mabalacat Town on Luzon

Manila Capital city of the Philippines on Luzon

Manus Island, part of the Admiralty Islands north of New Guinea

Marianas Island chain, including Guam, Saipan, and Tinian, in the Central Pacific

Marshalls Island chain in the Central Pacific

Masbate Island near the western entrance to the San Bernardino Strait

Midway Island in the Northern Pacific roughly midway between North America and Asia

Mindanao Island, part of the Philippines

Mindanao Sea Sea surrounded by Bohol, Mindanao, and Leyte Islands

Mindoro Island, part of the Philippines

Mios Woendi Island in northernmost New Guinea (Indonesia)

Mount Guinhandang Mountain near the landing beaches on Leyte

Mustang A commissioned officer who originally joined the military as an enlisted man

Negros Island, part of the Philippines

New Guinea Large island in the Southwest Pacific, north of Australia and southwest of the Philippine Islands (Indonesia and Papua New Guinea)

Okinawa Island, part of the Ryukyu chain

Palaus Island chain east of the Philippines

Palawan Island between the Sulu Sea and the South China Sea north between Borneo and the Philippines

Panay Island, part of the Philippines

Peleliu Island, part of the Palaus

Philippines Large island chain in the Southwest Pacific, northwest of New Guinea and south of Formosa (Taiwan)

Philippine Sea Portion of the Western Pacific east of the Philippine Islands and south of Japan

Point Fin A coordinate of latitude and longitude just off the entrance to Leyte Gulf; assembly point for American and Allied ships for the invasion of the Philippines

Ryukyu Island chain southwest of the Japanese home islands

Saipan Island, part of the Marianas Chain

San Bernardino Strait Channel separating southern Luzon Island from northern Samar Island

San Juanico Strait Channel separating southern Leyte Island from southern Samar Island

San Lazaro Magellan's name for the Philippine Islands

San Pedro Bay Bay between Samar and Leyte Islands

Seeadler Harbor Manus Island Harbor

Sibuyan Sea Small sea in the Philippines separating the Visayas Islands from Luzon

Solomons Island chain, including Guadalcanal and Tulagi, in the Southwest Pacific, east of New Guinea

South China Sea Portion of Pacific Ocean between Indonesia and the Philippine Islands

Southwest Pacific Allied theater of operations in the Pacific roughly comprising Australia, New Guinea, and New Zealand

Suluan Island in Leyte Gulf

Sulu Sea Sea north of Borneo and southwest of the Philippine Islands

Surigao Strait Channel between Panaon and Dinagat Islands connecting the Mindanao Sea with Leyte Gulf

Tablas Strait between Mindoro and Panay Islands in the Philippines

Tacloban Port town on Leyte

Tarawa Atoll, part of the Gilberts

Tinian Island, part of the Marianas

Tulagi Island, part of Solomons, north of Guadalcanal

CITIZEN SAILORS

RECRUITS

Japan's December 1941 attack on the Hawaiian Islands had, in three hours, reduced a good portion of America's Pacific fleet to sunken or burning ruins. Four U.S. battleships had settled, capsized, or disintegrated in the shallows of Battleship Row. Fourteen other ships had gone down in the deeper waters of Pearl Harbor's East Loch or been mauled at the piers, moorages, and dry docks along the rim of Southeast Loch. Across the islands more than three hundred military aircraft had been destroyed or damaged, most of them on the ground, parked wing to wing to protect against land-based sabotage. Nearly twenty-five hundred Americans had been killed and more than two thousand of these were U.S. Navy personnel. The toll exceeded combined U.S. Navy deaths in World War I and the Spanish-American War. Meanwhile, Japan had lost only thirty planes with forty-five airmen and five midget submarines with nine crewmen.

No one could overestimate the personal sorrow and tragedy of the losses of December 7. Yet the destruction left behind, as the Japanese bombers, torpedo planes, and fighter escorts returned to their carriers in the Northern Pacific, actually proved to be less than initially feared. Japan had taken a big bite out of a small apple. Even before the crippling attack, the U.S. Navy was a shadow of what it had once been and would need to become. Post–World War I naval treaties limiting construction, followed hard by a Depression economy, had done much more to dismantle America's fleets than the morning's torpedoes, bombs, and bullets. By 1941, the U.S. Navy had actually become smaller than Japan's Imperial Navy, at least in gross ship tonnage; Japan had used the postwar years to double its navy's size and fully modernize it. A revitalization of sorts began when Franklin Roosevelt became president; over one hundred new ships were launched, including two new aircraft carriers, sixteen cruisers, and nearly sixty destroyers. Despite this, the U.S. Navy still lacked for ships; it was still further behind when it came to the bases, fuel reserves, support craft, technology, logistics, and, above all, skilled and sufficient manpower to effectively operate a global wartime fleet.

All this soon began to change. The blow at Pearl Harbor put America finally, formally at war with an enemy it had expected to fight all along. In the next days and months, even as land, sea, and air losses in the Central and Southwest Pacific mounted, the enterprise of war—the methods and means of supplying all the missing resources—began gathering momentum. At the same time, because this was an effort defined by quantity and quality of manpower, the ranks of all the armed forces, including the U.S. Navy, began to swell.

⚓

Already, in the days before and just after Pearl Harbor, a trickle of early, sometimes eager, sometimes wary recruits had shown up at the military's door. More than a year earlier, Henry Burt Bassett, a courtly, lantern jawed Floridian, newly graduated from the University of Florida and selling industrial insurance in Southern Georgia, had run across his future while strolling in Monticello, Florida, his home town. "It was 1940. The war was brewing, of course, and I knew I'd be in it one way or another. Then I saw a big advertisement in front of the post office. It said 'Be a Naval Aviator,' $235 a month or something like that. Seemed like a lot of money. Flying appealed to me, though I'd never been on more than a few local jitney flights, and the training was in Pensacola, not too far away. From then on it was a matter of waiting: taking the physical exam, of course, and then waiting for orders to report."

Just three months before Pearl Harbor (and unknown to Burt Bassett), Burt's fraternity brother Tom Van Brunt, a graduate student and public school teacher, had begun the same road. "I was called up for flight training in September of forty-one at a Naval Air Station (NAS) in Chambley, Georgia. It was called elimination base—e-base—in those days. We didn't have uniforms except work khakis. We kept our college clothes because two out of three of us washed out and went home. That's why they called it e-base. There were just ten hours of training and then your solo flight."

Two sixteen-year-olds—Emmett Crump from Paris, Kentucky, and Tony Potochniak from Binghamton, New York—were among those swept up by the tide of emotion following the attack. Emmett's older brother was already in the Army and stationed in Hawaii. "Word got on the street around noon or thereabouts the Japanese had bombed Pearl Harbor. I went running up and down looking for my dad to see if he had word about my brother." Emmett soon learned his brother had survived the attack unharmed, but as vengeful feelings (both the nation's and his) continued high, he felt compelled to do something. Early in 1942, when he turned seventeen, Emmett left high school to join the Navy. Just after his seventeenth birthday several months later, Tony did the same thing. What drove Tony, as it drove so many others, was the helpless rage of losing friends: "Two family friends got killed early in the war, one at Pearl, one onboard *Lexington*.[1] No other way to put it, I wanted revenge."

Emmett and Tony were early and eager recruits. At age seventeen, with their parents' permission, they were also eligible to make the decision. Others tried to jump the gun. George Carbon had quit high school in Cleveland to sign up for the Navy. George passed his physical, tests, and interviews and was already in boot training at Great Lakes Naval Training Center when war broke out. He'd get to war sooner than most. The problem was, despite his mature appearance, George was just fifteen—an age when no one, and certainly not George, could consent to his enlistment. A call to his parents back in Ohio and George was on his way home, sentenced to continue his boyhood until he was at least sixteen and his parents could permit him to sign up. By 1942, when Vince Goodrich, a sixteen-year-old from Syracuse, tried to join the Marines, the services had wised up and were demanding proof of age. "They insisted on a birth certificate. By the time I was seventeen *I'd* wised up and decided to join the Navy."

Recruits like Burt Bassett, Tom Van Brunt, Emmett Crump, Tony Potochniak, George Carbon, and Vince Goodrich were just the vanguard of what the Navy and the other services needed. Meeting this need took time—more a matter of months than weeks, and often more a matter of years. When it came to manpower it would take the time required to register military-age men and call them up: time to process long, shivering lines of eager recruits and reluctant conscripts; time for cutting orders, for granting decent intervals of farewell; time for departures and travel on crowded rails across a continent; time for rousting, forming up, marching, drilling, yelling, pleading, browbeating, humiliating, and otherwise conspiring to squeeze (at least for the duration) civilian habits out of clumsy, stubborn, anxious herds of farm boys, factory boys, school boys, street boys, and boys on the dole; time for measuring, training, equipping, and graduating them—only to send them to more measuring, training, equipping, and graduating; and, finally, time for cutting orders and journeying with those orders to far-flung ships and air squadrons that, as often as not, were further behind schedule on drawing boards or in factories and shipyards than were the men being readied to use them. The stories describing these first passages toward war followed certain routes and patterns. Yet they were also as individual as the boys turned temporary warriors.

BASICS

Dick Rohde was still in high school and living in the rural countryside of Staten Island when war began. To Dick, the Navy and all things military breathed romance and adventure. His father and uncle had run a ship chandlery business (though it had been bankrupted during the Depression). Dick's mother had once dated a Naval Academy midshipman; during Dick's childhood this former "beau"—by then a naval flight instructor in Annapolis and by war's end an admiral—made it a point during summers to buzz Chesapeake Bay near the Maryland vacation home of Dick's grandparents, dropping gifts and greetings suspended from tiny parachutes. During a fleet visit to New York City in 1935, Dick, his parents, and his brother had been treated to a personal tour of the USS *Lexington,* one of the Navy's few aircraft carriers—and one of the first to be built as a carrier from the keel up.

After graduating at age sixteen from Curtis High School—and still too young to enlist without his parents' reluctant permission—Dick, who carried his compact frame with the breezy swagger of a Dead End Kid, began work as a page for Manhattan Bank Guarantee Trust, commuting daily on the Staten Island Ferry to his office job in lower Manhattan. Once he'd turned seventeen, though, Dick was primed to enlist, and his parents had been convinced to let him. One day he and another page decided on a patriotic impulse to offer themselves up. During their lunch hour, the two bounced resolutely into the downtown Marine recruiting office near South Ferry, half imagining they'd emerge looking just like the poster images that had drawn them in. To the snarling, salty recruiter they looked like something else—and something much less. The old Marine pictured no future in his Corps for either of the slender office boys and he bounced Dick and his friend out just as quickly as they'd bounced in. Momentarily humbled, though not deterred, the two went down the hall to sign up for a Navy with more need for brains and decent eyesight than heft or killer potential. Two weeks later Dick Rohde and his buddy were on a train and headed for boot camp in Newport, Rhode Island.

⚓

For other recruits who were less enthralled by heroic images, the war offered an unexpected, grudgingly welcomed deliverance from drift and poverty. The Depression had mercilessly derailed the lives of legions of American young men, forcing them out of school or jobs into a hard-scrabble life. If they were lucky, they might find subsistence work in government sponsored New Deal projects with names such as the CCC (Civilian Conservation Corps) and the WPA (Works Progress Administration). Then the distant threat of war followed by war itself ironically began to brighten their prospects. The war brought steady work, in factories and shipyards for the older and married, in the military for the young and footloose. It was the end of the Dole, the end of the Deal. This was the route for Glenn Parkin, a teenager from northern Utah and for two scrappy Midwesterners, Virgil Melvin and Ted Gurzynski.

Glenn, a fresh-faced boy with a pile of curly hair, had enrolled in the CCC in 1939 and spent the next twelve months working as a cook at a series of wilderness camps with austere names like Camp 940, Spike Camp F-49, and Camp F-6. When his CCC enrollment expired in 1940, Glenn returned to bleak prospects in Bountiful—a town whose very name mocked the struggling lives of many of its citizens. Then he found out the Navy was hiring; in February 1941 Glenn enlisted for six years. As war began, he was already a deck seaman on the cruiser USS *Northampton*—part of a task group of aircraft carriers and cruisers that missed the devastation at Pearl by hours. (Ironically, it was Glenn's father, newly arrived at Pearl to begin a job at the Navy shipyard, who was caught in the attack. It was days before Glenn could locate him and discover he'd escaped injury.)

Virgil Melvin, a seventeen-year-old farm boy from Hannibal, Missouri, had dropped out of high school to begin an unpromising career of hustling pool and setting pins in a bowling alley for 3¢ a line. Finally landing a WPA job, Virgil earned $16 a month wielding a star drill to manually bore holes in a concrete floor to mount machinery for a factory under construction. A landlocked boy intrigued by the parade of passing ships on the Mississippi, Virgil (Mel to his friends) had thought about joining the Navy. His father, a farmer turned struggling factory worker and a World War I Navy veteran, had staunchly refused permission. Mel's dad had had his fill of war and its consequences. "He saw another one coming and wanted to keep me out of it." But, once he'd turned eighteen, Mel was free to make his own decisions; he quickly enlisted in the Navy.

Ted Gurzynski, a Milwaukee native and, at age twenty-two, older and more battered by Depression times than Glenn or Virgil, had dropped out of school and worked in both the CCC and the WPA programs to escape joblessness. Combative and suspicious of authority, despite the infectious smile that could instantly light up his face, Ted had no romantic notions about the war or the military. "I came out of the CCC camps. When the war came I was just beginning to get back on my feet." He never considered enlisting. Then, in February 1943 when he was nearly twenty-three, induction finally caught up with him. "So I 'joined' the Navy. It was either that or get in the Army or the Marines. It was the lesser of the evils." Like many others about to be yanked from family, friends and familiarity, Ted also embarked on another life-changing path. "I got married exactly four days before I left for basic training at Great Lakes. Some honeymoon."

When it came to the process of joining the Navy, the experiences of Bill Wilson and Bob Hollenbaugh perhaps best illustrated the always murky line between outright volunteering and conscription. Bill Wilson was drafted after graduating from high school in Kalamazoo, Michigan. "I was eighteen. I got to the induction center and went through the physical and everything. A guy interviewed me after the exams. He told me I looked in pretty good shape and I could have my choice of the services. So it got to the point of making a decision. A sergeant asked me what I wanted, Army or Navy. And I said 'Well, give me the Army.' He stamped 'Navy' on my papers instead and said: 'You'll like it better there.'"

Bob Hollenbaugh, a native of Goshen, Indiana, was attending Western Michigan University in the spring of 1941 when his draft notice came. "My dad called me and said 'we have a letter here from the local draft board.' My dad was a tool and die maker and he spent time in the Navy during World War I. He worked below decks with the machinery gang, part of what they called the black gang on coal-driven ships. He told me, 'You go volunteer for the Navy, but stay topside. I don't want any son of mine working below decks.' Because I was going to college I guess I could have gotten a deferment. I just wasn't interested in college then, so I joined up."

⚓

In the spring of 1942, when Holly Crawforth walked into the Navy recruiting station in Reno, Nevada, hoping to volunteer, he was quickly rejected. Unlike Dick Rohde and Vince Goodrich, Holly had neither cared nor dared to try for the Marines. Holly knew his severe nearsightedness would make him more liability than asset if it ever came to close combat. He soon found out poor eyesight was also disqualifying to the Navy, at least in the first days of the war. Or, in Holly's case, nearly disqualifying: "When the recruiter found out I was working as an electrician's apprentice and I'd taken algebra, geometry and trigonometry in high school, my eyes didn't seem to be such a big deal." Holly was quickly signed up and shipped out the same night to a hurried basic in San Francisco. And once basic was over, Holly began three months of primary electronics training. Holly was then ordered to Stillwater, Oklahoma, where the Navy had commandeered much of Oklahoma A&M's campus.[2] It was at A&M that Holly began nine months of intermediate and advanced training on a technology so complex he felt perpetually adrift and baffled as he struggled to master it.

The technology was radar and though still highly secret, it was not brand new. The Navy was already beginning to install and use a rudimentary version on some of its newer ships. Six truck-sized installations had been deployed by the Army in Hawaii before the attack on Pearl Harbor; and one, perched on the northernmost cliffs of Oahu, had actually spotted, tracked, and reported the attacking Japanese, although the watch officer back at central station unwittingly dismissed the report. Radar was just one of many emerging technologies (radio communication, sonar, electronics, aerodynamics, engineering mechanics, and nuclear physics were some others) whose constant refinement and widespread production, would, in a steady accumulation of small, telling advantages, contribute tremendously to the war's final outcome.

These complex technologies required the Navy to recruit brains (even if connected to weakened eyes or other assorted frailties), often over brawn and ferocity. Holly Crawforth and Vince Goodrich fit this new mold and so did Don Bujold, a twenty-two-year-old machinist working for an aircraft hydraulics manufacturer in Detroit. Although Don's technical skills and his defense work entitled him to a deferment, he still leaned towards joining up. And, as was the case for many, the allure was as much about fitting in as it was about patriotism or bloodlust: "I thought, hey, my buddies are all in the service now. So I went down to the draft board and told them I wanted to go in the Navy. Even then they made me wait, and I didn't go in until January '43. At Great Lakes they put me in charge of my recruit company, what they called the granny knot admiral.[3] Then from boot camp they sent me to the University of Kansas. I was the recruit chief there also, and I was taking a freshman course in engineering."

Dick Rohde, who'd been so quickly snubbed by the Marines and then received with open arms by the Navy, was another in this mold. Following boot camp in Newport, Dick had tried one more volunteer tack—this time putting in for submarines. The submarine service also rejected him. "It was for something you'd never think of. I had an overbite. My mouth just didn't fit the breathing apparatus they used for underwater escape." Instead, because the Navy knew he'd taken typing in high school and had been a member of its fledgling radio club, Dick had been sent up to Boston for communications training. He and hundreds of others like him were housed in the dormitories and hotels near Boston University. Each morning they formed up to march along Commonwealth Avenue as it skirted the Back Bay, angled through Kenmore Square, and intersected with Boston Common. Turning (by column) south onto Charles Street and emerging from the Common where it intersected Boylston Street, the formation ended its parade in the classrooms and electronics labs of a commercial radio school.

WONDERS

Oklahoma A&M and KU were just two of the colleges preparing men for war. With their classrooms, labs, and adjacent housing, they often were ideal places to train young men on the necessary concepts and technologies. Some campuses also became time-compressed finishing schools for the flood of new reserve officers—junior officer leaders who, in combination with the growing legion of trained enlisted petty officers, were needed to augment the much smaller core of military academy graduates. These reservists became known as 90-day wonders—though just as often, depending on the war's timetable, they might be 180-day, 70-day, or even 56-day wonders. Many of these penny-bright young men had just been rushed to early graduation from college, only to be sent to another college campus.

Often the "wonders" left small campuses near their hometowns only to wind up at huge, fabled campuses a continent away. Larry Epping, like many others, signed up for the Navy's V-7 program, which allowed college undergrads to defer service until they received their degrees. (V-7 was as much an accommodation for a military not quite ready to receive the volunteers as it was for the volunteers not quite ready to go.) Larry signed up in 1942 while still attending small Mount Angel College not far from his home in the foothills of Oregon's Cascade Mountains. After graduating in 1943, Larry—a laconic westerner who had never been further east than the prairies of North Dakota—received orders to report for training at Columbia University on New York City's Morningside Heights. There, along with eight hundred other new Midshipmen, Larry drilled, marched, and attended classes amid the sights, noise, and rhythms of uptown Manhattan—a city bigger than belief. "I was awed by just the size and activity of the city. But I was even more awed by my roommate who was kind of a learning genius and never had to crack a book of any kind. He ended up number two or three in the standings, even though he never seemed to read anything but magazines."

Edward Pfeiffer, a history major at St. Michael's in Burlington, Vermont, and Dudley Moylan, an English major at Duke and a transplanted Floridian with roots in upstate New York, were two more V-7 products from the class of 1943. Both got orders to report to the campus of Notre Dame for midshipman training. For Dudley it was a simple move from one large university to another; for Ed, the product of a small Catholic college, it was like being called up to the major leagues.

Verner Carlsen, a married, twenty-nine-year-old pastor of a Lutheran congregation in Grettinger, Iowa, got a different kind of call. As war began and many of the young men in Verner's congregation went off to enlist, train, and go overseas, he spent much of his time keeping up a correspondence that grew more and more like the summons to a ministry. Although he held off for as long as he felt he could—tending to the anxieties and fears of parishioners who had sent their boys off, and the deep anguish of those who would never see them return—the calling in Verner's soul persisted. Finally, in 1943, Verner enlisted and received a commission in the Navy's Chaplain Corps. Verner's first stop on his new journey was the Virginia campus of venerable William & Mary College—eight weeks attending classes and running obstacle courses in the ranks of an unlikely regiment of ministers, priests, and rabbis.

For some, like Tom Stevenson, it was a scramble to get in under the wire. Born in Brooklyn, Tom had been raised in Hollis, a sleepy Long Island town known mostly for its potato fields. He went on to attend Georgetown University in Washington, DC, where Tom helped form a rowing club. The club's crews were routinely trounced by the likes of Columbia and Yale, but the experience contributed muscle and toughness to Tom's tall frame and boyish Irish looks. His graduation from Georgetown was accelerated in the interests of the war, creating a dilemma. Tom was participating in the Army's Reserve Officer Training Corps (ROTC) program; now he found out early graduation left him six months shy of the requirements he would need to earn an officer's commission. Without it, Tom figured he would be heading for the draft and the harsh and dangerous life of an ordinary foot soldier.

Casting around for options in the spring of 1942—and knowing somewhere out there was a draft notice with his name on it—Tom was in the audience for a presentation given by a Navy recruiter trying to drum up volunteers. Talking up the recruiter afterward, Tom learned he had some things going for him. "My family owned a New York steamship company and I'd worked summers on a few of the company's ships." In the process Tom had earned his ordinary seaman's papers and even a helmsman's certificate—both tangible proofs of his seaworthiness. These credentials, combined with his newly minted degree from Georgetown, paved the way for a Navy commission. Outfitted with custom-made uniforms from Rogers Peat—and greatly relieved—Tom went off for six months of drill and radio communications training in the ivied halls of Harvard University.

⚓

In a war whose first blow had been struck from the air there was a burning need for a steady supply of flyers. For the Navy this meant more young men like Burt Bassett and Tom Van Brunt with the skills to pilot the mostly single engine torpedo bombers, dive bombers, and fighters flying from its aircraft carriers. Naval aviation was clearly the business of very young men with the judgment, coordination, nerves, assurance, and controlled recklessness it took to launch and land on heaving decks just eight hundred feet long. For carrier pilots, the adrenaline-pumping takeoffs and recoveries were just the entrances and curtain calls to every operational or combat mission. The carrier pilots defied death even before they got to fire a shot, launch a torpedo, or drop a bomb.

The pilot recruiting effort began well before the war at airstrips, college campuses, and even high schools across the country. The training had to begin young. The students had to be readied and put in action before the softening effects of maturity—and awareness of mortality—began to take hold. Full preparation took nearly two years—a long time in the pressing calendar of war and an eternity in the time frames of young men trying to get over the hurdles.

For Jim Lischer, the journey began in the fall of 1941 when he enrolled in the U.S. government sponsored Civilian Pilot Training Program at tiny St. Ambrose College in Davenport, Iowa. CPTP, a program started in 1939, financed seventy-two hours of ground school and fifty hours of early flight training for undergraduate volunteers like Jim at eleven colleges across the country, including St. Ambrose. Despite its uninspiring name, CPTP had an essential strategic purpose—to build an inventory of airworthy pilot recruits.[4]

Jim's CPTP hours were spent at Davenport's local airport, first in ground school and then flight training in high wing, tandem-seating Aeronca monoplanes. The Aeronca quickly earned the nickname Grasshopper.[5] Perhaps it was because of the Aeronca's gawky profile and spindly undercarriage; perhaps because of the small country airstrips from which the planes often flew; perhaps because of the student pilots' bounding, chaotic takeoffs, and landings.

Jim's flight training went well; before the school year was out he'd earned his private pilot's license. Then the journey almost stopped. With his freshman year completed and the war underway, Jim left Davenport, intending to postpone school, and went to St. Louis to sign up for the Navy Air Corps. What seemed like a routine process came to halt when he failed his flight physical; blood tests showed Jim has too much albumin—a milk protein—in his blood. Jim returned to Davenport despondent and it took him several days to work up the courage to break the news to his dad. Jim's father, the owner of a chain of drug stores, heard the verdict—and had a simple solution for his Iowa son: "Stop drinking so much damn milk—it raises the albumin level." After a summer of working at the airport—and curtailing his dairy intake—Jim Lischer got retested and this time was accepted for active duty. In the fall he was on his way to Navy preflight school at the University of Iowa.

Further east, in upstate New York, Joe McGraw's flight training began without college. "I got out of high school in Syracuse in June of forty-two, signed up for naval aviation in September and got called up right away. I got into the beginning of the NavCad (Naval Aviation Cadet) program. There was a group of us from Syracuse called the 'Syracuse Avengers,' a name dreamed up by some publicist. In those days they really needed pilots badly. We had to take a test to prove we could qualify under the two-year college rule. In other words, we had to show college-level skills. The test had a lot of math. I was always good at math and so I passed it." Joe and the other teen-age Avengers were ordered to the University of North Carolina at Chapel Hill for three months of preflight training.

MAKESHIFT

Braced at attention on the shoulder of a dust-choked highway leading from Houston into Corpus Christi, holding a wooden rifle at port arms, Virgil Melvin grew tired of acting like a real warrior with a real weapon. Spaced to his right and left (and probably as far in either direction as he could see, had the dust cleared) were other men like him from the training companies of Corpus Christi Naval Air Training Center.

When they first arrived at Corpus for boot camp, there were no uniforms to issue to them. In the weeks since, there'd been musters, roll calls, hygiene lectures, and marching with wooden rifles, yet none of the training he'd come here expecting. Instead the recruits stood, sat, waited, marched, went to chow, even slept without a sense of purpose. This roadside charade was just one more example of a fouled up Navy unprepared to train, house, clothe, or feed its men—never mind fight. They were awaiting, and expected to impress, the occupants of a motorcade that never seemed to arrive. Scuttlebutt claimed it would be Roosevelt himself passing by, traveling with Secretary of War Stimsen. Who knew and, after all these hours, who cared? All in all, it was a hell of a way to get ready for war.

For Mel Melvin and thousands of other new sailors and naval airmen their first training seemed makeshift—as if they'd come early to a party that was starting late only to be bullied by a loud, frustrated, and impatient host. It was always a mismatch: either they weren't ready to do what the Navy expected; or the Navy lacked the ships, planes, guns, or equipment the men needed to put their training to work. It was, in the classic phrase of the time, hurry up and wait.

During his first days of his pre-flight training in Opa-Lacka, Florida, Burt Bassett was trained for things he wasn't sure he'd ever get to use. "I remember we learned a lot of Morse code during the first month. And at each stage of training we'd get more Morse code. They tried to get my keying speed up to sixteen words per minute, but I could never do it. They also taught us a little about aircraft construction and even gave us a few lessons in how to sew aircraft fabric. In every plane we carried a kit with fabric and eight-inch sewing needles. In case we ever had trouble landing and tore up a wing, I guess they thought we could repair it ourselves."

⚓

Occasionally hurry up and wait became wait and hurry up, something Holly Crawforth found out while still in San Francisco in October 1942, just beginning electronics training. One night, a few hours after falling asleep in his barracks bunk, exhausted after another long day, Holly was abruptly awakened, a flashlight beam flooding his face. It was one of the school chief petty officers ordering Holly to wake up, pack his gear, and get ready to travel. Holly remembered saying he couldn't because he had class the next day, but his drowsy objections didn't have much impact. During the night Holly began a journey taking him to Nouméa on New Caledonia, a Pacific island east of Australia. When he arrived, Holly got assigned as a radio technician to the USS *Enterprise.*

Within days, carriers *Enterprise* and *Hornet,*[6] surrounded by a screen of cruisers and destroyers, were steaming north from New Caledonia to a point four hundred miles west of the Solomon Islands. In the Solomons U.S. Marines on Guadalcanal were defending a precarious foothold—America's first offensive thrust of the war. *Enterprise* and *Hornet* and their air groups were being sent to challenge any Japanese carrier force moving south to dislodge the Marines. Toward the end of October, American scout planes spotted just what they were looking for: a southbound Japanese task force led by three carriers.

During what was called the Battle of the Santa Cruz Islands, Holly had his first brush with combat at sea. For him it meant sweating it out in darkened interior radar and communications spaces; meanwhile, above decks, *Enterprise* was rocked by explosions as her gun crews and covering fighter planes battled swarms of attacking Japanese aircraft.[7] It was a terrifyingly helpless sensation (as it was for countless other vulnerable "left arm" rates[8] throughout the war's sea battles). Their jobs required them to concentrate on running, tuning or repairing finicky gear while death could be as near as a bomb or torpedo explosion ripping through a bulkhead. Meanwhile, topside on *Northampton,* one of the screening cruisers, Glenn Parkin had a clearer view, frightening in a different kind of way: dozens of Japanese torpedo and dive bombers dropping out of a cloudless midday sky into a welter of fire from *Nora*'s forest of 40-mm, 20-mm, and 1.1-in. antiaircraft guns.

⚓

For some others still in stateside training, the war's early days of confusion, misdirection, and general lack of readiness actually offered a welcome, idyllic breather between the first days of training and the real business up ahead. By the beginning of 1943, Tom Stevenson had been commissioned an ensign in the Naval Reserve and completed six months of training in radio engineering and communications at Harvard. Most of Tom's Cambridge classmates were older Navy officers; they'd been detached from fleet ships and sent stateside to learn the new technologies that were quickly transforming just about all they knew about operating ships at sea. They had grim stories to tell.

Unlike these older salts, Tom was starting with these new technologies and still (his ordinary seaman papers notwithstanding) had a lot to learn about ship handling. So, instead of getting a ship assignment, Tom got orders to report to Fort Schuyler in Throgs Neck, New York—the home of the New York State Maritime Academy. Tom and a group of other green reserve officers spent a vacation-like late summer at Fort Schuyler, climbing onboard one of the Academy's two oceangoing yachts each day to practice piloting and navigation in Long Island Sound. The arrival of fall took them south for more training at sub chaser school in Miami. There Tom got his first experience aboard some vintage Navy combatants—two-hundred-foot Eagle Boats (PEs) built by the Ford Motor Company and intended for use in World War I. Dudley Moylan also trained briefly on the PEs in Miami before going to sonar school in Key West.

Duty aboard these older, outmoded PEs and other vessels like them was not unusual in the first months of the war. Just as politicians, admirals, and generals seemed always to plan for the last war, young officers and sailors often used the last war's leftover equipment. And not always just for training. After basic, Emmett Crump was billeted as a ship's coxswain to the USS *Decatur*, a 1920-vintage destroyer based out of Brooklyn, New York. *Decatur* was a "four-stacker," so named for the four perpendicular smokestacks that made the ships of this class look like seagoing calliopes. *Decatur* was small, a little over eleven hundred tons and three hundred feet long with a shallow draft of less than ten feet. Its 4-in. open mount guns, the rows of portholes along the length of its hull (one row just above the waterline), the vertical line of its bow, and the turtle-back slope of its stern gave *Decatur* a frail, antiquarian look—as if it had been built for ceremonies and goodwill cruises rather than blue water combat.

Decatur was also lightly manned—she carried barely 120 souls. Even so, she was cramped and some of her spaces served double duty. Emmett and his crewmates slept in hammocks suspended by hooks from the overhead of the mess hall, creaking and rocking like a coven of canvas-skinned albino bats in the quiet before *Decatur*'s 0500 reveille.

Emmett rode *Decatur* as she escorted empty tankers down the U-boat-plagued eastern seaboard from Norfolk to Caracas where the tankers loaded up with Venezuelan crude oil. "In the Caribbean we got a submarine—a German U-boat. We dropped depth charges and the concussions must have forced the boat to the surface. The crew abandoned ship through the sub's conning tower, jumping from the tower to the water. The sharks got most of them pretty quick."

As the war continued and the need for men and equipment in Europe climbed, *Decatur* eventually took deeper and more perilous gulps of ocean. During 1943, she ventured as a convoy escort on four Atlantic crossings to ports on the Mediterranean Sea, even fighting off coordinated attacks by German aircraft and U-boats—a vessel intended for the last war pitted against weapons built for the new war.

WINGS

Jim Lischer and Joe McGraw made their first carrier landings over the choppy waters of Lake Michigan in 1943. Flying from Glenview Illinois Naval Air Station north of Chicago, Jim, Joe, and other trainees made their carrier qualification landings—CarQuals—on the USS *Wolverine*, the first of three ships to be converted into "freshwater carriers." *Wolverine*— formerly the SS *Seaandbee*—had been a coal-burning, side paddle, wheel-propelled Great Lakes excursion steamer. She was a plush, decorous lady doing work her designers could never have imagined.

Wolverine was a make-do response to a nagging reality: attack carriers such as *Enterprise, Lexington, Saratoga* and *Yorktown,*[9] fighting almost nonstop in the Central and Southwest Pacific, could not be spared to return to friendly waters even to train desperately needed new flyers. So this prewar excursion boat was transformed into a wartime practice aircraft carrier. Stripped of her plush interior accommodations and top-heavy superstructure, *Wolverine* instead mounted a narrow 550-foot long wooden flight deck, capped by a small island superstructure on its starboard edge. The flight deck stretched fore and aft, like the leaves of a tabletop, well past *Wolverine*'s bow and stern.

Each morning *Wolverine* shoved off from a berth at Chicago's Navy Pier and steamed out into Lake Michigan, belching clouds of sooty smoke that in summer blackened laundry hung on the clotheslines of apartment buildings and hotels along Lake Shore Drive. *Wolverine* headed into the wind; aircraft landing on carrier decks needed headwind to slow their approaches; launching aircraft needed the same wind to get lift. Just as soon as *Wolverine* gained enough velocity over her deck, flight operations began. Often *Wolverine* operated so close to shore that gawking motorists created traffic jams and rear end collisions as they watched the fledgling pilots' landing adventures.

During 1943 new pilots like Jim Lischer and Joe McGraw made these landings (six successful landings and launches were needed in order to qualify as carrier pilots) in SNJs, the Navy's version of the low wing two-seat aluminum monoplane used by both Army and Navy advanced flight training. The planes usually left Glenview in groups of five to rendezvous over the white, bullet-shaped dome of the lakeside Baha'i temple in Wilmette, a northern suburb of Chicago. There the pilots got a range and bearing to *Wolverine* and began circling to wait for a "Charlie"—the signal to drop down and make an approach.

Although Lake Michigan waves were far gentler than the Pacific's waves would be, this was small consolation for pilots attempting their first flight deck landings. Lake Michigan wasn't the Pacific; still it was big, *Wolverine* looked incredibly small, and, angling towards a rolling flight deck three hundred feet shorter than an attack carrier's riding barely twenty-seven feet above the lake's surface, there was no room for miscalculation.

Planes making carrier landings required tail hooks—rods suspended from the planes' tail section. During a landing the tail hook hung down to grab one of the steel arresting cables spanning the flight deck; hook and cable then yanked the plane to an abrupt stop short of disaster. Because SNJs weren't designed for carrier flight, tail hooks for these CarQual landings often had to be improvised. The improvisation made for Joe McGraw's SNJs showed real ingenuity. "Some smart chief up there welded a tail hook under the tail. They had a couple of pulleys and a line just like a clothesline running along outside the SNJ's fuselage and into the cockpit. I remember there was an armrest three times right above the throttle that folded down below the edge of the canopy. You pulled in this line and wrapped it smartly around the armrest and your tail hook was up. So we had to fly with the canopy open all the time during CarQuals on the *Wolverine*."

Despite having two days to practice landing techniques ashore with the help of landing signal officers (LSOs), each of the first landings was ultimately an act of faith. You couldn't know how to land an airplane on a carrier deck until you actually landed an airplane on a carrier deck.

To make an approach with the *Wolverine* headed into the wind, each pilot flew his plane upwind to a point even with the carrier's extended bow, and then banked steeply left. The pilot then dropped wheels and improvised tailhook as the SNJ leveled out—now moving abeam of the carrier on the opposite downwind heading. When *Wolverine* began to drift out of his periphery, he once again banked steeply left, this time to come up *Wolverine*'s wake, engine racing, nose up, flaps down, wheels and hook dangling. An LSO standing on the port quarter of the flight used two hand paddles (though bigger and fabric-covered, they were remarkably similar to ping-pong paddles) to signal wing, nose, and speed adjustments. When the LSO flagged the plane to land, the pilot cut throttle and his plane dipped onto the deck.

Each time Jim Lischer brought his plane around to make these first approaches his eyes would be glued to the LSO's signal paddles while his heart would be in his mouth, pounding so furiously he imagined it might leap away. Then suddenly he would land. The SNJ would drop and bounce, the tail hook would trap a wire, and it would be all over—down safely. If he landed with enough room to take off again, crewmen would signal Jim to turn up the SNJ's engine to full throttle. Once it reached 2,000 rpm, Jim would begin his free run down the deck. At take off it would be flaps up, wheels up, and heart up as Jim orbited the SNJ to get ready for the next approach.

Joe McGraw suffered a bout of self-congratulation when he shot his first *Wolverine* landing. "Even though this was my first landing over water, I had a lot of time in SNJs by then and so I was pretty good. We were all pretty good, and the SNJ was a good stable airplane. When I made my first landing I trapped the number three wire and I'm sitting there saying to myself 'Man, a really hot aviator!' Then I hear this big pounding on the side of the fuselage. I look out the left side and there's an irate crewman down there. He's pounding on the side of the SNJ and he's pulling this rope screaming 'PULL THE ROPE! PULL THE ROPE!' So I pulled the rope to get the hook up, and out in front there's another irate guy and he's got two fingers up in the air, waving them and screaming 'GO! GO!' " Joe's triumph was only slowing the merry-go-round of anxious pilots orbiting overhead, each waiting heart-in-mouth for his next chance to land.

⚓

By the end of 1942 three major Pacific War battles—Coral Sea, Midway, and Santa Cruz—had been fought and decided almost exclusively by carrier-based aircraft. Not surprisingly, the most prized targets in these aerial showdowns were the carriers themselves. Sinking carriers became the principal measure of victory; losing carriers became the principal measure of defeat.

At Midway, the second, biggest, and most decisive of these three battles, the Japanese had lost *Kaga, Akagi, Soryu,* and *Hiryu,* four of the six fleet carriers used in the attack on Pearl Harbor. At the same time, the United States had lost *Lexington* (at Coral Sea) and *Yorktown,* nearly half of its entire Pacific carrier contingent. It was painful attrition for both sides, but, even this early in the war, the United States could sustain the resulting losses of pilots and aircraft better than Japan could.

When carriers *Zuikaku* and *Shokaku* returned "victorious" to Japan's home waters following the Battle of Coral Sea, the public triumph masked the reality that both ships had lost so many aircraft and pilots they would be pulled from the upcoming invasion of Midway. Their absence at Midway may well have tipped the scale toward America's victory. But the United States wasn't just gaining advantage in victory. Even America's first humiliating and painful defeats continued to work a relentless math. On its side of the equation, win or lose, Japan faced the next conflict with fewer carriers launching fewer planes piloted by less capable aviators. As the unfavorable odds mounted, Japan's naval leadership increasingly hungered for a ship-to-ship confrontation—a showdown in which they could bring the massive and superior firepower of their battleships and cruisers to bear. And, later, as the conditions for a triumphant showdown continued to elude them, naval leadership would be forced to entertain other, more sacrificial and more personal ways to meet the demands of *Bushido.*

PIPELINE

Meanwhile, America's side of the equation—in pilots, aircraft, and carriers alike—was slowly, inexorably scaling in its favor. Thousands of recruits coming out of college or, like Joe McGraw, even out of high school, were being funneled through a training pipeline encompassing Navy pre-flight, basic, instrument, tactical, and pre-operational flight. Often their instructors were pilots like Burt Bassett and Tom Van Brunt with little more flying experience and no combat experience. While they prepared others to fight, the instructors stayed behind, quietly building their flying skills through the accumulation of flying hours. Burt was stationed as a flight instructor at Corpus Christi when war broke out and, following graduation from flight training in June 1942, Tom became an instructor in St. Louis. "There was a real crush for primary instructors. That's all I did for a year and a half."

To the ambitious crops of new young aviators who'd been selected, at least in part, for their egos and brash self-assurance, their place in the big equation didn't matter much. In their personal calculus, each stage of training only seemed to stoke their impatience to get into real airplanes. The light at the end of this tunnel promised to be the CarQuals on *Wolverine*. When those were completed, they would get their squadron assignments and finally get in on the show. In their minds, then, and only then, would things begin to change and the war's balance begin to tip.

Following Navy preflight training—in Iowa City for Jim Lischer, in Chapel Hill for Joe McGraw—the next step was three months of primary training and soloing in N3N biplanes. This was basically the same aircraft on which Burt Bassett learned the basics of patching and sewing fabric and which Tom Van Brunt flew as an instructor in St. Louis. The N3N, known as the Yellow Peril to an entire generation of naval aviators, was a two-seat (instructor forward, student pilot aft) open cockpit plane. Its fabric fuselage was painted a bold canary yellow—a partial explanation for its name[10]—with a splash or swath of Navy blue. With its slow speed and simple cluster of instruments, the N3N and its successor the Stearman N25 were both easy to handle and forgiving of student errors. But the Yellow Peril also made for tricky takeoffs and landings in any kind of crosswind, a quirk Tom Van Brunt learned to respect. Tom logged more than 1100 hours in Stearmans. "It was a fun plane to fly. It gave me a leg up on the feel of an airplane that pilots who went directly from flight school into the fleet didn't always have."

Next came three months of instrument training and the switch from the two-wing N3N to the closed cockpit monoplanes: first the Vultee Vibrator and then the more advanced SNJ, the only type of aircraft most would fly until they got to the fleet. At this stage, pilots began jockeying for operational assignments and the type of fleet aircraft they'd eventually be assigned. The options were really three. Although the Navy had multiengine, land-based aircraft such as the PBY,[11] and even some lighter than air ships, most aircraft were single engine and carrier-based: torpedo bombers, dive bombers, or fighters.

⚓

Each aircraft type called for a specific pilot psychology and specific skills. Dive bombing and torpedo bombing required icy restraint and single-minded focus to block out the approach of imminent destruction. In a vertical dive or in a wave-skimming torpedo run, Navy bomber pilots were like boxers limited to one punch. While waiting for the instant to throw the punch (and never sure it would connect), they exposed themselves and their crews to lethal punishment. They couldn't flinch or heed the urge to pull up and away into safety.

Already in the early stages of the Pacific War this fearlessness, teamed with inferior equipment and faulty tactics, had cost dearly. At Midway all but two of fifteen carrier-launched torpedo TBD Devastators and all six new TBM Avengers flying from airstrips on Midway, were lost in attacks against Japanese carriers. Nearly all of their flight crews were lost during these attacks, and most had never gotten to throw a punch. Rigid, doctrinaire torpedo delivery tactics had played a big part in the massacre. To protect the fragile mechanics of their torpedoes, pilots had to come in straight and level on their targets, exactly 200 feet above the water and flying at 180 knots. In effect, they became perfect targets for the ships they attacked.

Navy bomber pilots also carried the extra burden of responsibility for other men—usually a crew of two in addition to the pilot. Sidestepping this weight (a heavy burden indeed for many teenage pilots still just learning to take responsibility for themselves) was just one of the attractions of becoming a Navy fighter pilot. Another was that, in the brutal business of modern war, fighter pilots came as close as was possible to fighting one-to-one, skill-to-skill with another opponent. Air-to-air combat was a defining concept. It was the opportunity to prove your worth in a struggle that still had some sense of chivalry about it—certainly more chivalry than the impersonal carnage on the ground.

This opportunity demanded unusual qualities: piercing eyesight, trigger-quick instincts, and the ability to be ever-oriented, ever-anticipating, ever-reacting. (Burt Bassett had learned early on he would never be fighter pilot material. He experienced nausea whenever he flew acrobatic maneuvers. The problem briefly grounded him; eventually it pointed him to becoming a torpedo bomber pilot.) If Navy bomber pilots were stone-nerved one-punch boxers, then fighter pilots were boxers throwing punches at a kaleidoscope of opponents, most approaching from behind, while bobbing and weaving through an infinite arena of sky.

Both Jim Lischer and Joe McGraw convinced their instructors they displayed these qualities. Jim was a strapping hulk, brimming with Midwestern assurance. Joe was blessed with amazing eyesight, a trait that seemed evident in his high cheekbones and piercing gaze: "In the air I always seemed to see things before anybody else did." Both earned tickets to fighter pilot training in Kingsville, Texas, followed by pre-operational training in Pensacola and Opa-Locka, Florida. Through it all, Jim and Joe continued to fly SNJs. "I *still* hadn't flown a real Navy fighter. None of us had. They had SNJs on the line at Kingsville. Each aircraft had a rather loosely mounted thirty-caliber machine gun up on right hand side of the cowling. It fired through the prop. The airplane wasn't built for that, they had just added it on. The gun had a terrible dispersal pattern. At three hundred yards it was about the size of a hangar door. You had to fly up close to the target sleeve—just shoot and duck in order to hit it. You had to get ten percent hits in order to qualify as a fighter pilot and a lot of guys ended up nearly wearing the sleeve."

In Opa-Locka, while they still flew mostly SNJs, some pilots finally got a brief taste of flying an actual fighter aircraft. Unfortunately it was a bad taste. The aircraft were the notorious and deeply flawed Brewster Buffalos, then nearing the end of their brief and disappointing operational lives. It was not a plane you wanted to take to a fight. Like the Douglas Devastators, the stubby, short-wing Buffalos had made a dismal showing at Midway: thirteen Marine-piloted Buffalos launched from the airstrip at Midway had attacked and then been methodically splashed by vastly superior Mitsubishi A6M Navy Type Zero carrier fighters. To Joe McGraw, the reason for the failure was obvious. "The Buffalo didn't have much of a tail so it flew in a skid all of the time. Whenever you made a turn it blanked out the tail. I don't know how guys ever hit anything with it." After months of Yellow Perils, Vultee Vibrators, SNJs, and now the sour taste of a Brewster Buffalo, Joe wondered if the Navy would ever get him in the cockpit of a real combat aircraft.

RESURRECTIONS

Bob Hollenbaugh arrived at Pearl Harbor in the last days of December 1941, as part of a destroyer repair unit. The unit had been formed in San Diego the previous summer. "The whole South Bay in San Diego was covered with World War I four-pipe destroyers—what they called Red Lead Row.[12] Our job was to get those ships ready to go to England and Russia for Lend-Lease.[13] I was assigned to the rigging loft where most of the guys called in from the reserves had worked in high-rise construction. Jesus, they were fearless! They scared the hell out of me the way they climbed rigging.

"Along came December seventh and the unit CO, a Mustang Lieutenant Commander, called us all together on Sunday afternoon: 'Boys let's keep our gear packed, there's a couple of destroyers we might be working on at Pearl.' By the time we got to Pearl Harbor, they had flooded the dry dock where the *Pennsylvania* and the *Cassin* and *Downes,* two destroyers, were stuck. They'd pulled *Pennsylvania* out, which left the two DDs off their keel blocks and leaning over against one another. They were just covered in oil. It scared me even more to be climbing up and down on those ships. Finally, my boss the First Class Boatswain Mate said 'Hollenbaugh, I'm afraid you're going to kill yourself. You go up on the dock and help wash the coveralls the guys are using.' They'd use three or four pair in a day.

"Eventually I made Second Class Boatswain Mate and became coxswain on a fifty-foot motor launch taking repair crews and equipment out to the ships nested in the harbor. Mostly destroyers and smaller ships— some of them damaged at Pearl, some of them in the Coral Sea. One day the CO said 'Hollenbaugh, you're gonna have to do one of two things because we don't need a Second Class running a motor launch. One option is you can go to diving school back on the East Coast and return here because we need a diver. Or you can go to new construction.' So I chose news construction. I was bound and determined to go to sea. I shipped back to the West Coast with orders for the *Johnston,* a new destroyer. I joined her in Harbor Island in Seattle six weeks before her commissioning."

⚓

By December 1943, the U.S. Navy's power in ships, planes, manpower, and logistics was finally on the way to eclipsing any other navy on the globe— including the Japanese. That was when John Montgomery, a slightly built eighteen-year-old newly graduated and transported from basic training at Great Lakes Naval Training Center, reported dockside to the USS *California,* a potent symbol of the Navy's resurrection and a doughty relic of its past.

During the Pearl Harbor attack, *California* had been a ready victim as she sat in Battleship Row's southernmost berth. Many of her watertight doors—doors sealing off warship compartments to limit internal flooding— were already open in preparation for a walk-through inspection scheduled for the next day. Within the first few minutes of the attack, a trio of aerial torpedoes had torn open two massive gashes in *California*'s port side. Two vertical bombs hits followed, both of them penetrating and exploding below decks. One explosion set off an antiaircraft ammunition magazine, the other ruptured the seams in the ship's bow plates. Oil fires raging on the surface of water enveloped *California* and continually ignited shipboard fires fueled by teak deck planks and painted surfaces. With no watertight integrity, onrushing seawater poured on top of internal flooding from *California*'s own fuel tanks and lines. Listing eight degrees to port, *California* quickly settled into the mud of East Loch all the way up to her superstructure. Ninety-eight of her crew lay dead on her decks or in her flooded compartments.

Now, almost two years later to the day, *California* was finishing a final refit in Bremerton, Washington, and about to go out in January on a shakedown cruise. Looming over John Montgomery as he stood on a pier bustling with sailors and shipyard workers, a full continent away from his neighborhood in Baltimore, *California* was easily the biggest thing he'd ever seen. Within a few days he learned more about her dimensions: 32,300 tons distributed over a 625-foot length and a 97-foot breadth; a crew of more than 2,000. Guns spiked in every direction from fortress-strength turrets on *California*'s main deck and superstructure: twelve 14-in. guns; fourteen 5-in. guns; four 3-in. guns; an uncountable forest of 40-mm and 20-mm antiaircraft guns. John also learned *California* was slow; with her flank speed of twenty-one knots she couldn't keep pace with much of a fleet newly built or still building for the war. For all her size and visible might, there was a limit to the types of battles she could enter.

John hoisted a sea bag nearly his size—and weighing not much less than his 113 pounds—and struggled up the incline of *California*'s midships' gangplank. As he stepped breathless onto *California*'s deck, an indignant chief petty officer in dress blues told Montgomery to get his sorry little ass back down. He'd walked onto the sacred, ceremonial quarterdeck—not the way a new and lowly seaman should ever dare to come onboard. Instead, John was ordered forward where he would have to scale another, even more sharply inclining gangplank to the ship's forecastle. For a few minutes, after wrestling his sea bag to the foot of the forward gangplank, John stood and tried to gather a new reserve of strength. Instead, he found himself filled with doubt he and his heavy gear would ever make it to the top. Just then John got welcome deliverance. A woman ship fitter—herself waiting to go onboard—had seen his dilemma. This angel of strength, whose name John didn't think to ask, heaved his sea bag in one swift motion across her trim shoulders and began striding up the gangplank. With a smile and a nod the angel motioned John to follow her.

Forming Up

SMALL BOYS

After working nearly two years as a ship fitter apprentice in Charleston's Navy Shipyard, Leon Wolper felt he had invested a lot of himself in the Navy. When his deferment was up and his draft notice arrived, Leon made it clear he wanted no part of the Army. "I went to Fort Jackson, South Carolina to be inducted. Only I refused to take the oath to go into the Army. I told them I was a Navy man because I had worked on the ships. They had to get an officer to speak with me. Finally I talked them into it. They let me take the oath for the Navy and I took my boot camp in Bainbridge."

By September 1943, when Leon left Charleston, the Navy Shipyard's ways, docks, shops, and sheds were humming around the clock with new construction. Its workforce had swelled to a new high of twenty-six thousand employees, up from two thousand at the beginning of the war (and barely two hundred during the worst of the Depression). Charleston and ten other shipyards, spaced along both coasts and the Gulf of Mexico, were now steadily launching and commissioning Fletcher class destroyers. Fletchers were a new generation of the small, fast warships (often called DDs) designed to protect supply convoys and groups of large warships such as aircraft carriers and battleships against the threat of submarine attack.

Construction of Fletcher class destroyers was first authorized by Congress in mid-1941. During 1942, twenty-eight Fletchers were launched, and a handful were completed and put into service before the year's end. A few, including *Fletcher* itself—the lead and namesake of the class[1]—even saw action in the battle for Guadalcanal. During 1943, Fletcher construction accelerated: more than fifty were launched and average construction time was reduced to less than six months. By war's end, 175 Fletchers were delivered to the Navy—the most ever for any one major warship class.

As the war in Europe swung in the Allies' favor and Atlantic convoys suffered fewer U-boat attacks, more and more of these new DDs were ticketed to the Pacific, either to augment U.S. fleets or replace aging DDs. In addition to protecting aircraft carrier groups from submarine threats, the DDs served as plane guards, positioned close astern of the carriers during launches and landings to retrieve pilots whose aircraft crashed or ditched. Destroyers also escorted supply convoys and, as the United States began island-capturing offensives in the Pacific, became offshore artillery platforms to pound Japanese beach defenses ahead of amphibious landings. Charleston had already produced seven Fletchers and three more were being completed as Leon left for boot camp. One of the last DDs Leon worked on before leaving was the *Albert W. Grant;* among the crew putting *Grant* in commission in November 1943 were Lieutenant (junior grade) Ed Pfeifer, assigned as *Grant's* torpedo officer, and Coxswain First Class Emmett Crump.

Although destroyer production was only one segment of a huge maritime construction program, DDs and other specialized combat ships were critical to the U.S. Navy's resurgence in the global conflict. The keys to resurgence included the Navy's ability to project airpower across wide stretches of ocean, keep sea-lanes open, and deliver men, weapons, and other war supplies. The DDs played a role in all these missions; they might also be key players when the time came for America's navy to confront Japan's navy in decisive sea battle.

DDs and other, even smaller, more specialized vessels also symbolized the particular character of the Navy's resurgence. When sailing in company with vastly bigger aircraft carriers, battleships, and cruisers, these vessels often were called "small boys." They were temporary ships with simple, uniform designs, mass-produced, quickly outfitted, and hustled into action. The useful lives of most of them would not much outlast the war. Some were even left behind in the Pacific; not worth the expenses of returning them to the States, they were purposely sunk or burned to the waterline. And although each usually went to sea with a nucleus of experienced officers and crew, the temporary ships were mostly manned by temporary sailors—reserve seamen, rated petty officers, and junior officers assigned to their first ships and going to sea for the first time. (In fact, the smaller the ship, the greener the crew.) Life aboard such craft defined the war experience for a generation of sailors and naval airmen; if not for the war, most would never have gone to sea or been in harm's way.

⚓

Among these small boys, DDs had the longest tradition. Destroyers originated in the nineteenth century as "torpedo boat destroyers" (designated

TBDs), designed and built to counter the emergence of small attack boats mounting deadly new weapons: self-propelled surface torpedoes.[2] In 1891, during an obscure Latin American civil war, a Chilean Navy attack boat torpedoed and sank a rebel armored vessel. Although the maneuver showed more daring than purpose (the torpedo was launched at a range of one hundred yards, there was no element of surprise and gunfire would probably have been more effective), the world's navies took enough notice to build or buy torpedo boats of their own.

At the same time navy planners, hedging their bets, also began casting about for a weapon to counter the torpedo threat. This turned out to be the TBD. The TBDs' two indispensable requirements were that they carry guns big enough to sink torpedo boats and travel fast enough get within firing range of their prey. Within a few years, the distinctions between the TBD and torpedo boats blurred—in speed, maneuverability, and even armament. The TBDs' growing tactical parity with torpedo boats, combined with the decision to arm them with their own torpedoes, inevitably dropped a curtain on further torpedo boat construction. TBDs became known simply as destroyers. To battleship and cruiser sailors, DDs also became known as "tin cans." The DDs were light and fast, but they also carried little armor protection. Well-placed shells could easily rip one apart. (Despite this, destroyer crewman quickly embraced the reputation of being tin can sailors.)

⚓

By the beginning of the war in the Pacific, DDs were firmly established as resilient fleet workhorses. Like the dependable Model T, the new Fletcher proved to be the classic design for a classic ship. The Fletchers were fast, well sized, well equipped, and sturdy.

A Fletcher class destroyer's main deck ran flush all the way fore and aft, a design feature revived from destroyers of twenty years earlier. (The old four-stack *Decatur* was flush-deck.) This increased the ships' longitudinal strength. The Fletcher's beam was also wider—close to forty feet amidships—a feature that reduced the tendency to roll in rough seas. The Fletcher was large: At 2,100 tons and 376 feet, a Fletcher weighed more than twice what earlier destroyers such like *Decatur* weighed, and was more than 25 percent longer. A Fletcher also carried more than twice the crew of earlier destroyers—295 enlisted and 34 officers. And, although accommodations were tight, every crewman got his own bunk—no one had to strap a hammock.

Below decks Fletchers' crew spaces were divided in half, separated amidships by propulsion gearing, auxiliary machinery, and four boilers housed in two fire-rooms, each supplying a separate, self-contained engine room. These propulsion spaces were named "snipe country" for the engineering crew that operated and maintained the equipment. Deck crewmen and engineering crewmen rarely mingled, and snipes seldom came top-side underway. Probably because of this, although snipes were creatures of flesh and substance, they also took on mythical qualities, like trolls or leprechauns. The sobering truth was that snipes had the most difficult and dangerous shipboard jobs; often trapped below decks, as many had been at Pearl Harbor, snipes suffered the heaviest casualties when a ship was damaged or sunk.

The separation of engine and boiler equipment improved the Fletchers' chances to continue fighting even if one of its power plants got knocked out (but made it no safer or easier for the snipes to escape.) The plants were powerful: a combined sixty thousand horsepower driving two screws was able to deliver flank speed of thirty-six knots, and more in a pinch.

Connecting the below deck halves was a deckhouse extending from the bridge beyond the two boiler stacks. The deckhouse had interior passageways for crew movement; it also contained ship's offices and the officers' wardroom. The bridge superstructure climbed three levels above the deckhouse. The superstructure contained the pilothouse, a closed space for steering and engine controls capped by an open weather bridge. On either side of the pilothouse and extending around the front were exposed bridge wings, places to position lookouts. Astern of the pilothouse were darkened interior spaces containing radar and radio communications transmitters and receivers. As respect for these new technologies increased, the spaces were transformed into Combat Information Centers (CICs), nerve hubs for coordinating the DDs' battle capabilities.

In the forward part of the ship there were three deck levels below the main deck: crew berthing quarters; compartments for communications, sonar, and fire control gear; and ammunition storage magazines. Aft, the taper of the Fletcher hull left room for only two levels: the lower one contained the after ammunition storage magazine; the upper level was split between crew quarters and the after steering compartment. A helmsman positioned in after steering could carry out steering orders should the bridge control signal fail. In the event of a power failure, the ship's rudder could still be moved (though slowly and with murderous difficulty) from after steering by hand-pumping oil through a transversely mounted hydraulic ram.

⚓

Fletchers' armament expanded as new ships in the class were fitted out, usually by adding clusters of 40- and 20-mm antiaircraft gun mounts (by now air attacks were the biggest threat to warships at sea). However, Fletchers' main gun batteries always consisted of five 5-in. 38-caliber[3] Mark 12 guns. After their introduction in the 1930s, the 5-in. 38s quickly became the standard main battery cannon for smaller combatants and the standard secondary battery for cruisers and battleships; they were the dependable car models of naval artillery.

The Mark 12 guns were dual-purpose, used for either surface-to-surface or surface-to-air combat. Ammunition was semi-fixed; the two elements of a 5-in. 38 round were a fifty-four-pound projectile and a separate twenty-eight-pound shell case containing a fifteen-pound powder charge. Rounds could be fired with accuracy at surface targets nine miles out or aircraft six miles up.

Each gun, along with its slide assemblies, gun-laying gears and controls, and fire-control electronics and hydraulics, was enclosed in a steel gun house. Although armored, the gun house enclosure afforded more shelter from wind and water than incoming fire. In tropical waters the enclosure was an oven; in northern latitudes, an icebox. The gun house rode atop a short pedestal attached to the deck and rotated on a roller bearing-propelled base ring. A central column extended below the gun house to a "ready ammunition" room one level down. Suspended in a carousel arrangement beneath the base ring were projectile- and shell-hoists. Projectiles and shell casings were hauled to the ready ammunition carousels from the ships' fore and aft ammunition magazines.

The DDs' 5-in. 38 mounts were numbered from bow to stern: there were two mounts forward of the bridge (the 51 gun on the main deck, the 52 gun on the deck house just forward of and below the bridge); two on the after portion of the deck house (the 53 and 54 guns); and one (the 55 gun)[4] on the fantail. Gun controls were linked by a network of electronics, mechanics, and hydraulics: to the ship's air and surface search radars; to a fire control director (in its own enclosed pedestal mount) perched atop the pilot house; and, below decks, to the plot room.

Plot contained a waist-high steel case that housed the ships' fire control computer. This control computer was the artillery system's nerve center, its electro-mechanical brain. Plot operators entered firing data on hand dials: target range and bearing; ship speed and course; air density and temperature; wind direction and force; gun barrel temperature. The computer resolved these entries into solutions of elevation and deflection for each gun barrel, and signaled them to the mounts. This arrangement enabled each gun to be fired either locally (by direct control of a gun captain in the mount) or remotely, as long as the firing circuit (the connections between radar, director, plot computer, and gun mounts) remained intact.[5]

During firing, a ship's gun mounts would be operated by eight-man crews drawn from among the ship's seamen and deck rates—a sweating, grunting, profane corps de ballet of gun captains, pointers, trainers, sight-setters, fuse-setters, loaders, hot shell men, and ammunition handlers. An experienced gun crew could maintain a firing rate of fifteen rounds per minute—and perhaps, in a sprint, as many as twenty-two rounds per minute, if the firing solution was steady and the loading angle ideal. (Experienced gun crews learned that when a ship was under fire—aircraft overhead, the ship maneuvering for its life, rounds coming in as well as going out—these firing rates and ideal conditions were unlikely.)

⚓

Tin cans also carried torpedoes, a total of ten housed and launched from two quintuple tube mounts, one mount behind each of the ships' two stacks. The mounts could be controlled by ship's radar from either the gunfire director sitting atop the bridge, or by one of two smaller torpedo directors mounted, one level below, on either wing of the bridge. (As a last resort, the torpedoes also could be launched manually from the tubes.)

The Fletchers carried Mark 15 torpedoes, new models designed to be an improvement over the dismally performing Mark 8s used in the first days of the war. The Mark 8s were plagued by appalling shortcomings, whether launched from surface ships or submarines. George Carbon, who'd gone from boot camp at Great Lakes to torpedo training in Norfolk, Virginia, and Newport, Rhode Island, was all too familiar with the baffling behavior of the Mark 8's gyroscope: "The torpedo gyros would go crazy; they'd either dive to the bottom or they'd surface and porpoise along the top." The Mark 8s were also equipped with a tricky magnetic detonation mechanism apt to go off prematurely or not at all. Perhaps most frustrating were the Mark 8's firing pins, which behaved as if operated by an onboard gremlin. When a torpedo managed a straight-on hit, the pin might be crushed by the contact, disarming instead of detonating the torpedo's explosive payload.

Despite improvements in propulsion, guidance, and overall reliability, the Mark 15 made for no more than an adequate weapon. It was certainly no match for the long lance—Japan's sophisticated and dreaded ship-to-ship torpedo. The long lance's reputation was nightmarish. It was powered by pure oxygen; as a result, the long lance wake was barely discernable as it approached a target, even in daylight. By contrast, the Mark 15 was still fueled by a temperamental mix of alcohol, steam, and compressed air. The long lance could both outdistance and outrun the Mark 15, hitting targets as far away as eleven miles at speeds nearing fifty knots. It arrived with an explosive payload thirty percent bigger than the Mark 15s.

Glenn Parkin, now stationed on *Hoel*, one of the new Fletchers launched and commissioned in San Francisco, knew only too well the long lance's effectiveness. Within weeks of surviving the air assaults at Santa Cruz, his former ship *Northampton* was slammed by two well-placed long lance shots during the Battle of Tassafaronga. Listing to port, her fantail consumed in flames fueled and accelerated by aircraft gasoline, *Nora* had gone down by the stern. *Nora*'s evacuation was orderly; the crew, donning kapok life jackets and inflatable belts, took rafts and floater nets into the nighttime waters bounding Guadalcanal, Florida, and Savo Islands. In the morning Glenn was among six hundred *Nora* survivors to be plucked from the sea by the *Fletcher*. The experience earned Glenn thirty days of survivor leave and a billet on *Hoel;* it also erased for him the notion that life on a ship was safer than life as a foot soldier.

⚓

Fletchers were new ships needing new crews. The crews were drawn from "new construction pools" assembled at fleet training centers such as the one in Norfolk, Virginia. Sailors in the pools included new rates coming out of specialty training schools as well as seamen fresh from boot camp. As ships got closer to being commissioned, individuals or groups were assigned. Mel Melvin got his assignment to *Monssen* this way; following basic in Corpus Christie, Mel had first attended shipboard gunnery training in Dam Neck, Virginia. Mel then spent Christmas 1943 in Norfolk before going north to join *Monssen* for its commissioning in Brooklyn on Valentine's Day 1944.

Arriving in advance of most of the pool crew was a core of more experienced senior officers, chiefs, and petty officers responsible for shepherding ship construction through to commissioning. For many sailors, such as Emmett Crump on *Grant,* assignment to a Fletcher was a step up in the world: a newer ship, a promotion to more responsibility. Other arrivals, though, might be wary survivors from sunken ships—like Glenn Parkin on *Hoel.*

In November 1943, Bill Robie joined *Melvin* when she was under construction in Jersey City. Only two years out of "Trade School" (Navy shorthand for graduates of the U.S. Naval Academy at Annapolis), Bill had already served nearly two years aboard the *Boggs,* an ancient four-stacker operating as a minesweeper out of Pearl Harbor. "I arrived at Pearl in January 1942. The entire harbor still had a layer of fuel oil about an inch deep and they were just beginning to pull the ships up. I was on *Boggs* for twenty months with various assignments—first lieutenant, gunnery officer, minesweeping officer." Detached from *Boggs* and sent back to San Francisco in September 1943, Bill received orders to *Melvin*. After training briefly with the crew as it formed in Norfolk, Bill went out ahead as part of *Melvin*'s pre-commissioning nucleus. Bill was impressed as he watched the manpower pieces fall into place. "It amazed me. Even with such a young crew, and a ship as complicated as a Fletcher was, we were still able to get 320 officers and men in shape to fight a war, to fight the ship." One of the seasoned crewmembers was Red Barth, a high-spirited first class signalman from Milwaukee. Although just twenty-one, Red was already a four-year veteran. When the war began, Red was completing a year of duty on the ancient cruiser *Milwaukee;* he then served two more years in Navy Armed Guard gun crew contingents on Liberty Ships crossing the Atlantic and the Mediterranean.

Pulled from the Norfolk pool and assigned to *Richard P. Leary* under construction in Boston Navy Yard, Leon Wolper got one last opportunity to steer himself to where he wanted to be. "The Navy sent me to Norfolk, Virginia, awaiting a ship. First they wanted to assign me to the USS *Texas;* they needed fifty seamen. I found out they were also looking for men for destroyers. I told them I preferred being on a destroyer because I'd worked on several, and was familiar with them. I got on the *Leary* three or four weeks before commissioning. They put me on the deck division, but only for one day. I told them I had ship fitter experience, so they assigned me there."

To officers and crew like Bill, Red, Emmett, and Glenn, who served on older ships during the first desperate stages of the war, the fighting capabilities of the Fletchers fueled pride. Assignment to the lethal new ships also fueled notions of revenge. Some of these notions were embedded in the lineage of the ships: *Monssen* and *McDermut,* for example, took their names from destroyers sunk barely a year before in the struggle for Guadalcanal. For some, revenge was even more personal. Commander Ernest E. Evans, a short, balding Trade School graduate whose demeanor, fireplug build, and Cherokee heritage earned him the nickname "Chief," became the new CO for *Johnston,* one of twenty-one "square-bridge" Fletchers built in Seattle. When Pearl Harbor was attacked, then-Lieutenant Evans was aboard *Alden,* a four stacker assigned to the Southwest Pacific. In January 1942, *Alden* and three other aging destroyers rushed into the strait separating Borneo and the Celebes due south of the Philippine Islands to surprise and sink three Japanese transports. The engagement gave *Alden*'s crew an exhilarating taste of victory, but the taste was short-lived: less than a month later, after participating in a task force that failed to stop the Japanese invasion of Java, *Alden* and her squadron mates were forced to flee under cover of darkness to the safety of Australia.

Johnston was laid down within two months of this galling retreat and launched in March 1943. During *Johnston*'s October 27, 1943, commissioning ceremony, Evans reflected on the differences between attack and humiliating withdrawal. "This is going to be a fighting ship," he promised *Johnston*'s new crew (among them Bob Hollenbaugh, the lead boatswain mate for the 2nd Division) gathered around him in a horseshoe formation on the ship's fantail. "I intend to go in harm's way."

⚓

A hasty or undiscerning eye could have mistaken a Butler[6] class destroyer escort (DE) for a Fletcher class destroyer. Bow to stern, a Butler DE displayed a similar lean, elegant hull line. As with the Fletcher, a topside deckhouse ran two-thirds the length of the Butler main deck; the deckhouse was capped forward by the same sort of bridge structure (though, to be sure, it was lower and more compact). Both the bow and fantail of the

Butler carried the same 5-in. 38 dual-purpose gun mounts carried on the Fletcher. Midships, the familiar profile of a torpedo mount perched behind a raked smoke stack.

From there, the similarities began to break down. First impressions aside, it was clear the DE carried less of just about everything. Where the Fletcher mounted five 5-in. 38 guns, the Butler mounted only two. Instead of two stacks, the Butler had one. Behind the single stack there was a lone torpedo mount; although it looked similar in profile, the mount carried just three Mark 15 torpedoes, not five. The Butler hull, so similar to the Fletcher in line, was nearly one hundred feet shorter, its draft a full yard shallower. Additional details drove home the differences: a displacement of 1,350 tons, less than two-thirds the heft of the Fletcher; two propulsion boilers instead of four; 24,000 combined shaft horsepower compared to 60,000 for the Fletcher; a maximum speed of 24 knots compared to the Fletcher's 33 (though it, too, could squeeze out a bit more); a crew of 186 officers and men, just over half the Fletcher complement of 330. The DE was less in nearly all respects: shorter, lower, lighter, slower, much less formidably armed, and much less versatile. In fighting capability the DE was probably more like the four stackers it was replacing than the Fletchers. Its one basic mission was to shield groups of larger combatants and service ships against submarine threat. If the DDs were small boys, the DEs were (and were sometimes called) "small small boys."

As Fletcher-class destroyers were mass produced in yards on both coasts and the Gulf of Mexico, DE construction went at its own torrid pace; Butler class DEs were built almost exclusively in coastal and inland shipyards in and around Houston, Texas. During the first months of 1944, in Orange, Texas, a town fronting the muddy Sabine River northwest of Houston, Consolidated Steel Corporation workers launched a new Butler class destroyer escort about every eight days. *Dennis, Samuel B. Roberts, John C. Butler,* and *Raymond* were four DEs built during this time, *Butler* and *Raymond* by Consolidated, *Dennis* and *Roberts* by Brown Shipbuilding in Houston.

⚓

For crewmembers with no experience with any other type of warship, the new DEs were impressive and deadly weapons, regardless of their limitations and the fact that they were never designed to fight in big naval engagements. Because most DE crews contained an even smaller nucleus of experienced officers and sailors than did the DDs, the men carried outsized views of the damage a DE could unleash, and the punishment it could withstand. When Dick Rohde reported to *Roberts* in April 1944 as it neared completion in Houston, he, like most of his new shipmates, was naively impressed: "It looked huge and dangerous to me."

Roberts' handful of regular Navy officers and senior enlisted personnel included its commanding officer Lieutenant Commander Bob Copeland and executive officer Lieutenant Bob Roberts, both in their thirties. Copeland, a Tacoma, Washington, attorney and naval reservist called to active duty in 1940, had previously commanded three other ships, including a DE. Roberts was both Trade School and a Mustang—an officer with experience as a Navy enlisted man. Among *Roberts*' very few senior enlisted was a communications chief named Tullio Serafini. Serafini, a Falstaff-proportioned sailor in his fifties, was by far *Robert's* oldest crewman. Serafini had served in the Navy during World War I, been discharged, and then reenlisted for World War II.

Bob Copeland brought with him lawyerly formality, meticulousness, and demand for precision; for his part, Roberts was a quick-minded navigator and tactician. Because of his background, Roberts also possessed credibility among the enlisted. Copeland, Roberts, and Serafini formed an island of age and experience in an ocean of young, green officers and rates like Dudley Moylan, Tom Stevenson, George Carbon, Vince Goodrich, Dick Rohde, and Bill Wilson. It was impossible to gauge (though Copeland and Roberts constantly tried) how these men would respond—individually and collectively—when the chips were down. The best they could do was to insist on discipline, practice, and preparation.

Copeland and Roberts ran a tight ship. Almost from the beginning, *Samuel B. Roberts* showed the discipline and formality of larger ships. Dudley Moylan, who joined *Roberts* as its antisubmarine warfare (ASW) officer after training in Key West, found it intimidating and perplexing at first: "When I first reported to Norfolk I ran into lots of trouble figuring out just what junior officers were supposed to do to stay in step with the senior officers. Copeland was smart and tough. The thing about our DE, it was very well organized; it always looked better than any other DE we tied up against."

Like most ships, *Roberts* also began to organize itself around the functional divisions that defined ship operations. The strikers, petty officers, and chiefs in departments such as Communications, Deck, Engineering, Sonar, and Ordnance became small fraternities within the ship. George Carbon, all of seventeen and fresh from torpedo school, was part of the crew nucleus reporting to *Roberts* during construction in Houston. George joined *Roberts*' Ordnance gang along with two more senior torpedo men, Rudy Skau and Ralph Dyke. "Skau was an A-1 person. He and Dyke were buddies. We were like brothers. All of us in the Ordnance Department pretty much kept together and looked out for each other."

⚓

Smallest of the small—at eighty feet in length and forty-five tons of mahogany and plywood—were the Patrol Torpedo (PT) boats. The size of PTs defined them as boats, not ships; they were, in fact, reincarnations of nineteenth-century torpedo attack boats. Design and testing for this latest torpedo boat version[7] began in the late 1930s—first as a craft for a small-boat navy proposed by Douglas MacArthur to defend against a Japanese invasion of the Philippines, then (coming full circle) as a quick-strike craft able to torpedo large warships under cover of darkness. If it had not been for one crucial design difference, PT planners might have been accused of losing sight of the torpedo boat's demise barely half a century before.

This crucial difference was the new PT's hull: in technical terms, a warped V-bottomed, reduced transom immersion, stepped hydroplane. Starting nearly halfway aft, the PT hull's backbone or chine swept up and into a raked, spoonlike stem. With the right dose of speed—supplied eventually by three high-octane gasoline-powered Packard engines—the PT hull became a lifting body, defying its own element to skim above the surface of the water. Hydroplaning, speed, and maneuverability were design features intended to make the boats so elusive that they could never be hit.

The majority—about three hundred of the five hundred PTs produced during the war—were being built at the Elco (Electric Launch Company) Boat Division in Bayonne, New Jersey.[8] Elco's PT boat design won out over its main competitor Higgins Industries, during Navy-sponsored East Coast sea trials in the spring of 1941. The competition was capped by a 190-mile performance run, an ersatz regatta kicked off from New London, Connecticut. Contestants in this "Plywood Derby" raced through fifteen-foot seas on a course rounding Block Island, Fire Island Lightship, and Montauk Point before returning to New London; the winning Elco finished the course in just under six hours at an average speed close to 40 mph.

By year's end, two squadrons of Elco PTs were on their way to the Pacific fleet. During the attack on Pearl Harbor, some members of Squadron (Ron) 2's crews joined in the harbor defense, firing machine guns at Japanese planes from PTs still perched in storage cradles on cargo ships that carried them across the Pacific. In the Southwest Pacific, Ron 3 boats fought gallantly in futile defense of the Philippines; before the fall of Corregidor, a section of PTs whisked MacArthur and his entourage south to Mindanao for escape by air to Australia. These exploits, and their retelling in the 1942 book *They Were Expendable,* spurred interest in PTs. For many of the eagerly volunteering boat captains and crews, PT service held the same reckless allure as piloting fighter aircraft.

Bill Brown, a Brooklyn native, Villanova University graduate, and a ninety-day wonder from Dartmouth College, was one the officer volunteers. "PTs were a real tricky outfit to get into. Before deciding to go to Villanova I'd gotten an appointment to Annapolis; and as a teenager I'd also been to sea during the summer on vessels of the Red D steamship line. So I thought these experiences helped get me into PTs. Then I found I didn't make as big a splash as I thought with the people who selected me. Actually it was my mother who got me in. And that surprised me because my father was killed in World War I, and I figured she wouldn't want me in any dangerous type of program. But she worked for an admiral in the Third Naval District and she got him to pull some strings, although I didn't find out until later."

Another officer volunteer was Terry Chambers. "I grew up in Southern California, pretty close to the ocean and spent summers on Catalina Island teaching swimming, life saving, and sailing at a Boy Scout camp. Unlike some people from the East Coast who'd grown up with their Daddy's yacht, I'd grown up a product of the Depression. My family's orange ranch went flat-ass broke." After working his way through his junior year at Pomona College, Terry dropped out to enlist in the Navy just after Pearl Harbor. Out of boot camp, Terry's small boat experience got him rated as a boatswain's mate, a boat coxswain, and (like Red Barth) head of a Navy Armed Guard gun crew assigned to a civilian Liberty Ship delivering supplies to the Southwest Pacific.

With one year of enlisted duty under his belt, Terry got orders in summer 1943 to Midshipman school at Northwestern University. "Off duty I hung out at the Chicago Yacht Club, cadging drinks and crewing on some of the members' boats. Near the end of training, a guy named Murray Preston came out from the PT school in Melville, Rhode Island, looking for PT volunteers. Ultimately I got assigned to Melville and ended up in Ron 33, which Murray commanded. Melville was a great place to be, at least until it started to get cold."

Terry Chambers was not the only one recoiling from the winter extremes in Narragansett Bay as experienced on the open decks of a PT. Harley Thronson, a boat officer and a Preston recruit from the University of Wisconsin, was accustomed to the extremes of Midwestern winters in Chippewa Falls, Wisconsin. But Harley was appalled by the conditions on Narragansett Bay. "I was used to the cold, just not this soaking wet kind of cold." Tom Tenner, a quartermaster third class born and raised in Pittsburgh, first volunteered for PT duty in August 1943, but his PT training didn't begin until fall. "I spent October, November, and December in Melville training on boats in the North Atlantic. It was freezing and damn rough. So my first impression of the PT boat was I hated it.

"When it came time for assignment, about half of the guys were scheduled to go right away as replacements to the South Pacific while the other half waited in Melville to pick up new squadrons. I was selected to stay and pick up a new squadron, which meant I'd have to be in Melville for the rest of the winter and maybe in the North Atlantic afterwards—something I didn't want. And I was restless. I'd been in the Navy for a year and hadn't even been shot at.

"It just so happened I was talking with another quartermaster who was scheduled to go to the Pacific. He was married and hoped to spend more time in the States near his wife. I was just the opposite; I wanted to get out of there. So we asked about switching places, and they let us do it. So I was off by train to California."

WILDCATS, AVENGERS, AND COFFINS

When Jim Lischer and Joe McGraw reached the unlikely outpost of Astoria, Oregon, they finally got to fly a real Navy fighter. Both were assigned to VC-10, a squadron forming at rural Clatsop County Airport near where the Columbia River emptied into the Pacific. The "V" in VC-10 stood for "heavier-than-air" aircraft and the "C" stood for "composite." Composite meant that some VC-10 pilots would fly torpedo bomber aircraft while others, like Jim and Joe, would fly fighter escorts.

At first VC-10 fighter pilots flew patched up F4F Wildcats, dubbed "War Wearies," returned from combat in the Pacific. (One F4F had arrived with a simple explanatory tag: "Found under a canvas tarpaulin on Guadalcanal.") The Grumman Company–manufactured F4F had been the Navy's primary carrier-borne fighter aircraft since the invasion of Guadalcanal. While it stood up better in combat than its hapless predecessor, the Brewster Buffalo, the F4F still couldn't fully match up against the lighter, faster, and more maneuverable Japanese Zero.

In time, new Wildcat versions, called FM-2s, began to replace the F4Fs. Joe McGraw became a Wildcat connoisseur—especially of the version he eventually flew in combat. "The Navy wanted the next generation F6F fighters real badly, so they made Grumman turn over F4F production to General Motors. Meantime Grumman had been advancing the design and performance of the F4F—by then they'd gotten to the F4F4 version. When they got to the F4F8 version, the designers decided to jerk out the old heavy Pratt & Whitney engine and put in a lighter weight nine-cylinder Wright radial engine. They took out some of the armor, two of the guns, and a lot of the ammo to lighten it up. They also put a higher tail on it. Those were the plans Grumman turned over to GM, which cranked out the FM-2. So actually what we were flying were F4F8s, only they were made by GM."

The FM-2 was a Wildcat, but a wilder Wildcat: "It could climb faster. It was lighter and it could turn tighter. And the word was if you didn't let a Zero sucker you below 180 knots, you could stay right with it." Lighter and tighter, the FM-2 was also stronger: "The old Pratt & Whitney engine only had 1,250 horsepower. They boosted the Wright radial engine up to 1,350 and chief mechanics on the line claimed they could get the horsepower up to 1,400. I don't know if they really did. But it sure could consume a lot of fuel."

Although the squadron had better airplanes, it was clear to Joe and to other pilots who'd spent so much time honing individual skills, VC-10 still lacked something just as important—its cohesiveness, its soul. "We were really a small air group, but didn't learn to become an air group until we left Astoria and got down to California."

⚓

The bomber piece of the composite squadrons was the TBM Avenger— another General Motors manufacture of a Grumman design. The Avenger was a big, lumbering aircraft with a three-man crew: pilot, turret gunner, and radioman. At nine tons fully loaded, the whale-bodied Avenger was the largest and heaviest-single engine airplane ever flown from a carrier deck. The Avenger's air combat virtues would turn out to be its rugged simplicity, reliability, and stability as a weapons platform—although its tragic first baptism under fire offered little first evidence of this. Five of six early version Avengers operating from Midway Island were shot down during a sortie against Japanese main force carriers at the Battle of Midway. The one surviving Avenger was severely mauled and its gunner killed. Its return to the airstrip proved only that the Avenger could absorb a lot of punishment before being disabled or splashed.

Tom Van Brunt got his first introduction to the Avenger at torpedo bomber training in Fort Lauderdale. "I didn't have a choice. You went where the need was. Even so, I hated it because I really hoped I'd get back in PBYs—I'd done quite a bit of time in them. The TBM was a powerful plane. It was also pretty slow." One of the frustrating things Tom learned as he began training was the difficulty the TBM had in successfully launching the Mark 13 aerial torpedo. "It was so discouraging. I remembered dropping several fish that porpoised and went in circles towards the beach instead of at the target."

Fortunately, by 1944, the Navy had learned some important lessons from the disastrous aerial torpedo attacks during the Battle of Midway; changes were on the way. An astonishingly simple modification to the torpedo made new tactics possible. Tom was one of the beneficiaries: "By the time I got to the fleet, they'd invented a Rube Goldberg device that really worked. They put a plywood cylinder—it was called a pickle barrel— on the nose of the torpedo and a plywood box on the stern to stabilize it in flight. It allowed for a smoother entry at a higher altitude, which reduced the danger for pilots coming in. The plywood nose guard just cracked off, which softened the landing. You got a much truer run. The torpedoes didn't porpoise or wander in circles."

Tom did his carrier qualification landings on *Wolverine* flying a greatly modified TBM. "It didn't have any armor on it and it was lighter than a regular torpedo bomber." Tom got down successfully on his first approach. Even with the lightened TBMs, the technique after landing was to unhook and pull the big aircraft to *Wolverine*'s stern to give the pilot adequate deck space for take off. Here Tom's own case of CarQual nerves kicked in: "I got ready to go, then the signalman on deck told me to cut my engine down and listen to my radio. The *Wolverine*'s captain was on the circuit telling the signalman to hold me. My rudder was fluttering so much there was no chance of taking off successfully. My feet were out of control, disconnected from my brain: just pumping up and down on the rudder pedals. So I had to catch my breath, stop my dancing feet, and get ready to go all over again. I did dozens of carrier landings afterwards, but I can't say I ever got completely comfortable with it. There was just such a small margin for error."

⚓

For composite squadron pilots like Jim, Joe, and Tom, landing on the *Wolverine*'s short, narrow flight deck was to be important preparation for their combat flying. Rather than being assigned the prestigious fleet carriers, composite squadrons were headed to escort carriers, new, small, and decidedly unglamorous types of aircraft carriers.

Like DDs, DEs, and PTs, the escort carriers (designated CVEs[9]) were temporary ships designed for specific wartime needs. CVEs combined the capabilities of providing mobile airborne antisubmarine defense for Atlantic supply convoys (an idea concocted by President Franklin Roosevelt) and, in the vast Pacific, of shuttling replacement aircraft between the U.S. mainland, fleet aircraft carriers, and captured island airstrips (the brainchild of Pacific Fleet Admiral Chester Nimitz).

In April 1943, at the Henry Kaiser Swan Island Shipyard in Portland, Oregon, First Lady Eleanor Roosevelt christened the USS *Casablanca*, the first of seventy-eight escort carriers built during the war. The CVEs were constructed around thin-skinned merchant class hulls, a concept that spawned a lot of nicknames, including "Baby Flattops" and "Jeep Carriers." To their crews they were known as "Kaiser Coffins"—a morbid tribute to their builder, their slow speed, and their frightening lack of armor protection.

The CVEs may have been slow, but their construction was swift. *Casablanca* was built from scratch in nine months. By early autumn of 1943, it took only six months to build a new CVE, and, by November, only seventy days. In December, as a Christmas present to President Roosevelt, Kaiser Shipyard workers even accelerated this schedule to launch *Gambier Bay*, one CVE ahead of the 1943 construction quota. By the end of the year, a whole new use had devised for the escort carriers. They would accompany Pacific island invasion fleets, freeing up larger attack carriers to roam freely and launch first strike missions closer to Japan's homeland.

Like *Gambier Bay*, most CVEs were named for American lakes and for coastal bays. Several others, including *Casablanca*, were named for a growing list of U.S. Army, Navy, and Marine Corps campaign victories.

Perhaps the most prestigious of these names went to *Midway,* a CVE commissioned on October 23, 1943.

Casablanca, Gambier Bay, Midway, and other escort carriers could carry and launch thirty aircraft. Composite squadron aircraft were a roughly two-to-one mix of FM-2s and TBMs. At sea the TBMs provided antisubmarine protection for escort carrier task groups, whereas the FM-2s flew covering combat air patrols (CAPs). For amphibious landings, Avengers and Wildcats also provided close-in aerial bombing and strafing support for troops ashore. Unlike the bigger, faster, but scarcer fleet carriers, the escorts could be deployed to support the amphibious forces during the full duration of an island invasion: the CVEs came to stay.

The CVEs looked like boxy, swarming insect hives when seen from a distance during flight operations. A small, open island superstructure—the equivalent of a flight tower at a small dirt airstrip—sat well forward on the ship's starboard side. The space for takeoffs and landings was menacingly short: barely half the length of flight decks on the newer fast attack carriers. When Tom Van Brunt reached the Pacific he had an opportunity to experience the difference. "I got permission to land on *Essex* one day while it was operating in a rest area. I visited a friend onboard and had lunch. Before my approach I'd started to ask *Essex* flight control which runway I should take. My friend and I had a good laugh over that. It really was a much bigger ship."[10]

SHAKEDOWNS

The year 1944 marked America's third year of fighting in the Pacific. America's Navy—its ships, aircraft, and manpower—had become both substantially bigger and strikingly different from the aging, inflexible force crushed at Pearl Harbor. Navy and private industry shipyards along three coastlines had already produced more than five hundred surface combat ships. Although the roster of these new ships included some of the biggest types of combatants—five fleet carriers, six battleships, and twenty cruisers were launched or commissioned in 1942 and 1943—the roster was weighted, in number and tonnage toward the temporary ships. By the end of 1943, with a momentum that continued until the end of the war, 210 destroyers, 233 destroyer escorts, and 35 escort carriers had been launched.

Before the war, many of the boys reporting to these ships had never glimpsed or sensed an ocean: Bob Hollenbaugh from Indiana, for example; or Verner Carlsen and Jim Lischer from Iowa; Emmett Crump from Kentucky; Mel Melvin from Missouri; George Carbon from Ohio; Don Bujold and Bill Wilson from Michigan; Holly Crawforth from Nevada; Glenn Parkin from Utah; Ted Gurzynski and Harley Thronson from Wisconsin. Others, like Bill Brown, Terry Chambers, Dudley Moylan, Tom Stevenson, and Leon Wolper, who grew up so close to the ocean that it barely dented their senses, soon began to experience the ocean with new intimacy.

Boys mostly accustomed to living in one place and perhaps contenting themselves with dreams about travel became true itinerants. They traveled often, singly or in groups, usually packed into crowded, cross-country trains for trips of days and sometimes weeks. Through boot camp, officer training, specialty training, replacement pools, and final assignments, sailors and aviators, enlisted and officers, often traced convoluted paths. (Many first trips actually took them further from the ocean than where they began before finally depositing them at its shores.) These included Larry Epping: from rural Oregon to New York City for Midshipman training, on to Philadelphia for damage control training, and then back to Oregon to join *Gambier Bay;* Mel Melvin: from heartland Missouri to coastal Corpus Christi for basic, to Virginia and finally to Brooklyn to join *Monssen;* John Montgomery: from Baltimore always west, first to Great Lakes Naval Training Center near Chicago for basic and then on west to Bremerton and duty on *California;* Ed Pfeifer: from Vermont to South Bend for Midshipman training, then to torpedo school in Newport, then south to Norfolk and Charleston to join *Grant;* Dick Rhode: from New York to Rhode Island for basic, then to Boston, then down to Norfolk and west to Houston to join *Roberts.*

Most joined ships for the first time, while others brought experience; some had even reached the war's most remote outposts. Before being assigned to *Melvin,* Red Barth saw action in the Atlantic and Mediterranean, as did Emmett Crump on *Grant.* Bill Robie had served in the Central Pacific; Terry Chambers, Holly Crawforth, and Glenn Parkin in the Southwest Pacific.

The Navy's pilots seemed to be the most nomadic, although their itineraries were hardly glamorous. Since the beginning of the war (and even before), Burt Bassett, Jim Lischer, Joe McGraw, and Tom Van Brunt were posted to a string of remote airstrips in Illinois, Missouri, North Carolina, Florida, and Texas. In pursuit of becoming real naval aviators flying combat aircraft, they learned to fly a succession of always memorable, often inferior airplanes. Burt joined the Navy in 1940. Tom joined soon after and, by the end of 1943, both had already over one thousand solo flying hours. But all this experience hardly seemed to matter: none of their stops and none of their hours had been with the fleet. In the war's third year neither had combat experience.

As 1944 began, the lives of the men, their ships, and units began pointing to common coordinates.

⚓

The next steps for the freshly commissioned ships and newly assembled crews were sea trials, shakedown, and deployment. Where, how, and how long depended on ship type and where it was built and commissioned. Ships launched on the West Coast (in San Pedro or San Francisco, Puget Sound or Seattle) with few exceptions were bound for the Pacific. Ships launched in East Coast or Gulf shipyards (in Bath, Maine; Boston; Brooklyn; Staten Island; Kearney; Charleston; Chickasaw, Louisiana; Orange; or Brownsville) might go either way.

Readying new DDs and DEs with new crews to fight at sea was quite complex. It was a work in progress—always more preparation and more practice. The purpose of sea trials was to reveal and correct the inevitable, sometimes minor, sometimes ghastly malfunctions, missing parts, and flaws of hasty construction. Shipyard workers and technicians came onboard at night to correct what the day's activity revealed. Crews also began running through the routines—in Navy parlance, drills and evolutions—that would one day enable the ships to operate (and to fight) instinctively. It was rough going at first, and sea trials were often marked by episodes of excruciating embarrassment played out in full view. Dick Rohde and others on *Roberts* recalled how the ship first backed into the Sabine River from her berth at Brown Shipbuilding—and promptly plowed stern-first into mud flats on the opposite bank. During the first stages of sea trails, poorly executed evolutions like this were the norm. On some days, it seemed some ships could just barely get out to sea and back, barely avoiding collision, grounding, or sinking. Inevitably, though, things improved as the cans got ready for shakedown.

At sea, the crews' lives and routines were warped into complex schedules of conditions, watches, and special details. Condition levels described how much of a ship's crew and weaponry stood ready at a given time: all during Condition I, half during Condition II, one-third during Condition III. Watches—shifts, usually four hours long, formalized in assignment schedules called watch bills—specified crewmember stations for each condition, for each special detail, and for each moment of the twenty-four-hour day. Special details were teams cobbled together for specific situations with names like Sea and Anchor Detail, or Boarding and Recovery Detail, or Provisioning and Stores Detail. In this mosaic of conditions, watches, and special details, almost everyone onboard had many assignments. On Navy ships, only the CO filled just one role.

Crewmen were assigned to ship divisions, and divisions were consolidated into departments. Within these departments and divisions, officers and crew had their day jobs: their ranks, rates, and seniority in departments such as Communications, Ordnance, Supply, or Engineering. Although there were exceptions, men were often assigned to watch conditions, stations, and special details having little to do with their day jobs. Men adjusted to a patchwork of responsibilities.

The day job for Dick Ralstin, an eighteen-year old Indiana native and a third class motor machinist mate in the Engineering Department on *McDermut,* was to operate *McDermut*'s topside auxiliary diesel generator.

But Dick also stood throttle watches in *McDermut's* after engine room, was assigned to a damage control party during repair emergencies, and operated the ship's whaleboat for the Boarding and Recovery Detail. Although Emmett Crump was the primary whaleboat coxswain on *Grant*, he also stood Condition I as a loader in *Grant's* 51 mount. The exceptions included sailors like Dick Rohde on *Roberts* and Glenn Parkin on *Hoel*; Dick always worked and stood watches in the Communications Shack; Glenn both worked and stood watches in the 52 mount.

Ship COs, XOs, and department heads also adjusted watch bills to suit particular circumstances. Because of their antisubmarine roles, *Roberts* and her sister DEs tended to be top heavy with sonar operators. To balance this bounty with other manpower shortages, CO Bob Copeland mingled sonar and radar personnel during standard watches to keep them alert and to make them interchangeable should a battle leave missing pieces. Watch-standing sonar petty officers like Vince Goodrich were in constant motion: "The radar men stood sonar watch and the sonar men stood radar watch. You'd spend half an hour on the air search radar, half an hour on the plotting table, half an hour on sonar, and half an hour on surface search radar. Then you'd repeat the cycle. With every fifth watch we wouldn't be in sonar or radar at all: we were on lookout, then helm, then back to lookout, and then bridge talker."

General Quarters (GQ) or battle stations (the practical names for Condition I) was the all-hands, no exceptions evolution—the pinnacle of shipboard readiness. Although crews might walk to other details or drills, everyone ran (feet pounding on steel decks, moving forward and up on the starboard side, downward and aft on the port side). With time, crew response to GQ trumpet or bell alarms was little short of Pavlovian. GQ was get to your station. GQ was dogged down doors. GQ was helmets and life jackets, shirts buttoned at necks and wrists, pants tucked into socks. GQ could be called in an instant, and last for minutes or hours. GQ was the moment of the ship's utmost power—and her utmost vulnerability.

⚓

Bermuda was the shakedown destination for East Coast–built Fletchers such as *Grant, McDermut, Melvin,* and *Monssen,* and Gulf Coast–built Butler-class DEs such as *Dennis, Roberts, Butler,* and *Raymond.* Although the island's tranquil seas and temperate climate were welcome, Bermuda was no cruise ship paradise for the tin cans and their sailors. Each day of their four-week shakedowns, the ships left Great Sound at first light for full schedules of drills and scored exercises, not returning until well after darkness.

Although the DD and DE crews endured the same day in, day out rigors, the two ship types pursued different shakedown agendas. For DDs, the emphasis was surface warfare, particularly the use of the guns—the 5-in. 38s, their 40- and 20-mm—and the Mark 15 surface torpedoes. (As coxswain of destroyer *McDermut*'s whaleboat, Dick Ralstin spent much of the ship's shakedown trawling to recover practice torpedoes. One elusive missing torpedo was found only when it surfaced to punch a hole in the whaleboat's hull.)

DEs also tested guns and torpedoes, but submarine detection using sonar was most critical training for them. Listening for submerged subs was slow, frustrating work requiring reserves of patience and perseverance that came hard to young men. Vince Goodrich recalled the tedious routine: "Sonar worked like an underwater sound searchlight—you pinged, trained the transducer, and listened for the echo. Starting on the port or starboard beam, you'd ping in small segments up to the bow, ping there twice, and then slew to the opposite beam. Once you found a target, you pinged, listened, and trained to get closer." Under real combat conditions, once a target was acquired, tracked, and cornered, tin cans dropped cylindrical explosive depth charges from their fantails, and fired smaller explosive charges called hedgehogs to destroy the opponent. During the shakedowns in Bermuda, practice opponents were most often Italian U-boats, captured when Italy surrendered to the Allies in 1943.

DDs and DEs had considerable success using these tactics and weapons, in both the Atlantic and in the Pacific. The fabled sub killing exploits of *England,* another DE, were particularly inspiring for the DE sailors. In May 1944, operating near the Solomon Islands in the Southwest Pacific, in less than two weeks' time *England* detected and destroyed six Japanese submarines.

⚓

Despite the short stay, the restrictions, the long days, and infrequent opportunities for liberty ashore, Bermuda was still the first "overseas" stop for most of the ships and their crews—a rare chance to be out in the world. Briefly released from shipboard confinement and discipline, the temporary sailors tried to cut loose, though their antics fell well short of the legendary exploits of hardened seamen returning to shore after months of danger and deprivation. During *Melvin's* December 1943 shakedown, for example, Bill Robie and two buddies stole the officers club Christmas tree. "We decided the club's tree would look better on our ship. So we took it back and set it up on *Melvin*'s bow, right up in the eyes of the ship. There it was for all to behold on Christmas morning—including the base admiral." *Melvin*'s crew got confined to the ship for the rest of its stay in Bermuda.

Detailed for Shore Patrol duty during *Roberts*' stay in Bermuda, Dick Rohde sported an unloaded forty-five-caliber handgun and rode the streets of Hamilton clinging to the back of a caged pickup truck to collect drunken sailors. When his own turn for liberty came, however, Dick, along with a Mormon shipmate from Utah, chose a tamer pursuit: they rode a narrow gauge railroad to the far side of the island and, in what seemed to both an exotic moment, sat, gazed at the Atlantic, and downed bottles of ginger beer.

Roberts' first stop following shakedown was Boston, where she went into dry dock for final repairs and alterations. The day after her arrival at Charlestown Navy Yard, Jack Roberts, a second class seaman, reported onboard for duty. Virtually no one on the crew knew that Jack was a brother of the ship's namesake, a Navy coxswain and Navy Cross recipient who died on Guadalcanal trying to rescue some pinned-down Marines on an embattled beach. Two other crewmen—the executive officer and one of the enlisted firemen—also were named Roberts, and this helped preserve the secret. No one found out for two or three months.

Off Long Island, on the transit from Boston to Norfolk, *Roberts* stuck a gray whale. The collision killed the whale and unleashed a torrent of blood; it also damaged *Roberts'* sonar transducer and warped its propeller. *Roberts* limped into Norfolk and was delayed for repairs. The delay changed *Roberts'* destination; her assignment to the Atlantic—most likely to support the imminent invasion at Normandy—was cancelled. While *Roberts* sat in dry dock for repair she also was repainted in the "dazzle" camouflage pattern[11] standard for Navy ships in the Pacific.

⚓

For the smallest and largest of the temporary ships—the PTs and CVEs—shakedown experiences were less orchestrated and more makeshift. In Brooklyn, personnel from Melville and PT boats fresh from construction in Bayonne were assembled into crews. "We were thrown into a replacement pool," Bill Brown recalled. It was a bit like picking sides for a sandlot game—a process at once casual and closely studied: "A squadron officer would say, 'Well I'll take Brownie . . . or I'll take this guy.' It went like that."

Bill Brown and Terry Chambers were both chosen for Ron 33. At first Terry got no boat: "We were two boats short in the Squadron—ten boats instead of the usual twelve; at two officers to a boat, we had more officers than boats to assign to them to. There were obviously going to be ten skippers and ten execs. So I became the 33's senior Ensign and its ordnance officer and scrounger.

"I ran into an enlisted quartermaster with some experience in the Pacific and who also happened to work at the supply depot in the Brooklyn Navy Yard. Through him I cadged equipment I knew we'd need in the Pacific and other squadrons would have a hard time getting. All I needed to do was admire something in the depot and it would be assigned to Ron 33.

"When we left Brooklyn Navy Yard heading south I was on the 493 Boat as a supernumerary. Bill Brown was the skipper. We traveled as much as we could down the Inland Waterway. We went though Chesapeake Bay to reach Norfolk, and one night we tied up next to somebody's farmhouse. In the morning the topside was covered with chicken shit and we had to scrape off the entire boat off before getting underway. We worked our way down on the inside to Jacksonville and then on to Miami for shakedown."

In Miami boat crews learned new realities about the use and misuse of PTs in combat. Some of their instructors were Guadalcanal veterans, including a scrawny jg named Jack Kennedy. Kennedy was known to the bigger world as the second son of the U.S. Ambassador to England. To the smaller world of PT crews he was known for having his 109 Boat carved in half during a nighttime tangle with Japanese destroyers—and returning to tell about it. The lesson from these actions was that PTs were neither torpedo knockout punchers nor the untouchable phantoms they were supposed to be. They carried inferior Mark 8 torpedoes; in the usual confusion of an attack, there was no time to line up a good shot. Later engagements in the Central Solomons and along the coast of New Guinea were demonstrating how PTs operated more effectively as opportunistic gunboats, coordinating with ground forces and working close to shore to shoot up coastal barge traffic, troop concentrations, and gun emplacements.

After shakedown in Miami, Ron 33's boats leapfrogged to Cuba, Jamaica, and Bogotá, Columbia, on their way to the Panama Canal. The boats often encountered heavy seas; when Terry Chambers took the wheel of the 493 Boat he tried his best to let it ride like a surfboard. "Every other boat was climbing up and then plunging into the troughs. They kept telling me to keep in formation, keep in formation. Instead I'd go off to the right and to the left, letting the boat follow the shape of the wave."

On the west side of the canal, the boats were hoisted onto supply ships for transport to the Pacific. The 493 was one of four Ron 33 boats cradled on the deck of a gasoline tanker. To Bill Brown, the long journey to the Pacific, with the boats strapped to a floating volcano, seemed to have fate written all over it. "We were all anxious. We felt like we were ripe for plucking."

⚓

Shakedowns for the first crop of CVEs were brief. Beyond hauling aircraft, it seemed as if the Navy lacked a precise idea of what the escorts should be prepared for. To Tony Potochniak, an aircraft machinist mate assigned to *Gambier Bay* from the CVE crew pool in Seattle, it seemed the ship went directly from commissioning to work, with no preparation in between: "Our shakedown consisted of going up to Bremerton where they degaussed the ship and we picked up supplies."

Larry Epping was an Ensign in *Gambier Bay*'s Construction and Repair (C&R) Division. His first ride into open water was both jarring and reassuring. "When *Gambier Bay* first got ready to go to sea, we crossed the bar at Astoria—kind of a rough bar to cross. It was also my first time at sea, it was storming, and it was almost night. The ship was light because there were no planes aboard and we were going up to Bremerton to stock up on torpedoes, bombs, and other explosives. It was bouncing around a lot, and just about everybody onboard was sick. But I had my sea legs already. I never got sick." Another of *Gambier Bay*'s young Ensigns was not as fortunate. Fred Mallgrave, a twenty-three-year-old from suburban Philadelphia and a Drexel graduate, was assigned to the Mechanical (M) Division. As Fred stood watch in the after engine compartment—a throbbing inferno in snipe country well below *Gambier Bay*'s waterline—he couldn't remember ever being so sick.

After taking on supplies, *Gambier Bay* and Tony's aviation gang went right to work. "We loaded 90 aircraft for a ferrying trip from San Diego to Eniwetok and Kwajalein, to replenish airplanes lost by the CVAs, mainly the *Enterprise*. Every space was occupied going out: the hangar deck was full, the flight deck was full. On the way home we picked up a bunch of War Wearies in Hawaii. We took all kinds of derelicts from Ford Island— fighters, bombers, even a PBY. They'd seen their last days; when we got back they all had to be taken off by crane. Back in San Diego we loaded planes from our squadron VC-10 and operated with them for a few days off the coast. Then we headed back to the Pacific."

Arriving from chaplain school in time for *Gambier Bay*'s commissioning, Verner Carlsen noticed he'd come up short on an essential piece of equipment. "The usual custom was if you came aboard ship as a chaplain you'd expect to find a field organ. Well, there was no such thing; these small carriers didn't get the deal some of the others did. So, in Astoria, I'd gone ashore with another fellow who said he was interested in forming a ship's band. We found some instruments and brought back two saxophones, a couple of clarinets, even a drum. *Gambier Bay* was the only escort carrier with a band. When we arrived in Pearl Harbor on our first trip out, the band assembled on deck to play."

ODD COGS

Burt Bassett and Tom Van Brunt didn't cross paths after college, but their pilot careers were remarkably similar. Because of his chronic motion sickness, Burt was limited in the aircraft he could fly. Tom had originally qualified on multi-engine PBYs, but the Navy had little need for more PBY pilots. By 1944, both were pilots with lots of flight time yet no fleet combat experience; they were out of synch, odd cogs in the Navy's increasingly efficient system of keeping ships and air groups replenished with manpower to fly single-engine fighters and bombers. With the war in the Pacific finally at full throttle, Burt and Tom were only now headed where so many of the younger pilots they'd trained had already flown and fought.

In September 1943, when Burt Bassett left Corpus Christie with orders to San Diego, he expected to be assigned to a few months of familiarization training in multiengine aircraft. He and his wife Louise drove their Ford coupe east to Florida to deposit their young child with grandparents and then hustled west to San Diego, wondering all the way whether their gasoline and tire rations would get them the distance.

"When we got to San Diego I went to the assignment office and found out they'd discontinued the program—there was no more need for multiengine pilots. They told me I'd be going to a Corsair Squadron—a fighter squadron." That assignment only lasted twenty-four hours. "I had to go back and tell them about my motion sickness troubles, so they said okay, you're going to torpedo bombers."

Burt's first introduction to the TBM Avenger came when he reported to VC-10 in Astoria. "At that time the Avenger was the most fearsome of all planes. I'd never seen one before I got to Clatsop. It looked like a giant to me. I was pretty impressed when I saw it fly." VC-10 was assigned to *Gambier Bay,* then undergoing final fitting in the Kaiser Shipyard upriver in Portland. As *Gambier Bay* was being readied for sea, VC-10 prepared to become a squadron.

"We received planes in Astoria, and the men began to gather from many different points. The airport was right near the beach, at the end of the Lewis and Clark Trail. Most of the squadron members lived down in Seaside in cabins. Ed Huxtable, the commanding officer, was already there. He was an Academy graduate. He turned out to be a good leader, quiet, informal. I happened to be the next senior by a few numbers, a Lieutenant. So they made me Executive Officer. At 27 I was older than most."

VC-10 also became home to several other senior Lieutenants and former instructors like Burt, including two twenty-four-year-old fighter pilots. Gene Seitz, a transplanted Californian, a self-confessed "airplane fanatic" and an instructor at Pensacola, had been in naval aviation since 1938. Dick Roby, a Corpus Christi instructor like Burt Bassett, was a New Jersey native who joined the Navy out of Drew University. "I was sent to Corpus along with a heck of a lot of other people and all of us spent most of two years there as instructors. When I got to the West Coast they assigned me to three different squadrons. The first two took me out because they had too many lieutenants. When I got to VC-10 I discovered there were actually more lieutenants than in the other two squadrons, all of them fighter pilots, except Burt."

Two of VC-10's older officers, neither of them fliers, ended up being Burt Bassett's best friends. One was the VC-10 flight surgeon Wayne Stewart, and the other was air combat intelligence officer (ACI) Vereen Bell. "The ACI was a prominent young man. He'd written a couple of popular books and one of them was made into a movie called *Swamp Water*[12] Vereen was off to a fast start. And of all things he was from Thomasville, Georgia, twenty-five miles from my home. My wife Louise was also from Thomasville and she went to school there. Louise and Vereen shared a lot in common and, though he was six years older, they both knew many of the same people."

Burt got no special training on the Avenger itself. "It was just another single engine airplane. We got a short cockpit checkout, with somebody looking over your shoulder. Everyone was expected to get it off the ground and get it back safely."

In its roughly assembled form, VC-10 moved from Oregon down to California where, over the next weeks, both the FM-2 and TBM pilots learned to fly as a team. The fighter pilots learned how to provide cover for the TBMs, while the torpedo bomber pilots practiced attack maneuvers. "We practiced bombing, using one-hundred-pound water filled canisters, and torpedo runs. Finally we learned how to fire wing-mounted rockets: HVAR, High Velocity Aircraft Rockets. Having them gave us three buttons on the stick: one for the machine guns; one for the bombs or torpedo; and one for the rockets."

Meanwhile, an important matter loomed: landing the FM-2s and the ponderous TBMs on the short, sea-tossed flight deck of an escort carrier. Burt Basset recalled: "We began to get some practice in carrier-type landings. This was practicing on land; we hadn't yet tried to land the thing on a carrier. Taking the TBM in slowly was the hardest part. You almost stalled the aircraft to make a carrier-type landing, maybe five, six, seven knots above stall speed."

For Burt it got no easier at sea. "We went out for two weeks of carrier practice. The first week on another escort carrier, the *Altamaha;* the second on *Gambier Bay.* This was March and April, and the Pacific swells were so high it caused a lot of problems and a lot of damage to the aircraft, especially the big TBMs.

"Both weeks were disastrous. We lost our first TBM pilot out there. He came in too fast. He was waved off from his landing and pulled straight up, but he pulled too hard, and the plane went up and over. His crew got out, but he didn't. Another pilot had to ditch his aircraft on two consecutive flights. Though the reason both times was engine failure, he was finally relegated to the beach and gave up his wings—it was just too much for him. On one of my landings both wheels collapsed; the rims were shattered. This was typical of what was happening."

⚓

It was much the same story for Tom Van Brunt: more than one thousand hours in his flight log, but most of those hours were in Stearmans; some

TBM training but no operational experience. Like all the other instructors, as Tom moved up in rank he moved down in the ways the Navy could use him. Unlike Burt, though, Tom had not yet found his way to a squadron home. As the war surged forward, he seemed to be left further behind.

"When I got to San Diego to be assigned to a squadron, I was a Lieutenant (jg). I expected to be on the West Coast for three or four months at squadron training, so I'd brought my wife and baby and a house trailer. By then they had lieutenants coming back by the dozen from the fleet, and they were turning them around and sending them back as replacements. So they said they were going to make me a replacement pilot too, which meant going out to the Pacific by the first available ship. I ended up saying goodbye to my family and headed out."

Opening Shots

MARIANAS

The division of four FM-2s circled over the cane fields, jagged ridges, and caves of northern Saipan. Gene Seitz was division leader; Chuck Dugan[1] flew on Gene's wing; Dean Gilliatt,[2] a Coral Sea veteran, led 2nd section; Joe McGraw, the formation's "tail end Charlie," flew last, on Dean's wing. "We were frustrated being on CAP. We wanted to have at 'em. The closest we could get that day was circling over the island." Gene Seitz shared Joe's frustration. "We all felt pumped up, saying to ourselves 'Here come some tough customers.' We wanted to draw first blood; we were ready to start the war. As far as we were concerned, because we'd just arrived, the war was just starting."

Each pilot carried a six-shot thirty-eight-caliber pistol tucked into a shoulder holster. Later, the four of them talked about what happened next. "It wasn't a formation thing," Joe remembered, "but we all did it." It was easy to open a Wildcat canopy part way—three or four inches—and lock it into position. "All we had to do then was roll, point the thirty-eight out the window, aim so you didn't punch a hole in the wing, and pull the trigger."

Gene fired first. "I pulled back my canopy, took the pistol from my holster, and fired six rounds into the island of Saipan. So did the others." Joe McGraw was surprised at the noise, "It was the first shot I fired in combat and it was a hell of a lot louder than I thought it would be."

⚓

During the first months of 1944, the sailors and airmen on temporary ships finally began joining the two streams of U.S. power converging through the islands and sea-lanes of the Western Pacific. In one stream were Army and Navy forces under the overall command of General Douglas MacArthur. MacArthur's forces surged up through the Equator in the Southwest Pacific, mounting a series of amphibious assaults up the long coastline of New Guinea. MacArthur's campaign pointed northward—both strategically and emotionally—to the retaking of the Philippine Islands.

In the other stream were Navy and Marine forces commanded by Admiral Chester Nimitz. These forces pressed westward in a giant plunging scoop across the vast Central Pacific, pointing directly to Japan's home islands. On the way they wrested islands in the Gilbert, Marshall, and Caroline chains from Japanese control. As the spring and summer months of 1944 brought MacArthur's stream of power to the Vogelkop—the "bird's head"–shaped northwestern tip of New Guinea—so they brought U.S. Central Pacific forces to the doorstep of Japan's three island strong-holds in the Marianas archipelago: Saipan, Tinian, and Guam. The Japa-nese faced a sobering challenge in the Marianas. Just as America's spring 1942 naval victory at Midway kindled its hopes for ultimate victory in the Pacific, so Japan's loss of the Marianas would be more than a strategic step back. It would all but extinguish any prospect for holding the remnants of its Pacific empire.

The fifteen-island Marianas chain, named for Spain's seventeenth-century Queen Maria Anna, stretch in a four-hundred-mile north-south arc across sea lanes connecting China, Japan, the Philippines, and Hawaii. At the chain's southern end are the Marianas' four principal islands—Saipan, Tinian, Rota, and Guam. Rota and Guam were touchpoints in Magellan's voyage of exploration The larcenous behavior of Guam's Chamorro natives prompted Magellan's crew to name the islands *Las Islas de los Ladrones,* the Isles of Thieves.

The Marianas were a testament to the shifting winds of global dis-covery, conquest, and colonialism. Spain ceded control of Guam to the United States following the Spanish-American War. After World War I, Japan displaced Germany's rule of the rest of the chain and aggressively colonized Saipan and Tinian—fertile, mountainous islands separated by a narrow three-mile-wide channel. Japan also seethed at the nearness of U.S. interests barely two hundred miles to the south in Guam;[3] within two days of the attack on Pearl Harbor, Japanese troops stormed and captured Guam. To Japanese eyes, the islands were not merely Japan's possessions; they were its substance, controlled by its army but also populated by its citizens. When U.S. invasion forces gathered in mid-June 1944 to threaten Saipan and Tinian, Japan's thirty-thousand-strong army and navy defend-ers prepared to hold native soil. Putting aside memories of two years of bloody, stubborn concessions and retreats—the Solomons, Gilberts, Mar-shalls, Carolines, and now New Guinea—Japan's occupying army and her naval and air forces braced for a decisive showdown.

⚓

Many of the temporary ships assigned to the Central Pacific campaigns—especially the new CVEs and DDs—had brushed some other action before their crews saw the uplands of Saipan, Tinian, and Guam surfacing on the western horizon. But Operation Forager, America's invasion of these island strongholds, was the first occasion for many ships to fire gun batteries at hostile targets; for their crews it was the first full immersion in the grim process of Pacific island invasion.

Among the new crop of Fletchers, *Hoel* and *Johnston* probably saw the most action and their crews saw much of it together. *Hoel* arrived in the Pacific first, and in mid-November 1943 took part in the invasion of the Gilberts. A week before Thanksgiving her crew rescued a handful of survivors from escort carrier *Liscome Bay,* the quick victim of a single Japanese submarine torpedo hit to her ammunition magazines. Less than three hundred of *Liscome Bay*'s crew were pulled from the sea by *Hoel* and other ships; more than six hundred were lost.

For *Hoel*'s crew, including Larry Morris, a Kentuckian and a seaman in *Hoel*'s deck division, it was an occasion to rethink his breezy reasoning for joining the Navy: "I figured I wouldn't have to walk to war. The ship would get me there and back." It was a blunt reminder of the reality of war at sea—when the ship goes, the world goes with it. It was also a tragic, necessary reminder to the Navy of the vulnerability of the thin-hulled CVEs. In the next months, the CVE fleet (including *Gambier Bay* and *Midway*) was pulled into dry dock; ships' ammunition magazines were encased in coffer dams filled with fuel oil as a way to better shield them against torpedoes.

At the turn of the year both *Hoel* and *Johnston* participated in shore bombardment, escort, and picket duty for the invasion of the Marshall Islands. During March, both ships cruised the northern Solomons. In May, *Johnston* got credit for the probable sinking of a Japanese submarine. As summer approached, *Hoel* was assigned to training and convoy duty, whereas *Johnston* was assigned to a task force preparing to invade Guam as soon as Saipan and Tinian were conquered.

Albert W. Grant's journey to Saipan and Tinian followed her participation, as part of Destroyer Squadron (DesRon) 56, in the first big invasion of coastal New Guinea and as a screen ship for air assaults on Truk (one of the Carolines). Then, beginning in mid-June, *Grant* spent over a month with invasion forces cruising in sight of Saipan's volcanic Mount Tapotchau and, across Saipan Channel, Tinian's northern lowlands. *Grant* was joined there by other new Fletchers, including *McDermut, Melvin* and *Monssen,* each now part of DesRon 54. Almost every day, the tin cans' crews stood marathon GQs, moving between the relatively quiet routine of offshore nighttime screening and radar picket duty and the noisier, deadlier daytime rhythms of inshore bombardment and call-fire missions. Days also were punctuated by frantic antiaircraft bouts with incoming Japanese aircraft.

⚓

On D-Day, June 15, 1944, *Grant, McDermut, Monssen,* and *Melvin* (her crew buzzing with excitement over a possible submarine kill[4] just the day before) were all on station with the Northern Attack Force off Saipan's western beaches. Coming barely a week after the Allied invasion of Europe, the invasion of Saipan was to be crowded from war headlines by the exploits half a world away on the beaches of Normandy.

As the land assault began, the DDs' COs maneuvered their shallow draft ships within a mile of the landing beaches, searching out trenches, concrete pillboxes, blockhouses, camouflaged gun batteries, and other targets of opportunity. Optics and rangefinders on the basket (the Mark 37 gunfire director mount swiveling atop the pilot house) methodically scanned beach escarpments until a target was spotted and pinpointed. Target coordinates transmitted electronically from director to plot were converted to barrel elevation and deflection settings for relay to the 5-in. main battery guns. Depending on the ship's angle to the shore, firing data might go to one battery, to several, or even all five.

With breeches loaded, the 5-in. mounts pivoted in jerky unison under director and plot control, steadying once a target was in its crosshairs. During the lurching ride, the gun crews stood by and balanced themselves as best they could in the sun-cooked gun housings, sweating hands kept away from the breech and carriage between loadings, ears plugged futilely with wads of cotton. Gun muzzles rose, dipped, and finally steadied, moving as much or as little as the target. When all was set, a firing buzzer—a jarring, unmistakable standby signal, earplugs or no—sounded in the mount. Perched on a metal bicycle seat, and staring out through his own set of prism optics, the gun pointer squeezed a hand-held firing key to complete the firing circuit. A heartbeat of silence might then pass as the plot computer delayed firing until the precise instant when guns and ships—hulls swinging in the water through metronomic arcs of pitch and roll—were exactly on target. Then a jarring clap, like thunder breaking in your ear and an explosion and recoil that seemed to hammer the ship's every plate and seam. Topside, brackish-brown smoke peppered with flakes of explosive debris drifted over the water and back onto weather decks. As soon as mount hydraulics returned the guns to loading position, crews filled breeches with new packages of projectiles and powder casings and waited the fine-tuning of elevation and deflection before the next shot.

For *Grant, McDermut, Melvin, Monssen,* and the other DDs standing off Saipan and Tinian, this was the ear-splitting, bone-jarring, often days-long process of gunfire support. The ships became floating artillery platforms until the Marines could get far enough ashore and stay long enough to bring in their own artillery. During the landings, those standing GQ on the weather decks could watch the drama unfolding on the reefs and beaches before them. They could see troop landing craft—LCIs—plunge into clouds of dust and smoke raised by the impact of the gunfire, and then return once the Marines disembarked. When the clouds settled or dispersed, the destroyer crews could see the Japanese shellbursts coming from inland (sometimes reaching offshore to bracket or hit ships) and the dots of men on the beaches scrambling for cover.

At H-Hour on D-Day, *Monssen* took up position off Red 1, the northernmost of what would soon stretch to ten landing beaches, standing just south of the bulk and big guns of *California*. At his mount captain station on *Monssen*'s starboard 40-mm, gunner's mate Virgil Melvin, called Mel, had a front row seat for the assault's first days. "Saipan was our first real engagement and we had all new gun barrels. The other ships had more service on their barrels, so we used ours a lot. During the landing we were close enough to see the landing craft beach and the Marines duck for cover."

⚓

Looking up, Mel and others on weather deck stations would also see echelons of FM-2s and TBMs launched from CVEs further offshore— *Gambier Bay* and *Midway* among them—streaking through a clear daybreak sky and swooping in full-throttle just ahead of the landing craft. After months of CPTP, e-base, preflight, ground, and flight training, of flying the least and oldest aircraft, of CarQuals, of stints as instructors, of forming up and shakedown, *Gambier Bay*'s VC-10 pilots and *Midway*'s VC-65 pilots were finally joining the war.

Gene Seitz's VC-10 division was one of the D-Day echelons. "We were pretty new at the business of going into Indian Country. Here we were on D-Day, H-Hour. We all dove down just ahead of the boat landings to strafe the beach and keep the Japanese down. Everybody was scared to death. Then you did it once and didn't get shot, it was 'hey, let's do it again.' There wasn't much return fire."

⚓

As the Marines ashore battled inland from the landing beaches, bombardment stopped until the ships could establish radio contact with Marine fire-control shore parties. Once they made contact, the ships guns became "call-fire" batteries to take out inland targets holding up the Marines' advance. On *Grant*, the wait dragged on for hours and was punctuated by a close glimpse of war's carnage and by a real but unseen tragedy. As they stood by, guns silent, prowling closest to shore of any of the invasion DDs, *Grant*'s crew took aboard a returning landing craft's cargo of eight wounded Marines. In the officer's wardroom—converted to an aid station and operating room— *Grant*'s medical officer C. A. Mathieu,[5] pharmacist mates, and mess stewards tended to the victims: stopped bleeding, cleaned wounds, removed shell fragments, treated shock, administered morphine, changed bandages, comforted, and consoled. (For some Marines the trauma of combat was itself the wound. They could be sedated but not comforted.) Meanwhile, after hours of fruitless attempts to establish radio contact with their shore fire-control party, *Grant*'s crew learned there would be no contact: the party—men they never met and never heard from—were wiped out during the assault. *Grant* would be assigned to another fire-control party the next day.

⚓

Mel Melvin and the rest of *Monssen*'s crew built days around the business of barraging Saipan and Tinian: "We were constantly shooting—hours at a time. The gun barrels on the five-inch got so hot the paint burned off them. One time we had a 'hang fire.' To keep the projectile inside the gun from cooking off, a damage control party stuck a firefighting applicator nozzle right in the muzzle of the gun and turned the water on. Steam came pouring out. Other times the grease in the gun slide actually melted. When we had a break in firing we'd have to pump new grease in. It seemed like we'd be on station two to four days at a stretch, just lying to in the area or slowly cruising. We'd bombard and then take up a position to screen while somebody on screen would go in to fire."

On June 16, D-Day plus one, *Monssen* shifted north to a station off Mutcho Point and used its guns to help drive back counterattacking Japanese tanks. "We seemed to shoot at everything with one exception. Garapan, the main town on Saipan, had a building with a spire on it (it was a bell tower, built during the German occupation). We had instructions not to shell it because we were using it as a navigation aid." Meanwhile, *McDermut* moved even further north to Tanapag Harbor, using both its 5-in. and 40-mm guns to destroy Japanese demolition boats attempting to set fire to Navy supply craft.

When ships' magazines were depleted, the DDs would pull alongside anchored freighters and LSTs to rearm. On *Monssen* and the other ships, ammunition resupply was a hot, hasty, nerve-racking, all-hands project. "We weren't very safety conscious," recalled Mel Melvin. "When we'd go alongside the Ts, their main decks rode much higher than ours. They rigged wooden chutes and their men just dropped the projectiles and the casings in the chute to slide down. Amidships and on the fantail we put down big mats made out of old mooring lines. The projectiles and shells would come down and bounce on those."

As these provisioning operations demonstrated, the dangers of simply handling large caliber ammunition were often greater risks to ships and crews than incoming rounds from Japanese shore batteries or air attacks. One day in July, when *Melvin*'s main battery guns shot over eight hundred call-fire rounds at Saipan, a powder casing in Mount 53 ripped open as it moved into the breech from the loading tray. A live explosive projectile had been rammed into breech ahead of it, leaving smokeless powder and priming compound scattered throughout 53's gun housing. *Melvin*'s Chief Gunner's Mate John Macalosa acted quickly. The 53 gun was cranked up to its maximum elevation—eighty-five degrees—and the breech mechanism was cautiously opened. Macalosa scrambled to the top of the gun shield where other crewmen handed him one of the solid steel practice projectiles used for loading drills. Macalosa cautiously lowered the practice projectile down 53's barrel to dislodge the live projectile, and then jumped back down and climbed into the gun housing. He soon emerged, cradling the live round like a lethal baby in his arms. He brought it to the ship's railing and tossed it overboard.

⚓

A month after beginning its work off Saipan, *Monssen* shifted south to Tinian to do call fire for Marines who had just gone ashore. The Japanese were losing their grip on Saipan; Tinian's proximity made it a convenient platform from which to throw harassing fire at the backs of the Marines. On Saipan and Tinian, while Japanese soldiers hunkered down in intricate honeycombs of caves, civilians were urged or prodded to hurl themselves off island cliffs ahead of the advancing Marines, a measure of Japanese desperation. When "Wintergreen"—*Monssen*'s voice call—came over the circuit, it was often a request to take out a cave. With *Monssen* so close to shore and target trajectories so direct and flat, it was often the 40-mm, including Mel's, that got the target assignment. In contrast to the deep base-line thunder of the 5-in. salvoes, the exposed twin-barreled 40s fired with a mechanical slam-slam-slam; their barrels trailed curls of white smoke laced with the poisonous smell of ammonia.

Tinian yielded unexpected targets for both the 5-in. and 40-mm gun crews. On one morning, Mel and the rest of *Monssen*'s topside crew were confounded and terrified by incoming small arms fire. "We were sitting offshore and kept taking small arms fire. We couldn't figure out where in the hell it was coming from. Finally, somebody spotted a sniper sitting inside one of the navigation buoys. We put our forty-millimeter on the buoy and blew it up." On another day a cow was spotted grazing on a barren Tinian hillside. *Monssen*'s CO ordered the 54 gun to shoot the cow, reasoning it to be a source of food for the stubbornly resisting Japanese. Even though director, plot, and mount acquired and locked on the unsuspecting target, 54's first round carried high. When the round landed, however, the projectile set off a tremendous earth-ripping explosion that evaporated both hillcrest and cow. The round had hit an undetected ammunition cache just over the hillcrest.

TURKEY SHOOTS

For Joe McGraw and the other VC-10 pilots, "Saipan was something else. We headed in with sixteen fighters and twelve torpedo planes onboard. We were the fleet that came to stay and the Japanese didn't like it. Before Saipan, the fast task forces would go in, raid them before the invasion, and leave. But the CVEs came there and stayed to cover the invasion. The Japanese squadrons were in pretty bad shape, but by the time we showed they began to recover. The Japanese would send twin engine Bettys and Frans[6] down through the islands, hit us at Saipan, and then go south to Guam, which we hadn't taken yet. Then they'd re-arm and refuel and hit us on the way back north."

⚓

As the CVE pilots and aircrews operated in the skies above Saipan and Tinian, out to the west Japanese fleet squadrons were being decimated in the lopsided Battle of the Philippine Sea. The battle, part of Japan's desperate new policy to destroy America's Pacific Fleet "with one blow," began in earnest on June 18 (three days following the invasion of Saipan) and continued through June 24.

Like the battles at Midway, Coral Sea, and Santa Cruz, the Philippine Sea ended up being more about aircraft and pilots than sailors and ships. Although the American fleet that confronted two converging Japanese forces had more combat ships, the deciding differences were in aircraft and pilots. The U.S. Navy had double the number of combat aircraft—956 to Japan's 473. Japan hoped to offset pure numbers by operating some aircraft from the "permanent aircraft carriers" of islands still in their hands: Guam, Rota, and Yap. In the end Japan's strategy proved unworkable—air superiority was more than numbers or advantageous geography.

U.S. Navy aircraft (including the successor to the FM-2, the F6F Hellcat) were now able to match the speed, maneuverability, and durability of any Japanese aircraft. And the aircraft were being flown by legions of skilled, savvy, veteran pilots whose ranks had been bolstered by an influx of instructors (veteran pilots such as Burt Bassett, Dick Roby, Gene Seitz, and Tom Van Brunt) into operational squadrons. Although the very best Japanese pilots were still worthy opponents, they were fewer and had only themselves to rely on in poorly equipped and poorly trained squadrons. Whereas the new young pilots joining Japanese fleet squadrons may have been talented, few survived long enough to develop and display their skills.

In the run up to the battle, each side endured the frustration of trying to find its opponent first—close enough and early enough in the day to send out attacking aircraft. Burt Bassett was one of two VC-10 TBM pilots sent out to scour the ocean. "I went out on one sector, up north. We were told to go as far as we could. I left at 1500, never found anything, and didn't get back until just before dark. I was down to about twenty gallons in my tank when I finally touched down."

While patience and discipline made the Japanese better at snooping out their adversaries, it didn't change the outcome. It only brought novice Japanese pilots sooner to their destruction. When the battle was over, American aircraft as well as antiaircraft fire from screening ships such as *Monssen,* had laid near complete waste to Japanese Navy and Army air forces. On June 19—a day Navy squadron pilots dubbed the Marianas Turkey Shoot—American forces splashed 265 enemy aircraft. By the battle's conclusion, Japan had lost 90 percent of the aircraft, pilots, and crewmen it had sent into action. Although American losses of forty-one aircraft with seventy-six pilots and crewmen were tragic, Japan's were staggering and irreplaceable.

Three Japanese aircraft carriers were sunk during the Battle of the Philippine Sea, including *Shokaku,* one of the last two surviving carriers from the Pearl Harbor raids, and *Taiho,* its newest and largest. Although the Americans lost none of their carriers, what they did lose, critics believed, was a huge opportunity. American commander Admiral Raymond Spruance played his superior forces close to the vest, holding some back to protect against an "end run" by Japanese ships that might threaten the landings at Saipan and Tinian. Three Japanese carriers were destroyed, yet six others, in company with forty-six battleships, cruisers, and destroyers, escaped to Okinawa and Japan's home islands. The surviving Japanese Imperial Fleet was a wounded, proud, still potent adversary. In the months ahead, as Japan shortened its lines of interior defense and saw its strategy options dwindle, the Imperial Fleet prepared for another desperate lunge at victory.

⚓

As air engagements raged to the west in the Philippine Sea, the CVE aircrews were immersed in the skies and embattled ridges of Saipan. Just after D-Day, Joe McGraw, along with Jim Lischer, Gene Seitz, and four other VC-10 fighter pilots, ganged up to shoot down a Betty. "It took us a long time," Joe remembered. "We chased him way up to twenty-eight thousand feet, which was high in those days—we had to put on our oxygen masks.

I got into position to make a good run on him first and smoked one of his engines. We chased him though the clouds all the way down to the deck and between the bunch of us, and using most of our ammunition, we finally shot him into the water. I really respected him—he was a hell of an aviator." Joe later got credit for that kill and, despite the accepted wisdom that all skilled Japanese pilots were gone, he was convinced they still had their hands full. "I thought to myself, if their fighter pilots are as good as this guy, we've got some real trouble ahead."

In fact, Joe's first real trouble came from the guns of American ships rather than the Japanese. During the Marianas Campaign, the CVE air groups devised special tactics to counter Japanese aerial torpedo attacks that came in like clockwork against the CVEs and their screens each day at dusk. "We set up what was called Emergency Combat Air Patrol (CAP): two fighters on each deck of the four carriers, engines either ticking over or warmed, pilots strapped in, ready to go. If any Japanese torpedo planes got through the outer CAP and hopped over the picket destroyers, we'd launch emergency CAP. The deal was to just take off, leave gear and flaps down, canopy open, charge the guns, turn into the intruders, pick a target, and start shooting.

"One day I was flying wing for Gene Seitz and we were ready on deck for emergency CAP. It was coming dusk, torpedo planes were spotted and we launched—only we launched a little bit late. The deal was as soon as task force AA had the intruder within range they could also start shooting. And if our fighters happened to be in the way, AA could shoot right through us. So as soon as the flak started going by we'd have to pull up and get out of it." It was a necessary risk-reward calculation. "The Japanese were hauling these long lance torpedoes and they were really deadly on the CVE freighter hulls. One torpedo could take a carrier out. The idea was you might lose a fighter to flak, but you might also save a carrier." After pulling up, the emergency CAP fighters were supposed to turn and circle back, ready to pounce on any stragglers surviving the gauntlet of AA fire.

As Gene Seitz's plane charged down the deck ahead of Joe's, Gene could already hear the antiaircraft fire begin. "I saw this Japanese plane approaching from the right. I climbed and turned to the right." Gene's Wildcat was barely one hundred feet off the deck. "I had just enough time to pull up the lever to charge my two right guns. Then I held down my trigger and let him fly right through the bullets. It did him in."

Meanwhile, Joe McGraw got on a second Betty. "I was just starting to hit him when all the flak came and I had to pull up. I got one small hit in my right wheel, which didn't do much." Then something worse happened. "As I pulled up and turned to the right, some guy on one of the ships' forty-millimeters tracked me. Before anybody in the gun tub could get him off, he came up through me and put a round through my right wing tip." Ahead of him Joe could see more tracer rounds go up and begin to come back down.

"You had to time it just right. I knew one was going to come right through me, so I waited until the last instant and jammed the stick forward." A round exploded right behind the armor plate of Joe's cockpit.

Joe's Wildcat was hit badly. "Behind the cockpit armor plate was the radio and a vacuum tank for the flaps. The flaps came up and the radio went out. I was climbing out, close to stalling speed. I managed to keep flying speed, turned right, and went around to the back of the task force." The Wildcat's gear was still down and now stuck in place. Joe fought the Wildcat's balky controls. As he reached the back of the task force, a crippled and smoking Betty came out from underneath him. "I just pushed over and got on him and started to hit him when his right wing folded at the root and he went in the water. He'd been fatally hit by flak." Another Fran flew over. "I grabbed my radio and shouted 'Hey guys, there's a Fran coming over the top!' But there was no radio. So he got away and headed on down to Guam."

When Joe finally rendezvoused with the CAP fighters from the other carriers, he got a sobering, wordless appraisal of the damage to his Wildcat. "I pulled up alongside the guy who was leading the rendezvous. I think it was one of the guys from the *Kitkun Bay*. I pulled up on his inside and he looked me over and started shaking his head. He was giving me a signal about big holes. Then one of my guys pulled up on the inside of me. I think it was Dick Roby. His plane didn't look too good either—it had a bunch of holes."

It started to get dark. "They gave us a Charlie to come back to the ship and land." Joe's problems weren't over. "They'd land all the healthy chicks first. The Japanese were clever enough to leave a snooper outside the task force. We'd have him on radar, but he'd be too far out to shoot at. The snooper would wait until the fighters landed. If any light showed or there was a problem—a crash or a fire on deck—he'd have a target. He'd come closer and slip in a torpedo. So they let all the healthy airplanes land first and I ended up being the last guy in line to land."

Joe shot several approaches. Standing on a wind-shielded platform on the rear port quarter of the flight deck, waiting to bring Joe home, was Bill McClendon, *Gambier Bay*'s LSO. Bill, a Texan and a former pilot who'd flown Wildcats in the North Atlantic, had been trained as an LSO just before joining *Gambier*. "Bill kept waving me off, giving me 'wheels' and 'flaps.' I thought 'Jeez Bill, I know *that*. I just want to get aboard.' Bill just kept waving me off. They still had the snooper out there and they thought I was damaged enough to cause a fire."

Joe was briefly pointed toward *Kitkun Bay* to try landing there. But when Joe arrived, *Kitkun*'s deck was closed and he had to return to *Gambier Bay*. Joe continued circling, keeping his bearings from the dim red glow of a single light on the control tower. "I circled for about fifteen minutes. Dumb Ensign that I was, I thought 'Jeez, they're just going to leave me up here until I run out of gas.' It turned out they were still waiting for the snooper to leave. Finally he did, probably because he was also running low on fuel."

Joe was finally cleared for another approach. By then, Bill McClendon recalled, "It was pretty damn black." For night landings, fluorescent strips on Bill's flight suit and hand paddles were illuminated by a portable black light. Bill extended and moved his black-lit paddles, coaxing Joe to align his Wildcat for landing. "During landing approaches I looked at the aircraft's flight attitude. I had a picture in my mind of how the aircraft ought to look—especially where its tail ought to be relative to the landing gear. The problem was that Joe had no flaps, and without flaps he was coming in pretty fast." From his cockpit, Joe kept his eyes glued to the Bill's wands. "I was shooting my first and only night landing. Old Bill crossed the wands for an early cut. I was lined up but the ship looked a long way off. So in my mind I went—'one-thousand-one'—and then I took the cut. I should have listened to Old Bill."

Backing the six deck-hugging arresting wires used to catch aircraft tail hooks were a series of barriers; each barrier consisted of a pair of six foot high hydraulically controlled steel stanchions—one anchored to each side of the flight deck. Two arresting wires were strung between each of the stanchion pairs, one wire about three feet above the deck, the other six feet. The barriers were raised before each recovery; they were essential but unforgiving safety nets designed to block runaway aircraft from crashing into other aircraft parked on the bow.

Joe's Wildcat hit hard and roared down *Gambier Bay*'s deck. To Jim Lischer, sitting with other VC-10 pilots in the ready room just below the flight deck: "It sounded like a train crash." In fact, Joe's lurching Wildcat was nearly a runaway. Its tailhook sailed over the first five arresting wires, stopping only when it managed to snare the last wire. "If I'd taken Bill's cut I would have gotten the three. Instead I got the six wire and stretched it so bad I stuck my nose into the first hydraulic barrier." Joe's knees started shaking—a reaction of frayed nerves, relief at still being alive, and the utter shame of his miserable landing. "I thought 'How am I going to get up the nerve to get out of this airplane?' Just then my plane captain ran out—he was a skinny little guy from Kansas, a hell of a good plane captain. He beat the crash crew to the airplane. He climbed up on the airplane and looked in the cockpit. He screamed at me 'My God, Mr. McGraw, look what you've done to my airplane!'

"It just broke the tension, so I could get out of the plane. When I looked at the airplane later it had some thirty-five holes in it. I figured they'd managed to hit everything except the engine, the fuel, and me."

⚓

Practically every day of *Gambier Bay*'s stay off Saipan and Tinian, the VC-10 crews flew ground support strikes, often within yards of Marine forward positions and always within range of returning ground fire. Burt Bassett led his TBM division in bombing, rocket, and strafing strikes, paralleling the Marine lines as much as possible to reduce the risk of friendly casualties. "We avoided coming in from ahead or behind. When the Marines wanted really close support they sometimes marked their furthest line of advance with panels of reflective fabric so we didn't end up bombing them."

During one strike north of Saipan Tanapag Harbor, Dick Roby led two divisions of FM-2s. "We were given coordinates for a strike. We carried grid maps and I'm looking at this grid map to check the location. And I thought 'Wait a minute, the map panels for the Marines are right there, right where we were supposed to go in.' Then the controller came on the circuit and said: 'They're fifty yards from where we want you to hit.' What they wanted us to hit was the side of a ridge and the Marines were on the other side. I had eight planes and I told my people 'you guys have *got* to hit where you're told to hit, where they put the white phosphorous. If you don't, if you go over the ridge, you're likely to hit our people.' I don't know how many of them fired—not everyone did. But we didn't get any over the ridge."

On another strike further south, inland from the landing beaches, Joe McGraw encountered more incoming ground fire, this time from entrenched Japanese troops. "We were on a strafing mission north of Aslito airfield. There was a bunch of Imperial Japanese Marines on a ridge holding up the advance and we got called in to strafe. They really wanted to take that ridge bad. Four of us went in and strafed the heck out of it—we found out later there'd been something like twelve hundred Japanese Marines holding the position. During the strafing the Japanese brought out their AA from Aslito and there was flak around. During one of my runs I felt a 'thump.' Someone else looked me over and it didn't seem too bad—just a couple of holes. After the strike we climbed back up and were headed for the ship when they called us on the circuit and said there's a raid coming in. We dove steep for the water, and I mean we *really* dove steep. As we headed down I felt another 'thump' and half of my tail came off.

"We each carried extra fuel in fifty-gallon drop tanks under the wings, and it turned out one of those had turned sideways and come off. The weakened tail was hit by my drop tank and off it came—I lost control of the plane. In a dive like that it's hard to get out. If you're going to bail out and you've got any tail surfaces you pull up, roll it over backwards, and push out with your feet. The problem was we were doing nearly 350 knots in this dive and I didn't have much control. At that angle and speed you just don't step over the side. I had to get my feet up on the edge of the seat and give a hard shove to get out. I got about halfway out and then the wind pulled me the rest of the way. By the time I got out I decided it was time to pop my chute. Over water you have nothing to go by to tell you how far down it is. You can't tell if it's two hundred feet or two thousand feet. A little voice said 'you better do something,' so I pulled the chute. It popped open like a rifle going off. I swung twice and hit the water. A destroyer came by about four hours later. They delivered me back to *Gambier Bay* and traded me for fresh mail and twelve gallons of ice cream."

REPUTATIONS

By the time the Marianas campaign moved south for the capture of Guam and further south to the Palaus, the crews of the temporary ships had built enough experience with the war, their ships, and each other, to acquire reputations and nicknames. They also had enough time to brew the superstitions ever present in the closed communities of sailors and ships.

Monssen carried the reputation of a good-luck ship—along with the feeling its luck might be at the expense of others. For all the action it saw in its weeks off Saipan and Tinian and on picket duty in the Philippine Sea, *Monssen* somehow always escaped without a scratch, whereas ships around it weren't always as lucky. As far as Mel Melvin was concerned, "The good Lord watched after the *Monssen*. One day we were screening the *Colorado* off Tinian. We pulled out on rotation, and the *Norman Scott* relieved us. Just as soon as we left station, both *Scott* and *Colorado* took shore battery rounds. *Scott* took a shell hit to the bridge, which killed the CO along with about twenty officers and enlisted." Several weeks later it happened again. "When we were at Peleliu, the *Wadleigh* was out screening and we were sent to relieve her. Just before we got on station *Wadleigh* hit a mine. We didn't get a scratch."

Some reputations and nicknames were telling jabs at the demeanors, quirks, or officiousness of officers, especially COs. To Dick Ralstin and the other snipes on *McDermut,* her CO C. B. Jennings became "Jingle-Bell Jennings," a tribute to Jennings's obsession with minute (and, to the snipes, meaningless) speed changes signified by engine-order signals or "bells." "We used to joke about Jennings being a two-bell man," Dick recalled.

Other names, though, were more deferential. Even before *Johnston*'s commissioning, her skipper Ernest Evans was known as the "Chief"—a nod to both his Cherokee heritage and his warpath emotions. Evans' reputation soon rubbed off on the ship: By the time *Johnston* arrived offshore for the July 29 invasion of Guam, she was known to her crew as "GQ Johnny," a name built on Evans' eagerness to go to battle stations. *Johnston*'s stay at Guam deepened and burnished the reputation. Bob Hollenbaugh, by now a first class boatswain mate, was assigned as mount captain for the 54 gun. "It wasn't our first shore bombardment, but it was the biggest and longest. We went broadside for the landing so we could almost always fire five-gun salvoes.

"Just before the landings we took on about five or six Marines who communicated by walkie-talkies with Marines on the beach. Evans—I swear he was gonna put the thing on the beach! He kept telling the Gun Boss, 'If we get close we can do a lot better job.' I had a good crew. My projectile man Frank Nelson was even a baseball pitcher, a southpaw for the Sacramento Bees. He could handle those projectiles.

"The Marines would tell the Gun Boss Hagan[7] what holes, what caves to aim for. We were on the Orote Peninsula where there were cliffs. There was a lot of firing coming out of holes, out of caves up there. Any place these guys wanted to fire we'd put in rounds. We fired so much, so hard, and so heavy at times we had to let the breeches cool to prevent pre-ignition."

Cruising close to shore, *Johnston* took on wounded as had *Grant* and other DDs at Saipan and Tinian. During one lull, when Bob Hollenbaugh jumped out of the mount and went down on deck to check on his handling room crew, he encountered a badly wounded Marine waiting for treatment. "There was this kid laying there on the deck just below my gun with his right leg shot off below the knee. God, didn't he look young! I said 'How you doing there?' And he said 'Fine, sir.' He kept calling me 'sir.' I think I was all of twenty-two at the time. He was pretty doped up, waiting to be treated. I asked him how long he'd been in the Marines. He said 'About nine weeks, sir.' He was just out of boot camp, he'd made his first landing on Guam and now he was headed back home for good."

⚓

While Tom Van Brunt was being transported to the Pacific as a replacement pilot, he was promoted to full lieutenant. He now trailed the shaky reputation of being a senior aviator with no squadron experience. "They didn't know what to do with a lieutenant in a replacement pilot group. So they just kept sending me on: first to Kwajalein and then Eniwetok. I was standing by in Eniwetok when they put me on an escort carrier headed for Guam to supply replacement planes and pilots during the invasion. I was senior, so my plane was first on the catapult ready to be sent out. We got a message the *Lexington* needed a pilot and a plane. So I got in the plane on the catapult ready to go to the *Lexington* only to learn the engine mag[8] wouldn't check out. So they pulled me back. I went to the ready room while they fixed it. When the next order came in it was for a plane instead of a pilot. They were sending a pilot over to take my plane but not me."

Now without an aircraft, Tom stayed with the aircraft replacement carrier and watched from its flight deck as the invasion of Guam unfolded. "I remember playing ping pong in the ready room—it was a strange thing to be doing with the war right on the horizon." It was not until he returned to Eniwetok that Tom finally found a home. "The USS *Midway* pulled into port and was looking for a supply of pilots. So I was at last assigned to its composite squadron, to VC-65."

But when he got aboard *Midway*, Tom received a cool welcome. "I took my papers in to report to the Executive Officer. He saw I was a lieutenant, looked over my logbook and said: 'What the *hell* are you doing here?' I said 'Sir, I'm here because these are my orders.' I never liked him after that, but the truth was he'd seen what nobody else picked up on. I didn't have squadron training. A lieutenant in a composite squadron was next to the highest you had."

During his first days aboard *Midway*, Tom was relegated to the obscure role of squadron material officer and was getting no flying time. Finally VC-65's skipper Ralph Jones[9] brought Tom in for a heart-to-heart. "He told me: 'You got a problem here—a reputation for no real experience on carrier landings or squadron training. I've got to work with you, and we've got to make it work.' So he assigned me to fly wing with one of the squadron's best ensigns, a guy named Bill Brooks.[10] And when we got into port, Ralph got *Midway*'s skipper to take the carrier out so I and another guy who was in the same condition could make practice landings. I got in maybe ten or twelve landings and I felt much more competent afterwards. I never stopped feeling grateful to Ralph."

⚓

On October 2, 1944, a day after *Melvin* anchored in Seeadler Harbor on Manus Island, part of the Admiralties Chain located north of New Guinea, Commander Barry Atkins came onboard to take over command from Warner Edsall. Edsall had skippered *Melvin* since commissioning; he was an aloof, by-the-books skipper who was a stickler for constant drills and, despite the Central Pacific's withering heat and humidity, for ensuring the crew wear proper uniforms. Atkins, a compact figure with an ice-blue, appraising gaze, was a Trade School graduate whose first wartime assignment was gunnery officer aboard *Parrott*, one of the four-stackers escaping to Australia ahead of the fall of Java. (One of the *Parrott*'s squadron mates was *Alden*, on which Ernest Evans served.) Of more interest to *Melvin*'s crew was Atkins' experience as a former PT Squadron CO in the Solomons and New Guinea. Ever since the fall of Corregidor the exploits of the PTs had acquired a near-mythic reputation among sailors throughout the fleet. The reputation of the PTs continued to grow on New Guinea, where PT squadrons supported MacArthur's stream of power as it moved north toward the Philippines.

BUCCANEERS

In December 1942, America still struggled to gain a foothold on New Guinea, the continent-size island of mountains and jungle north of Australia.

MacArthur liked the PTs; he had advocated their development, they had helped him escape from the Philippines when it fell to the Japanese, and MacArthur saw a place for the PTs' speed, maneuverability, and shallow drafts in combat operations along New Guinea's rugged coast. At Macarthur's prompting, four Elco squadrons and a tender were assigned to his command. The boats' first bases were at Tufi, a missionary station, and at Morobe, both on the north coast of New Guinea's remote Papuan Peninsula. The following March, Barry Atkins led a ten-boat strike force against a Japanese transport column during the Battle of the Bismarck Sea, arriving to finish off a merchant ship.

In February 1944, when new squadrons and boats arrived, the PTs were rerouted to Finschhafen, a port town located up the coast from Tufi and across Dampier Strait from New Britain. From there, they followed MacArthur's campaign northwest along the shores of the Bismarck Sea, establishing bases at Aitape and finally at Mios Woendi, a small island guarding the entrance to Geelvink Bay in northwestern New Guinea.

Some boat officers and crewmen, like Ron (short for Squadron) 33's Bill Brown, Terry Chambers, Ted Gurzynski, and Albert Brunelle (at barely 115 pounds, a wisp of a motor machinist mate from Woonsocket, Rhode Island) and Ron 36's Walter Kundis (a nineteen-year-old gunner's mate from the coal fields of Pennsylvania), had been with their boats since commissioning in Brooklyn. All had accompanied their squadron boats as they were hoisted on tankers and hauled across the Pacific.

Others, like Ron 7's Tom Tenner, Don Bujold (a PT volunteer after he completed his training at the University of Kansas) and Jake Hanley (a radioman from Columbus drafted out of Ohio State) came separately as full crew replacements for boats that had been operating in the Pacific since the early days of the war. Still others, like Ron 12's Bob Clarkin and Andy Gavel, both torpedomen (Clarkin from Brooklyn and Gavel from New Jersey), trickled into Finschhafen, Aitape, and Mios Woendi as individual replacements during the spring and summer of 1944.

The experience of the PTs in the campaigns to capture the Solomon Islands and New Guinea forced changes in tactics and weaponry. The boats leaving New Guinea in the fall of 1944, bound for the Philippines, looked and performed much differently from the original Elcos. During the struggle of Guadalcanal, attempts to throw the PTs into nighttime torpedo attacks against Japanese cruisers and destroyers were usually disastrous and sometimes nearly suicidal for the crews. The attacks were too rushed and chaotic, the PTs' World War I–vintage torpedoes too unreliable, and the Japanese night fighting tactics too effective. PT boats were not destroyers, although, in the early shoestring days of Navy operations in the Pacific, they had been forced into that role.

Operating on the assumption that the boats' best defense was never getting hit in the first place, the first Elcos were built lightly armed to reduce weight, increase speed, and enhance aerodynamics. The PTs' spare topside profiles echoed the look of Elco's racy peacetime Cruissette motor launches. The Elco PTs carried themselves as if built for the gentlemanly weekend regatta that first earned Elco its contract to supply PTs to the Navy.

⚓

By mid-1944 the Solomons and the Bismarcks were taken and the long New Guinea campaign was nearing its end. Once-novice crews on once-novice boats were finally catching up with the realities of war and their place in it. The sleek profile of the typical PT deck had been transformed into a menacing arrangement of new deck guns, radar domes, whip antennas, and auxiliary equipment. When Ron 7's Don Bujold and Tom Tenner arrived in New Guinea in February 1944, they were assigned to the 127 Boat, then being overhauled. "It had the old World War I torpedo tubes and torpedoes. One of the first things was to get rid of the tubes and replace them with c-clamp shaped racks carrying newer Mark thirteen torpedoes. The tubes were inaccurate and had to be cranked out to launch. With the racks it was simpler to just aim the boat, pull a lanyard, and drop the torpedoes." Yet, even with the improved racks, torpedoes were seldom used; like wings on penguins, they seemed to have outlived the PTs' evolution. Some skippers even pulled two of the four racks in favor of more gun mounts or even rocket launchers.

The PTs emerged from these overhauls and modifications looking more like gunboats than torpedo boats. Tom Tenner recalled 127's armament: "We had two twin fifties, a thirty-seven-millimeter and a twenty-millimeter on the bow, a twenty-millimeter on the stern, four torpedoes, and two depth charges." And that was only the basic weapons package. In addition, boats increased firepower by adding mortars, rocket launchers, bazookas, cannons, and small arms—all according to each skipper's taste and his crew's ability to scrounge and install the equipment.

Like fleet ships, the customized boats gained personalities and the names to go with them. Names were usually the skipper's choice, a matter of his style and image. For example, Bill Brown named his 493 Boat "Carole Baby" in honor of his first born; ironically, 493's launch date was the same as her birth date: October 25, 1943.

Other boats were named in a racier fashion. Lieutenant (junior grade) J. P. Wolfe, a happily profane Texan and former college football lineman, at first named Ron 36's 524 "Stud," and arranged to have its bow display a rearing stallion with a torpedo thrusting prominently between its haunches. But this was too much for the sensibilities of Ron 36's CO Frank Tappaan.[11] The 524 ended up being named "Bet-Me," the lusting horse image replaced by a colorful, less provocative spray of playing cards showing a royal flush. Thoughts of lustful freedom (and frustration), however, were never totally suppressed. The 194 Boat Andy Gavel rode was called "Liberty Hound," while another boat—the 152 Boat ridden by Bob Clarkin—perhaps best described the frustrated prospects of New Guinea PT sailors: "Lacka-Nookie."

Because the PT boats were so small (compared to just about any other armed craft), their weapons looked more conspicuous and potent than they might on bigger vessels. As the boats' weaponry escalated, so did their crews' cocky views of their crafts' capabilities. In Tom Tenner's mind, "There was no fear. We were afraid of nothing that moved. If something happened at night, we would come back disappointed if we hadn't seen it. If we saw light, any movement on the radar, anything, we would tear right into it." When Jack Cady,[12] the 127 Boat's new skipper, upped the ante by replacing its stern 20-mm with a two-man 40-mm gun, the crew's swagger only increased: "When the forty was installed we thought we were a battleship. That was the way it was."

Of course the overhauls and modifications did nothing to reduce the boats' vulnerability to incoming fire. Underneath it all, the PTs were still incendiary packages of mahogany and plywood fueled by three thousand gallons of high-octane gasoline. To ensure their boats' survival (and their own), PT sailors often traded boat stations to be where they felt most comfortable—or imagined themselves least vulnerable. On the 127 Boat, Quartermaster Tom Tenner switched his GQ station from topside to the chartroom, while Radioman Jake Hanley moved to the port twin .50s. Tom welcomed the change: "Jake didn't like being down in the chartroom when the action was going on. He asked the skipper to change assignments and Cady said 'Okay, Ten can do it.' And I jumped at the chance to work with the radar." Jake, for his part, jumped at the chance to be topside. "I wanted to be in the game. I had to know what was going on."

On the 493 Boat, where he was the lead motor machinist mate, Ted Gurzynski also chose to sit behind the port twin .50s during GQ rather than being in the engine compartment. Ironically, he considered topside a safer place to be. "I never wanted to be in there when we were in any action. I felt I had a better chance of coming out alive if I was topside. I was the senior motor mac, so I told the other two if they stood engine watch when we went out, I'd stand watch there all the way back to the base."

Survival also required that the right men do the right jobs—regardless of rank or rate. Though Don Bujold was one of the 127 boat's motor machinist mates, his GQ station was at the stern 40-mm. "When they gave us the forty-millimeter, I knew the gunner's mate assigned to it couldn't hit the broad side of a barn. I told Cady if I couldn't shoot any better than him I'd turn in my ticket. He said 'Okay, we'll find out.' So, they put a bunch of oil drums out in the water and the skipper maneuvered the boat while I tried to hit them. Now I'd shot a few rabbits and pheasants in my day back in Michigan. I had Jake training the gun for me while I handled elevation.

I knew enough to fire on the up roll of the boat and I ended up hitting the drums pretty well. So Cady told me 'The gun's all yours.'"

⚓

A typical PT crew included two officers and twelve to fourteen enlisted men. These men grew close during construction, shakedown, and transit, and even closer and more informal during the New Guinea campaign. Successful boat officers were fiercely loyal to their crews; those who weren't got weeded out. "We didn't like our first executive officer," Tom Tenner recalled, "so he had to go. We got Dudley Johnson to replace him. He and the skipper Jack Cady were great. They listened and when we needed something we went to them. They didn't go for this ordering and demanding way of getting things done."

The key was mutual respect, whatever the skipper's style. Although Jack Cady and Dudley Johnson conquered the 127 Boat crew's hearts and minds with off-handed demeanors, others, like "Bet Me's" Texas skipper J. P. Wolfe, were undisputed top dogs. To Walter Kundis, Wolfe was "one big son-of-a-gun. There was no doubt about it—he was the boss of the boat, he was in charge. In fact when he first saw me—I was a skinny kid from Pennsylvania—he said: 'I have nothing against you, I just want to get rid of you. I want real men on my boat.' He ended up keeping me, though, and I stayed on his boat until the end. He was one good skipper. He knew how to take care of us." Each PT became a tightly guarded little world, loyal (though often also brutally caustic and frank) to its own and prickly toward intruders. Don Bujold remembered one of Cady's brushes with squadron staff following a successful coastal night patrol: "The personnel officer came aboard one time and told Cady, 'Give me the names of a couple of your good men and we're going to pass out medals to them.' Cady told him. 'What do you mean a couple? Give them all medals.'"

⚓

The PTs were thrown into the gritty business of coastal patrol, gunfire support, and interdiction during Sixth Army's advance up the New Guinea coast, as it captured strategic harbors such as Hollandia, Wakde, and Biak, and bypassed others.

The boats' baptisms of fire usually came at odd, unguarded moments, sometimes even unnoticed until they were over. The 127's baptism, Tom Tenner recalled, came on an early patrol out of Finschhafen across Dampier Strait and up past New Britain. "First a Japanese plane tried to drop a bomb on us. It exploded off our port bow, maybe fifty meters away. The explosion was the first we knew there was even a plane in the area." Later the boat began firing at shore positions. "Whenever I wasn't needed on the radar—like this day—I would go up topside to be a loader on the after twenty-millimeter. The gunner already had a full magazine on it, so I was just standing there ready to load. I heard this whistling sound and felt a blast of wind. Both the gunner and I turned our faces to look at each other. A three-inch shell from one of the Japanese shore batteries had gone right between us."

Unable to move troops and supplies through New Guinea's dense and mountainous interior jungles, the Japanese instead relied on barge traffic moving close to shore during the night. The PTs' primary role became "barge busting": detecting, cutting out, and mauling this traffic. In between they covered troop landings and extractions, fired at shore positions, evacuated wounded, and rescued downed fliers. Ron 33's Bill Brown became known as "Boy Scout Brown," recognition of 493's record for landing and retrieving Army scouts ahead of amphibious landings. In September, near the end of Ron 33's stay on New Guinea, its CO Lieutenant Murray Preston led the 489 and 363 boats in an audacious rescue of a Navy pilot shot down near Japanese-controlled Halmahera Island, east of the Celebes.[13]

The boats almost always patrolled at night, coming in close to shore expressly to shoot and be shot at—and sometimes even to rearm. "We hid caches of ammunition ashore," recalled 127's Don Bujold. "We would actually beach the boat and go ashore to rearm with ammunition we'd stashed away—fifties, twenties, and even forties." Jake Hanley had first been assigned to the 135, a boat which met its end stranded on a beach. "We lost the 135 up in New Britain in April. We chased some Japanese barges into a cove that was too small for us. When we turned hard left to get out, the surf caught us and we beached. Another boat tried to get a line to us, but that boat began dragging bottom and had to back off. We ended up destroying the 135."

In its action reports, Ron 36's 524 Boat logged the demolition of enemy freighters, luggers, landings barges, fuels depots, and ammunition dumps. During one night patrol Bet-Me's crew even managed to duel with a truck convoy. "We watched these trucks come by," recalled Walt Kundis. "They had their headlights off. Still, we could see them every once in awhile when they turned them on. We looked at our chart and figured out they would turn their lights on when they got ready to make a certain corner. So we waited. Soon enough, when one of them came around a curve, they turned their lights on and we shot them up."

The PT crews' lives more closely resembled the lives of front line army squads than navy crews. Crews lived in the cramped dual-purpose compartments of the boats. Squadron support personnel and replacements—the base company—lived in clusters of canvas tents connected by plank bridges suspended over a constant landscape of mud. The tents were perpetually wet, either dripping rain or sweating humidity. Everyone ate powdered food. Many were chronically sick in some major or minor way: bouts of dengue fever, running sores, jungle rot, prickly heat. One brief breath of relief from the nights' danger and the days' tedium was a visit to Mios Woendi by Bob Hope's USO tour. After staging a show, Hope, along with Frances Langford and Jerry Colona returned to Biak on Ron 12's 194 Boat.

Except for the rescues of downed fliers and stranded GIs, the PTs' New Guinea experience was a brutal, unforgiving business. The boats lacked the space or time to take prisoners, whereas the Japanese lacked the willingness to be taken. Survivors from Japanese barges who made it ashore might live to kill GIs. "Our job was to bust barges and take care of bobbing heads," remembered one crewman of his experience in New Guinea. "When the heads stopped bobbing, the mission was done."

In all, New Guinea was a great place to leave. As summer 1944 ended and the monsoon season arrived, the PT crews on Mios Woendi, along with the crews on hundreds of other ships staged in New Guinea's ports and in the Admiralty Islands to the north, relayed rumors about the war's next destination. They heard it might be the Philippine Islands.

Verner Carlsen, USS *Gambier Bay*

Tom Stevenson, USS *Samuel B. Roberts*

Virgil (Mel) Melvin, USS *Monssen*

Glenn Parkin, USS *Hoel*

Robert Hollenbaugh, USS *Johnston*

Evan H. (Holly) Crawforth, USS *Midway/St. Lo*

Theodore Gurzynski, PT 493

Albert Brunelle, PT 493

Joe McGraw, *USS Gambier Bay*, VC-10

Harley Thronson and Terry Chambers, PT 491

Gene Seitz, USS *Gambier Bay*, VC-10

Tom Van Brunt, USS *Midway/St. Lo*, VC-65

CROSSINGS

TARGETING LEYTE

Now that American forces under Douglas MacArthur controlled all of New Guinea, MacArthur was aggressively plotting his return to the Philippines. In the Central Pacific, the Americans held the key bastions in the Marianas and had simultaneously dismantled Japan's air armada. With Japan's carrier forces in disarray, what remained of the Imperial Fleet was its still-formidable battle line of battleships, cruisers, and destroyers.

Navy leaders were impressed by MacArthur's daring achievements in New Guinea, but didn't necessarily share his ambitions for an island-by-island liberation of the Philippines. Instead, they preferred a more selective strategy: capturing only those islands where they could establish strategic air bases to launch B-29 bomber strikes against the heart of Japan. This so-called Southwest Pacific ladder included the capture of the Philippines' southernmost island, Mindanao, the aerial pounding of remnants of Japanese air power on northernmost Luzon, followed by the conquest of Formosa, well north across the South China Sea. The ladder's rungs excluded other Philippine islands; cold logic argued a direct assault on Japan would end the war more quickly and liberate the Philippines sooner than would bloody island-by-island invasions.

But then two Japanese moves outflanked American ambitions to easily capture Formosa: the redeployment of most of the battered Imperial Fleet to Lingga Roads just across the strait from Singapore, and land-based advances in Southern China. These moves concentrated Japanese power due west and northwest of American positions. The Philippines beckoned again. With control of the Philippines, U.S. forces could choke off sea-lanes bringing food, fuel, and raw materials from the south to the resource-starved Japanese home islands.

Lingga Roads offered the Japanese Imperial Fleet access to fuel and the unhindered opportunity to train for the next—and likely final—showdown with America's Pacific Fleet. Although the Japanese planned other contingencies, they fully anticipated confronting an enemy assault on the Philippines. And they still dreamed of destroying the American invasion force in a swift and decisive nighttime assault. As the plan for battle took shape in Tokyo, the commander of the Lingga-based First Striking Force, Vice Admiral Takeo Kurita, prepared the crews of his battleships, cruisers, and destroyers to fight.

Kurita's two biggest ships, battleships *Yamato* and *Musashi,* were also Japan's newest. Each displaced sixty-eight thousand tons and could travel at twenty-seven knots. *Yamato* and *Musashi* also carried 18.1-in. main batteries—the biggest ship-mounted guns on earth. There were practical reasons for *Yamato*'s and *Musashi*'s proportions. Japan's naval planners knew America would limit the size of the biggest ships in its two-ocean Navy so that their hulls could clear the narrow locks of the Panama Canal. Japan's super battleships might be fewer, but they would always be bigger, faster, and, with their huge main gun batteries, more lethal in the ultimate showdown. There were also practical reasons for the towering, distinctive "pagoda" superstructures on First Striking Force's older, slower, and smaller twins, battleships *Fuso* and *Yamashiro*. The pagodas were exotic features to Western eyes, yet their real purpose was pure function: increased mast height improved spotting, range finding, and aiming for their main gun batteries.

⚓

To General MacArthur, retaking the Philippines was a matter of Philippine—not to mention Asian—faith in American honor. It was also a matter of personal honor. His father had commanded U.S. forces in the Philippines during the first years of U.S. occupation. In early 1942, at the insistence of the president and the joint chiefs, MacArthur fled the islands, leaving behind his troops to surrender to the Japanese. He always vowed to return.

Indeed, if the islands were to be bypassed, MacArthur went on record requesting the opportunity to state his views fully—and in person—to President Roosevelt. MacArthur got his chance when Roosevelt, in the midst of campaigning for an unprecedented fourth presidential term, combined strategy planning and politics in a trip to the West Coast and Hawaii. On July 27 (while the Navy and Marines mopped up Saipan and began the assault of Tinian), in a Waikiki private residence, MacArthur conferred with Roosevelt and the genial, courtly, but iron-willed Admiral Chester Nimitz, commander of U.S. Central Pacific forces. MacArthur was insistent and emotional but also logical and respectful, and his arguments won out. What emerged from this meeting was top-level accord to more directly target the Philippines, initially bypassing Mindanao for an assault on the islands of Leyte and Luzon.

⚓

Targeting Leyte, far to the southeast of the Philippines' largest island Luzon, made sense to naval planners. Leyte's deep, sheltered gulf faced east into the Pacific, making it easy for a U.S. invasion force to approach un-obstructed. Reaching Leyte from the west (as Japanese forces based near Singapore would have to do) was not nearly as easy. A maze of islands blocked the way and there were only two navigable passages for large warships to thread their way through the maze. One was San Bernardino Strait, a channel in the archipelago's midsection separating southern Luzon from northern Samar. From San Bernardino Strait it was a fifty-mile run south along Samar's rugged coast to Leyte Gulf. Further south was Surigao Strait, a channel connecting the Sulu and Mindanao Seas with Leyte Gulf.

Landing on Leyte also came with risks. Allied invasions in the Central Pacific were usually mounted against widely spaced island dots in a vast surrounding sea. Any serious Japanese challenge required the use of aircraft carriers, and most of Japan's carriers littered the ocean floor. In the Philippines, however, the Japanese still controlled many island airstrips and might launch air strikes to thwart the invasion. But this concern evaporated when U.S. air strikes against Mindanao and against the Palau Islands to the east of the Philippines encountered little Japanese resistance. Japan's air power seemed exhausted. As a result, the Leyte invasion date was stepped up to October 20, just at the onset of the monsoon season. The difficulty of building and operating new airfields on Leyte's waterlogged soil during the monsoon months could be offset by keeping escort carriers on station, as had been done in the Marianas.

⚓

Military invasions are vast endeavors that test the boundaries of both lo-gistics and destructive imagination. During World War II, U.S. amphibious assaults carried these endeavors to new levels of complex savagery. As Japan gained control of the Central and Southwest Pacific early in the war, and then as the Allies campaigned to recapture it, vast stretches of ocean had to be crossed before fighting could even begin. For two years, American success in one island chain pointed to new invasions requiring leaps of hundreds, sometimes thousands of miles: in the Central Pacific from the Gilberts to the Marshalls to the Carolines and to the Marianas; in the Southwest Pacific from the Solomons to New Guinea. As American oper-ations in the Central and Southwest Pacific gained momentum, invasions increasingly resembled vast, methodical business enterprises. In contrast, Japan's holding stands became sacrificial, holy missions.

The planning that specified all the minutia of the American enterprise to recapture the Philippines began in September 1944 and took five weeks; it took two weeks just to distribute the plan document to the necessary people in the right locations. The document was more than one inch thick. Twenty-five pages detailed the complex orchestration of movements; four pages listed addressees; six pages described reporting relationships among enterprise commanders; a twenty-five-page appendix listed all the radio frequencies and call signs to be used.

The enterprise was three-pronged. One prong was an expeditionary invasion force drawn from MacArthur's Sixth Army that had conquered New Guinea. The second was a bulked-up Seventh Fleet of transports, amphibious ships, surface combatants, and escort carriers to deliver Sixth Army troops and supplies to Leyte. The final prong included Third Fleet[1] fast carrier forces to support the invasion with air strikes, while blocking Japanese intrusions from the north or west.

Now, in the first days of the autumn monsoon season, the Allied streams of power combined and embarked to retake the Philippines under the enterprise name King II. From staging ports throughout the Southwest Pacific, an armada of nearly 700 ships carrying 165,000 troops and 50,000 sailors and airmen started ocean crossings—distances of 1,250 to 2,000 miles—all converging on "Point Fin," a coordinate of latitude and longitude just off the entrance to Leyte Gulf. The day of the landings, October 20, was designated A-day, an effort to distinguish the Philippines campaign from the June invasion of Fortress Europe.

SHELLBACKS

At dawn on October 6, *Samuel B. Roberts* cleared submarine nets to enter the broad oval basin of Manus' Seeadler Harbor. *Roberts,* detached from convoy escort duty with Third Fleet and assigned to Seventh Fleet, had left Eniwetok Atoll and traveled southwest through the Caroline Islands in company with five other DEs and two unarmed auxiliary ships—a salvage tug and a submarine rescue vessel. Hundreds of ships were already at Manus; they filled Seeadler's anchorages in a panorama of dazzle-painted hulls below a sky filled with towering, rain-heavy clouds. The harbor floated combatants of nearly all classes: the Kaiser-built escort carriers; older battleships of the *Pennsylvania, Mississippi,* and *Tennessee* classes; cruisers, including *Louisville, Nashville,* and *Denver;* and their screening destroyers. The moorings and anchorages also stocked an alphabet soup of amphibious, transport, service, and auxiliary vessels: LSTs with flat decks and towering superstructures aft; LCIs with circular castle turret-like conning towers; LSMs with deep, massive well decks and carrier-like starboard mounted island superstructures; massive fleet tankers called AOs; and smaller, more explosive gasoline tankers, AOGs.

The day before reaching Manus, *Roberts* made its first crossing of the Equator. It also was the first crossing for most of her crew, occasioning a ritual whose origins dated to warships under sail, when "crossing the line" truly meant stepping into a vast, treacherous unknown. In a "crossing" ceremony, "polliwogs" (novice sailors who hadn't yet crossed the line) were initiated into the privileges of Neptunus Rex's domain by "shell-backs" (those sailors, regardless of rank or other stature, who already had). Crossing was a rite of passage—to manhood, to a bond among shipmates, to the professions of sailor and warrior. Its ceremonies were often ribald, punishing, humiliating, and sometimes dangerous—a rare chance for shellbacks to pull rank, revenge grievances, and settle scores.

On *Roberts,* as on nearly all the temporary ships, polliwogs vastly outnumbered shellbacks. There were barely enough shellbacks to fill out the principal parts for King Neptune's bizarre court: Davy Jones (Neptune's chief courtier), a signalman dressed in a pirate suit made of black signal flag bunting; King Neptune, a boatswain mate sporting a yellow wig and a white mustache made of manila line, unthreaded to bare strands; Neptune's wife, a carpenter's mate, painted, powdered, and dolled up in a hula skirt; the royal baby, Chief Radioman Serafini, his huge frame tucked into a diaper fashioned from a mattress cover; the royal judge, *Roberts'* Chief Engineering Officer, in black bunting, silk top hat, wing collar, and a black bow; the royal devil, a ship's cook in skin-tight red bunting, horns, and a long forked tail; the royal barber and royal dentist.

Convoy ships conducted their crossing ceremonies in staggered sched-ules thirty minutes apart. Ships in the midst of their ceremonies stood limited deck, engineering, and sonar watches; for a time, *Roberts'* XO Bob Roberts, a shellback, single-handedly manned the pilothouse. As the cere-monies continued, the newly initiated shellbacks gradually returned to their stations until the ships were once again fully manned.

Roberts began her crossing ceremony at 8 A.M. Polliwogs (including CO Bob Copeland) stripped to shorts, soaked to their skins, and jolted by low voltage prods from the royal devil's fork, mustered on the fantail. Each polliwog stood before Neptune's court, to be read and respond to fanciful charges and specifications. And then the ritualistic, unvarying conditions for penance began: a visit to the royal dentist to chug a nau-seating mouthwash (diesel oil combined with vinegar and paprika); a chaotic hair trim by the royal barber's electric clippers (topped off by a splash of royal hair tonic/fuel oil); a kiss to the royal baby's grease-smeared belly; and a run through the royal gauntlet. The gauntlet, a length of canvas ventilation tunnel about fifteen feet long, its floor awash in garbage, was the final trial. Polliwogs entered the tunnel and crawled through on hands and knees while shellbacks laid into them with paddles. They emerged as shellbacks.

Although crossing ceremonies might be abbreviated or toned down because of battle conditions and passage through hostile waters, they were never abandoned. And although the ceremony on *Roberts* and the other convoy ships had the makings of disaster if a Japanese submarine attacked, the morning passed uneventfully. Although the war still waited, this ordeal was over for *Roberts*' new shellbacks.

⚓

Each of the nearly 700 ships involved in King II was assigned a number. Digits and decimal points brought a sense of order to Manus Island's Seeadler Harbor and New Guinea's Humboldt Bay as hundreds of ships arrived, anchored, loaded, and prepared to depart during the first two weeks of October. Nearly all the vessels in the Admiralty Island and New Guinea staging ports were Seventh Fleet vessels with Seventh Fleet designations—at least for the duration. The Seventh Fleet was nicknamed MacArthur's Navy because it was created expressly to support his Southwest Pacific campaigns. It began as little more than a paper navy: a few submarines, a repair tender, some troop ships, a handful of DEs and PTs. Now, beefed up for the Leyte invasion by the transfer of scores of ships like *Roberts* from Third Fleet, Seventh Fleet boasted enough ships to crowd the horizon of each King II staging port.

Every Seventh Fleet ship belonged to a Seventh Fleet Task Force (TF). For King II, Seventh Fleet was divided in three Task Forces. Two Attack Task Forces, the Northern (designated TF 78) and the Southern (TF 79), would land troops on Leyte. Collections of ships with specific missions for specific phases of King II, added a decimal point and more digits to create the finer detail of Task Groups (TG). *McDermut, Melvin,* and *Monssen,* for example, were all part of TG 79.11, the destroyer screen for the amphibious ships of the Southern Attack Task Force.

A third Task Force, designated TF 77, contained ships and aircraft to support the landings of both the Northern and Southern Attack Task Forces. Fire support battleships and cruisers comprised TG 77.2; its battleship contingent included *West Virginia, Tennessee,* and *California,* all resurrected from the debris of Pearl Harbor nearly three years before and now back in the show. Although their slow prewar speeds prevented them from running with Third Fleet's fast attack carrier groups, their 14-in. and 16-in. main battery guns were still potent offshore bombardment and callfire weapons, as proved during the Marianas campaign. The thirteen tin cans of DesRon 56, including *Grant,* formed 77.2's destroyer screen.

TG 77.4, a second Task Group within 77, provided carrier-launched bomber and fighter air support for King II. In all, 77.4 contained eighteen escort carriers and their screening tin cans. The 77.4 divided its 18 CVEs into Task Units (TUs) of six carriers each, along with a screen of destroyers. TU 77.4.3 held *Gambier Bay*, *Midway*, and four other escort carriers; its screen contained destroyers *Hoel*, *Johnston*, and *Heermann*. The screen also contained *Roberts* and three other DEs: *Dennis*, *Butler*, and *Raymond*. Despite the pace of new construction, the Navy was still starved for DDs. So smaller, slower, more lightly armed DEs (ships designed only for antisubmarine warfare) filled out the screens. If Seventh Fleet could be considered a massive trunk, with Task Forces as its broad lower limbs and Task Groups as its lithe, resilient branches—the DEs, perched at the extremities of the three Task Units, were the slenderest of twigs.

⚓

Ship departures from Manus and Hollandia began as early as October 10, with each sailing staged in relation to A-Day. Many of the amphibious and service ships plodded along at little more than single-digit speeds, much to the dismay of crews on the faster escort ships harnessed to them. To Dick Ralstin and the rest of the crew on *McDermut*, the unease was palpable. "It was one of those nine-knot deals. A destroyer's just not comfortable at nine knots."

TF 79—the Southern Attack Force—left Seeadler in a convoy of ninety-seven ships on October 11. The Task Force's amphibious, service, and support vessels outnumbered combatants nearly three to one. Staged ahead of its transports and amphibious ships were the minesweepers needed to clear the Gulf's approaches, the combat transports to infiltrate Ranger assault forces onto Leyte's offshore islands, and the hydrographic survey ships to measure and clear landing beaches ahead of A-Day.

This convoy's crossing was graced with mostly clear, hot premonsoon weather brushed by a light following wind. Occasionally the ships and their crews were shrouded in steamlike mist or bathed in lukewarm downpours visible miles ahead, hanging like gray curtains from the clouds. And always, traveling as they were within a degree or two of the Equator, there was oppressive humidity. Topside was hot, below decks was hotter, and engineering spaces were merciless, relieved hardly at all by ventilation from fresh air blowers. At night, where there was enough room and enough tolerance by ships' captains, sailors and soldiers dragged their sleeping gear to weather decks to sleep out in the open.

On the day before *Melvin*'s October 11 departure, VC-10's Dick Roby was able to visit with his younger brother Al, *Melvin*'s First Lieutenant. "We'd met up with each other about four or five times, including once in Tulagi and two times in Manus. I went over to his ship and took a photographer from *Gambier Bay* with me for *Melvin*'s change of command ceremony. We took all the pictures for that. Unfortunately they were on the *Gambier Bay* still undeveloped when *Melvin* went out."

Gambier Bay was due to depart on October 12, part of a convoy combining Task Groups 77.2 (the fire support battleships and cruisers) and 77.4 (the escort carriers) along with transport and service ships. That convoy would endure a much rougher ride.

⚓

As the October 12 convoy got set to go, a wave of superstition (always brewing beneath the surface of actual effects and plausible causes) pulsed through *Midway*. She'd been robbed of her name and given another. Tom Van Brunt, visiting with his brother, was among the first to learn the news: "The night before we left Manus to go up to Leyte, my younger brother was sitting with me on *Midway's* flight deck. He was in communications on one of the supply ships and could read code. He was able to decipher the blinkered messages when the light bounced off the clouds. He picked that one up when it came in. They changed the name of the ship from *Midway* to *St. Lo*. 'Goddamn, ill-fated ship,' I heard one of the boatswain mates moaning, 'You don't change the name of a Navy ship. We'll be at the bottom of the ocean in two weeks!' Nobody at home, of course, including my wife, knew it had happened."

Midway carried a proud iconic name,[2] one that defined U.S. triumphs in the Pacific war. Now it had to be surrendered—a larger fleet carrier to be named *Midway* was on the drawing boards. Along with superstition, the change stirred resentment and confusion. Confiscation of the name was humbling—a show of disrespect for the CVEs. Even through *St. Lo* was a storied World War I battle, it had been fought on the other side of the world and on land. A new name also meant a new mailing address—a perplexing disconnection for distant families and an annoying detail for clerks at the Fleet Post Office to wrestle with.

When the ships of Task Groups 77.2 and 77.4 moved into the Philippine Sea on October 12, they headed toward a refueling rendezvous. When fueling was completed, the three carrier units (Task Units 77.4.1, 77.4.2, and 77.4.3) with their escorting DDs and DEs pushed ahead; they were to arrive at Leyte on A-Day minus three (October 17) to begin softening-up air attacks on the beachheads. Although the formality of Task Force, Group, and Unit nomenclature still applied, ships' communications circuits increasingly used easier parlance to identify the Task Units; the voice calls for each of the three Task Unit commanders. TU 77.4.1 was Taffy 1, the others Taffy 2 and Taffy 3.

At first the convoy plodded through calm waters; then the monsoon season caught up with the Taffys. What hit them was no mere storm—it was the fringe of a genuine typhoon with winds gusting up to ninety miles an hour. In peacetime, the ships might have turned back or turned wide. Instead, for the greater part of a miserable day, the ships plowed on and plowed through. On the CVEs, the mountainous seas and raging winds made for rocky conditions and curtailed most flying. On *Gambier Bay,* though, Dick Roby's VC-10 division was launched on a futile search mission. "It was pretty rough even on the edge of the typhoon. As we heard it, a soldier on one of the transports decided to commit suicide and jumped overboard. I took my division up and we looked for him. In that weather and that sea there was no chance of finding him."

If conditions on the CVEs were difficult, they were miserable on the DDs. As far as Bob Hollenbaugh on *Johnston* was concerned, "It was the damnedest storm I've ever been in. Water came crashing over the bow. My division, Second Division, had responsibility for the deck aft of the number one stack, including the whaleboat hanging on davits on the starboard side just aft of the superstructure. In the middle of the night my boss, the First Lieutenant, woke me up. He shook me: 'Bob, Bob, wake up. We're just about to lose your boat.' By the time I got topside the whaleboat was loose from the aft davit and was bobbing up and down, being slammed by the water. John Longacre, a big nine-year boatswain mate from First Division carried a big knife on his ankle. He just took the knife out, hung over the side, and cut the lines. We didn't even try to save it—it was too dark and just too damn rough. The saying we had was 'one arm for you, one arm for the company.'"

On DEs such as *Roberts,* conditions were even worse. The typhoon's fury pinned much of the crew to their bunks. Most of the temporary sailors—new shellbacks, but scarcely more seaworthy because of it—became deathly ill, torn between the desperate fear the ship might sink and, after enough hours, the wretched hope it would. A handful of ships' officers, quartermasters, and deck ratings manned the wheel house and the open bridge while, below decks, engineering officers and a small gang of machinist's mates and water tenders manned the two engine rooms without relief. Exhausted, nauseated snipes could only lie down on the gratings, rest awhile, and then struggle back to work.

Topside, *Roberts'* skipper Bob Copeland and Lloyd Gurnett,[3] the First Lieutenant, relieved each other on the helm. XO Bob Roberts, Tom Stevenson, and Dudley Moylan, bundled in oilskins, took turns as officer of the deck on the open bridge. "At one point," Dudley remembered, "I had the deck and ended up being the only person on the open bridge. I watched the ship roll probably more than we were supposed to be able to and not capsize." The rolls—measured by an inclinometer on the open bridge—routinely exceeded forty degrees and on two terrifying occasions swung above fifty degrees. At the end of some rolls it was barely easier to stand on the deck than it would have been to stand on an adjoining bulkhead. Still, *Sammy B.* moved surprisingly well in the towering seas. The ship would heel a long way, then look for its balance and start back again. Through the worst of the storm *Roberts* didn't quiver or buckle—and continued toward Point Fin.

⚓

Roughly a quarter of the armed combatants bound for Point Fin were PTs. They were staged to arrive following A-day. The boats made the eleven-hundred-mile open-water voyage from their base at Mios Woendi Island, first traveling north to the Palau Islands and from there on a second leg west to the Philippines. Traveling in company with tenders, fleet tugs, and supply barges, some of the boats were able to refuel at sea, whereas others spent portions of the crossing under tow by tug. Ted Gurzynski, like many other men on the boats, began the journey without precisely knowing the destination. "Before we got underway, Bill Brown told us we were going into something big and to make out our wills. Just something basic, and then the lawyers would take care of it. Away we went, though we didn't know officially until we were underway it would be Leyte."

Ted, a motor machinist's mate, volunteered for PT duty after completing diesel engine training in Chicago, though not for its excitement or its risks. "They were asking for volunteers for submarines, lighter-than-air, and PTs. The recruiter said he wouldn't recommend PTs because it was rough duty and you'd be home in six months with your kidneys in your hands. When I heard I could be back in six months I volunteered." Getting back quickly was important—and getting more important all the time. As the 493 boat set off for Leyte, Ted's wife was home in Milwaukee awaiting the birth of their first child. The child might have already arrived. Ted got no word and expected none, located at what seemed the absolute end of the earth. Now Ted might have his own firstborn and here he was headed out on 493 for something very big.

Many of the boats made the trip with additional crew. Ted recalled: "When we left they were disbanding the base force and loading them up on the boats. Originally the 493 boat had two officers and ten crew. We ended up with fourteen crew and three officers. The new third officer was Lieutenant (junior grade) Dick Hamilton, a feisty former amateur boxer from North Dakota. Dick was a refugee from the 494 boat where, as XO, he'd battled with 494's skipper Joe Moran.[4] Bill Brown took a liking to him, despite Dick's combative reputation. "We always called him Dicky Dare because of his boxing background. He was a great little guy."

When they reached the Palaus, some boats, including the 491 skippered by Harley Thronson, anchored in sight of Peleliu Island before beginning the second leg of the journey. The Marines first stormed Peleliu on September 15; a month later, they were still battling to dislodge the Japanese garrison. "We could see the battle going on at Peleliu. It was terribly windy." It was a hot tropic wind, but it also felt chilling and unnerving, as if it were the labored breathing of the struggle ashore. "The guys on the boats felt screwy because of the wind."

Terry Chambers made the transit as XO on the 491 Boat and remembered riding through the remnants of the same typhoon that pounded the Taffys. "We traveled in a fleet of several squadrons and halfway up there we got into a horrendous monsoon-type rainstorm. Being practical sailors, we all stripped, stood out on deck, and got freshwater showers." For others like Al Brunelle, sitting in 493's engine room, the experience was neither practical nor pleasant. "It was the roughest weather I'd ever ridden in. The engines really revved up when we went down, came up, and the stern lifted out of the water. Those props were really spinning because they weren't hitting any pressure. I was sitting in a little chair on top of the engines. I had a bucket in front of me because I had the dry heaves."

Jake Hanley remembered conditions on Squadron 7's 127 Boat being just as rough. "No one was allowed below deck. The waves just dropped out underneath and the bow came slapping down so hard that below decks we would have been driven right into the overhead. We all just hung on. I spent most of my time in the cockpit, which was splashed with water. Jack Cady was on the helm for many hours. I remember he finally lay down in the cockpit. The water was washing over his face, but he was sound asleep."

KING II

On October 17, A-Day minus three, invasion preliminaries began in the waters and outer islands of Leyte Gulf. Minesweeping of Gulf approaches began at dawn. The minesweepers were a dog's breakfast of vessels—converted destroyers, some old, some new; square-bowed steel-constructed AMSs, about half the length of a destroyer; and shorter, wooden YMSs with high bows and high bridges. On that same morning, parked sixty-five hundred yards off Suluan, the outermost island in the Gulf, cruiser *Denver* fired the first rounds of a shore bombardment whose flame, noise, and devastation would puncture many hours of the next days and weeks. The DDs, including DesRon 56's *Albert W. Grant* and *Richard P. Leary* and DesRon 54's *McDermut* and *Monssen* once more took their turns at the firing line.

On October 17 and 18, Army Ranger battalions went ashore from fast transports to scour the four gatekeeper islands of Leyte Gulf: Dinagat, Calicoan, Suluan, and Homonhon. The Rangers fought and dispatched a thirty-two-man garrison on Suluan, while encountering hardly any resistance on the other three islands.

As the Rangers landed, worked, and then withdrew, invasion fire support ships stood outside the Gulf entrance, buffeted by wind and seas that threatened to delay the timetable for landings. On October 18, with conditions improving, these ships began a slow, cautious advance into channels still dangerously littered with floating mines. Three minesweepers led the way. By early afternoon battleships *Pennsylvania* and *California,* cruisers *Minneapolis* and *Denver,* and several destroyers, including *Grant,* traversed the channel. From *Grant*'s bridge, Ed Pfeifer watched one of *California*'s secondary batteries explode a floating mine. The line of ships then swung north to begin pummeling the six beachheads dotting Leyte where it curved north to its boundary with the mass of southern Samar.

Small destroyer transports moved to within fifteen hundred yards of shore to deploy teams of underwater demolition and reconnaissance specialists, supporting them with harassing gunfire as they prepared the beaches and then retrieving them. Surveys by the teams confirmed suitable landing beaches with few obstacles. The transports and fire support ships then withdrew as night came on, still fearful of floating mines. On the same day, the Taffys moved into operating areas outside the Gulf to launch softening attacks on ground forces, airstrips, and shipping; the FM-2s and TBMs of composite squadrons from *Gambier Bay, St. Lo,* and the other CVEs hit Leyte, Mindanao to the south and Cebu, Negros, and Panay to the west. Normally, this would have been the work for air groups attached to Third Fleet carriers. Instead, those carriers stood in waters well northeast of Luzon, anticipating and hoping to tangle with Japanese carrier forces whose whereabouts and intentions remained a mystery.

At first light on October 19, the fire support ships returned. Toward late morning they maneuvered into position offshore, southern units near the landing beaches at Dulag and Tacloban and northern units near San Pedro Bay. Each unit divided further into sections to spell each other as they soaked the beaches with continuous gunfire. As sunset approached, the ships withdrew to the expanse of the Philippine Sea south of the Gulf, where they steered zigzag courses to avoid submarine attack.

In the first hours of October 20, A-Day, transports began offloading troops and equipment onto smaller attack transports, landing ships, and amphibious craft in preparation for midday runs to the beaches. The morning sky was heavy with clouds above calm waters. It grew muggy as the sun arced over Samar's hills. Transports began crawling northwest into the Gulf, the Southern Attack Force heading for positions off the palm tree–lined beaches near Dulag, the Northern Attack Force into place off the docks of Tacloban Town. Sandwiched between the attack forces were cruisers and destroyers to provide both escort and fire support.

The initial order to deploy came at 6:45 A.M. Smaller landing craft, loaded or ready to be loaded with troops, were hoisted from the transports, stationed about seven miles from the beaches. Shore bombardment resumed, first with thirty or so high explosive rounds each from the main battery guns of battleships *Mississippi, Maryland,* and *West Virginia.*

A continuous barrage of 8-in. and 5-in. rounds then followed from cruisers and destroyers. Navy aircraft, this time launched from Third Fleet carriers standing well out in the Philippine Sea, began firing on shoreline troop entrenchments and continued the pounding of airfields on Leyte, Mindanao. and other islands. Meanwhile, CVE planes flew CAP for the ships in the Gulf.

At 9:30, amphibious craft began jockeying at the departure line, ahead of them a five-thousand-yard run to the invasion beaches. Each beach was named for a color: Beaches White and Red in the North, and Beaches Orange, Blue, Violet, and Yellow in the South. At 9:43, the run began. The cruiser and destroyer shore bombardment—salvos now whistling over the hunched shoulders of beach-bound troops—peaked and lifted to move inland. Replacing it were screaming sheets of 4.5-in. rockets hurled from some of the gunboat landing craft running less than twelve hundred yards from shore. Finally, Japanese mortars returned fire from hills behind the beaches.

For most in the Northern Sector it turned out to be an easy landing with nothing like the carnage at Tarawa and Peleliu. Wave after wave of boats made it to their designated beaches on or near schedule. There were gentle waves, no mines, and few beach obstacles. Troops advanced inland even as mortar fire began to take a toll on several exposed landing craft. Because of a shallow sloping beach, some larger landing craft were unable to get in close enough to unload heavy supplies; craft and cargos were diverted to the north and south.

In the south, assault troops landing at Orange, Blue, Violet, and Yellow Beaches moved through a broad, level plain of rice paddies, cornfields, and coconut groves interrupted by one-thousand-foot high Catmon Hill. Japanese mortar and light artillery fire from this and another much smaller hill offered virtually the only early resistance to the landings. Indeed, across the whole front, there was little indication the Japanese intended to hold this particular ground.

⚓

Early in the afternoon of October 20, General MacArthur made his personal return to the Philippines. Transferring from light cruiser *Nashville* to a landing craft that broached well short of the northern landing beaches, MacArthur and his retinue splashed ashore in knee-deep water. After walking inland to inspect the terrain and the results of the bombardment, MacArthur paused on the beach, delivered a rallying speech into a cluster of waiting microphones and then returned to *Nashville*.

As McArthur completed this first day's symbolic inspection, U.S. Army X Corp troops further north secured San Juanico Strait—the water separating Leyte from Samar—cutting off the possibility of Japanese reinforcements. Twenty-fourth Division soldiers to the south seized the crest of

strategic Mount Guinhandang and successfully repelled a Japanese coun-
terattack.

Transports and their crews worked furiously to get their cargos ashore
during daylight, so they could withdraw ahead of darkness and avoid dusk
air attacks. By day's end, U.S. Army forces in the north controlled Tacloban
Town. In the south they commanded the coast from bank to bank of two
flanking rivers. The beach assault now turned into a land campaign.

As the assault troops worked their way further ashore, the ships in the
Gulf began their first duels with Japanese aircraft. In mid-afternoon, earlier
than air attacks would normally be expected, cruiser *Honolulu* was hit
portside by an aircraft-launched torpedo. As the afternoon lengthened,
cargo ships still in the gulf shrouded themselves in smoke to hide their
positions, while destroyers stood by, ready to defend them with an umbrella
of antiaircraft fire.

SHO 1

Within minutes of the U.S.'s first minesweeping forays into Leyte Gulf
on October 17, news of the impending invasion was on its way to the
Japanese Combined Fleet headquarters. The moment the Japanese had
anticipated was at hand. On October 18, Fleet headquarters triggered the
seaborne portions of its *Sho Go* or "Victory Operation" plan. *Sho Go* had
several contingent versions, each a response to a different possible invasion
target. Most Japanese planners, however, assumed it would be the Philippines; the plan for the Philippines was *Sho 1*.

Japan's senior leaders did not delude themselves about *Sho 1*'s prospects. They knew their air strength was inadequate to support the plan;
success would require a supreme effort by Japan's remaining surface fleet.
Even success might not alter the war's ultimate outcome. They desperately
hoped the Americans, in grasping to retake the Philippines, had stretched
their lines of communications and supply too far. The Americans would
now finally be vulnerable against Japan's compressed lines of defense. As
the Americans attacked Japanese flesh, Japan would strike American bone.

Japan's slim hopes pointed to an earlier triumph over a different
Western foe: In 1905, during the Russo-Japanese War, the Imperial Navy
had annihilated a Russian Baltic Sea fleet that had traveled eighteen thousand miles to wrest Siberia's Port Arthur from Japanese control. The two
fleets clashed on a windy May afternoon in the Straits of Tsushima, the
frigid ocean passage between Japan and the Korean Peninsula. Maneuvering to windward of the Russians, the Japanese battle line managed to
pull ahead and cross the bow of the Russians' lead ship. The Japanese
formation became the horizontal cap of a "T" and the Russian ships its

vertical leg. The classic maneuver—known as "crossing the T"—enabled Japanese gun batteries to bear on the Russian ships all along their column, simultaneously masking many Russian batteries and limiting their ability to return fire. The stunning gambit sealed Japan's victory and established the Imperial Fleet's mythic reputation.

For the Russians on the losing side of the gambit, battle turned quickly to flight. In the following day and a half, six of eight Russian battleships were sunk and the remaining two captured; twenty-five other ships were sunk, captured, or driven to neutral ports; nearly five thousand Russian sailors died and another six thousand were captured. For a Japanese navy then barely fifty years from inception, Tsushima represented an instant coming of age.

In its Tsushima victory, Japan grasped the model of what it could do should Japan's interests ever collide with America's. When war came, the Japanese Navy would knock out the U.S. Asian fleet, seize the Philippines to control the Pacific (it eventually did both), and then await the return of a reinforced U.S. fleet bent on recapturing its possessions. The Imperial Fleet would then confront an American fleet (as it had Russia's forty years earlier) worn down from a long voyage, and crush it decisively near the Philippines.

⚓

Vice Admiral Takeo Kurita's First Striking Force, one piece in the *Sho 1* plan, sailed northeast from Lingga Roads in the predawn hours of October 18 and reached Brunei on the northwest coast of Borneo two days later. When he arrived, Kurita received orders to continue toward the Philippines, entering Leyte Gulf at dawn on October 25 to attack American amphibious and supply shipping. Fleet headquarters recommended Kurita make a two-pronged approach: While one group of his ships threaded through the islands of the Sibuyan Sea, entered the Philippine Sea via San Bernardino Strait, and struck at Leyte Gulf from the north, a second group would swing up from the south via the Sulu and Mindanao Seas, and sweep into Leyte Gulf through Surigao Strait.

Kurita decided to take most of First Striking Force through San Bernardino Strait. Staying to the north, these ships would be out a range of air attack as long as possible. He detached the second contingent—two battleships, a cruiser, and four destroyers under Vice Admiral Teiji Nishimura—to take the southern route. Both groups left Brunei on the morning of October 22, Kurita's group ahead of Nishimura. If the column of broad-beamed battleships sailing out of Brunei evoked the glory of Tsushima, it was also a reminder that such glory was fading. Command of the sea required control of the air above it: as First Striking Force set off no covering aircraft flew overhead. At the northern tip of Borneo the two contingents separated,

Kurita's twenty-nine ships continuing northeast, while Nishimura' seven ships diverged east.

Far north of the Philippines, Vice Admiral Jisaburo Ozawa commanded Japan's Mobile Striking Force, consisting of six carriers, three cruisers, and eight destroyers. The carriers were the survivors of Japan's pounding in the Battle of the Philippine Sea—among them they carried barely one hundred usable aircraft. Mobile Striking force was to be *Sho I*'s sacrificial lamb. On October 20, Ozawa's ships steamed south from Bungo Suido, the strait separating Japan's home islands of Kyushu and Shikoku; Ozawa was intent on being detected and luring America's powerful carrier fleets away from Leyte. If the deception worked, First Striking Force's battleships, cruisers, and destroyers, joining as pincers from the north and south, would find a clear path into Leyte Gulf.

A fourth key player in *Sho I,* Vice Admiral Kiyohide Shima, commanded a force of three cruisers and four destroyers anchored near Okinawa. Originally designated to be the vanguard of Ozawa's Mobile Striking Force, Shima's ships were detached and assigned instead to escort troop convoys from Luzon to Leyte. Shima vigorously protested being kept out of the decisive battle he knew was in the offing. He won his point: Designated as Commander Second Striking Force, Shima was ordered to continue south, refuel his ships, and then follow Nishimura through Surigao Strait into the Gulf.

BODY CRASHING

New Air Fleet Commander, Vice Admiral Takijiro Onishi, arrived in the Philippines on October 19 to organize air cover for the First and Second Striking Force forays into Leyte Gulf. Onishi quickly learned that providing air cover by traditional means would be impossible: He had fewer than one hundred operable planes to put aloft. He would need something else—a tactic to truly affect a battle certain to decide Japan's fate.

What Onishi proposed to his squadron commanders at Luzon's Mabalacat field was "body crashing"—organizing Japan's Philippines-based aircraft into suicide squadrons, each plane carrying a 250 kg bomb and each targeting an American aircraft carrier. The idea caught hold in an audience of pilots who had lost both comrades and honor in humiliating battles with American aircraft in the Marianas, the Palaus, and at Yap. Here was the opportunity to erase shame; it was the sacrifice of one pilot and one aircraft for the destruction of a warship with a crew of three thousand and fifty or more aircraft. Onishi's enraptured audience asked only to be allowed to organize the force themselves.

WAITING HOURS

Leyte Gulf, October 21–23

PT squadrons completing their open water journeys filtered into the Gulf accompanied by tenders, tugs, and barges. The tenders anchored in the Gulf and the boats also lay offshore while the shore bombardment and troop landings continued. Finally they revved engines and skimmed through the armada. Onboard the 491 Boat, skipper Harley Thronson felt they were on stage. "We were quite an attraction, the featured event. A lot of the battleship, cruiser, and transport guys had never seen a PT boat."

"We finally pulled into the harbor at about A-day plus two or three," recalled Terry Chambers, 491's XO. "My God, it was wall-to-wall transports, with destroyers racing around the outside edges." Without their tenders, the PTs lacked a foothold—they panhandled for food and stores from the bigger ships. "We didn't know what we were supposed to do. Finally we got wind the Seabees had arrived to build an airstrip at Tacloban. We heard they had a fuel barge and so we went to get gasoline."

Squadron 7's boats almost missed the Philippines. With the weather calmed, Tom Tenner took his turn at the helm on the journey's westbound leg. "All we had to do was follow a gang of boats ahead of us. I wasn't too concerned about having to navigate. Then we seemed to get lost. It was my turn on the wheel and I was just supposed to follow the wake in front of me. All of a sudden I saw another wake off to port. It seemed to be going the wrong way. Then, a little later, I saw *another* wake going the wrong way. This happened three or four times. Finally, the wake in front of me turned around, leaving us as the lead boat. It took awhile to sort things out and get our bearings. We breathed a sigh of relief when we finally saw the islands, the Gulf, and all the ships. We charged in as if we owned the place; by this time all the rest of the Squadron 7 boats were following us. It was October 20 or 21. The whole Gulf was filled—warships, freighters, anything you could think of. It was massive."

Leyte Gulf, Morning, October 22

By the time *Melvin* arrived at Leyte Gulf, most of her crew already had the measure of their new CO Barry Atkins. Red Barth's opinion was unequivocal: "We got a gem. I'd kiss that man's bare butt on Main Street at high noon. We all loved him. Just his demeanor, the way he treated everybody. He leaned towards the crew."

Bill Campbell, an ensign freshly graduated from Trade School, reported to *Melvin* just over a week before her departure from Manus. The last leg of his long journey out to the Pacific was a frigid ride in the belly of a B-26 bomber on a hop from New Guinea, and he arrived unceremoniously by climbing over *Melvin*'s fantail.

Campbell became one of *Melvin*'s assistant gunnery officers. On A-day plus two, as *Melvin* stood down from dawn GQ, Campbell climbed into the gunfire director basket to take over from Bill Robie for the first time. He was still taking a seat when a Japanese plane swooped down. "I let myself in through the hatch and was putting on the headphones. The bridge alerted me to a Japanese aircraft, a Val, headed our way. I ducked down to acknowledge and at the same time felt Bill Robie beating on my helmet."

Getting ready to climb off the basket as Bill Campbell took over, Bill Robie spotted the intruder. "I saw the goddamn Val come straight toward our bow. He didn't fire anything as far as I could tell." Red Barth saw the same thing from the port bridge wing: "Here came a damn Japanese plane skipping over the mountains—we never could pick him up. And he flew over us but nobody fired. I could have thrown a potato at him and hit him."

Bill Campbell scrambled to catch up. "I grabbed the slew sight, moved on target, and shouted, 'Commence tracking.' I'd practiced this so many times in training—director crew matches, plot follows, guns lock in and fire. Not this time. The gun barrels went up and down and swiveled in all directions—plot room and guns were changing crews. I was eyeball-to-eyeball with the pilot before he passed overhead without firing a shot."

Bill Robie watched helplessly as the attack unfolded. "The skipper somehow managed to slow the ship. The Val pilot pulled back his stick, skimmed over, and missed us. His gunnery problem was developing too fast. He figured our original speed and Barry's slowing the ship made the Val overshoot us." (On the bridge, Barry's assessment was more circumspect: "It happened so quickly. I can't remember if I gave an order or not.")

Red Barth saw what happened next. "As the Val flew away from us he made a right turn and was going to come back. The Good Lord takes care of dumb fools. There were two Navy fighters right on his butt. When he made his turn they blew the hell out of him. Then the smart asses came down alongside us off the starboard side maybe thirty or forty feet off the water, waggled their wings, gave us the high ball, and took off."

What Barry did next was undisputed. "I turned on the PA speaker and said, 'That was the most disgraceful gunnery I've ever seen!' I was disgusted." Barry called Bill Robie and the gunnery officers not on watch to the wardroom. Bill Robie recalled the meeting: "We didn't fire a shot, which gave Barry ample opportunity to have, as he says, 'a short fight talk.' A number of us got really reamed." No arguing that. Disgraceful didn't cover it. In one unguarded moment destruction and death flew right in on them. And for the Japanese pilot—who'd probably failed to fire or drop the Val's bomb because of his own surprise—the end came just as unexpectedly and quickly. His performance also was disgraceful—only he'd paid with his life.

South China Sea, Palawan Passage, Dawn, October 23

Under clear predawn skies off Palawan Island north of Borneo and west of the Philippines, American submarines *Dace* and *Darter* intercepted Kurita's force as it steamed northeast. Kurita's twenty-nine ships were deployed in five columns, cruisers and battleships flanked by three columns of destroyers. *Darter* and *Dace* separated and maneuvered at periscope depth until each lay east of a cruiser column. Aiming for the lead cruisers in each column, the two subs fired a total of twenty torpedoes, sinking two cruisers—including Kurita's flagship *Atago*—and severely damaging a third. Admiral Kurita jumped overboard from *Atago* and was pulled from the water by destroyer *Kishinami*. Leaving two other destroyers behind to rescue survivors and attend to the crippled cruiser *Takao*, Kurita transferred to *Yamato* and signaled his remaining ships to continue northeast toward the Philippines.

Off Samar and in the Skies above the Landing Beaches, Morning, October 24

A-day plus four found the Taffys deployed to provide ongoing air support to the advancing Sixth Army troops on Leyte; they were spaced roughly thirty to fifty miles apart along a north–south axis from the south end of Samar to the north end of Mindanao. Seen from above, the units of CVEs, DDs, and DEs seemed to pinwheel in two concentric circles. The inner circle, with a radius of twenty-five hundred yards, contained the carriers; the outer, with a radius of six thousand yards, the screening DDs and DEs. During the day the Taffys moved closer to land to attack Japanese bases, patrol for submarines, and provide CAP, both for their own ships and for the supply and service vessels in the Gulf. Each night the units moved east into the protective darkness further offshore.

October 24 proved to be a big day for VC-10's fighter pilots. At 5 A.M., two divisions of FM-2s, one led by Dick Roby, the other by Gene Seitz, launched on CAP from *Gambier Bay*. Until sunup, the eight planes orbited together inland from the Leyte beachheads; then the divisions split, Gene's four planes climbing while Dick's stayed low. As they did, Japanese twin-engine bombers launched from mainland bases to the west began filtering in. Dick and his wingman E. H. Courtney intercepted two: "I tallyhoed a Sally above me. I started to climb, but then Courtney tallyhoed another on our starboard beam. I turned into that one, fired a long burst, and saw it catch fire. Courtney followed behind me and shot off the Sally's right wing." Wrapped in flames, the Japanese bomber spiraled to the ground.

Meanwhile, flying above them, Gene's division intercepted four more Japanese bombers. "I made a high side run on the starboard side of a Sally. I fired a five-second burst, which shot off its port wing. The Sally flamed and crashed west of Tacloban. None of its crew jumped."

As Gene's target flamed and Gene's wingman C. A. Dugan took down a second bomber, the two remaining planes in Gene's division—one piloted by Joe McGraw—were still out of firing range. When Joe lost contact with his wingman, he briefly formed up with Seitz and Dugan. But both were low on fuel; they soon dropped out to return to *Gambier Bay*, leaving Joe on station with four wildcats from another carrier. "Just then a large formation of twenty-one twin engine Lilys was tallyhoed. They were in close formation at fifteen thousand feet, headed straight for Leyte Gulf." Joe climbed from ten thousand feet to intercept: "I just started shooting as I closed. I was at the right altitude—just below the bombers. I took out one with hits in the right engine and the wing root; he flamed and went down."

By then, Dick Roby's division had raced in from the west to leap into the bombers. "I pulled astern of a Lily and gave it a long burst. It caught fire, rolled over, and headed down." Dick pursued two other Lilys but had to break off when ground fire enveloped the Japanese planes and threatened his own. Dick returned to *Gambier Bay* with only four rounds of ammunition left in his wing guns and less than ten gallons of gasoline in his tanks.

Joe McGraw and several others continued to hammer the Japanese bombers. "There were some escorting Zeros hanging out at the back, about two thousand feet above and astern of the Lilys. I kept my eye on them, but they didn't see us until their airplanes were going down. Then they pushed over and dove down through us, taking out two of our guys. I made the call 'fighters coming down' and we all pulled up and headed up through them. I climbed pretty steep and corkscrewed a little, so I couldn't get a shot at them and they couldn't get a shot at me. As soon as they passed I rolled left and got on their tails, hoping to nail one. But the Zeros poured on the coal, went right down through their own bombers and almost hit some of them. They left the bombers behind and headed full bore toward the beachhead. They must have had a secondary mission to strafe the beach.

"I didn't get a shot at them. The order of the day was to stop all the bombers from hitting MacArthur's beachhead. So we pulled back in there and kept after the Lilys. I scissored out, came right back in again, and picked up another one. I got his left engine but he wouldn't flame. So I sucked around behind his tail and shot up his other engine. As he dropped off on one wing and started going down, I was sitting there looking right in the face of the rear seat gunner. The guy shot a few holes in my airplane, one through the wing, one through the prop, and one zinged off the top of my canopy."

Joe had splashed two and nearly got one more. "I was hitting another one in the same place on the right engine when another of our fighters came in from my left, shot at the same Lily, and damn near collided with me. I don't know who finally got it. It peeled off and went on down. It was a probable for me."

The Lilys had flown in tight formation; except for Joe's brief duel with the rear gunner, there'd been little return fire. By the time the hapless bombers got to the beachhead there were only two left. "One was smoking bad and on the way down, the other was being attacked by a crowd of fighters. Then up came a wall of flak so I pulled back." The last two Lilys went down near the beaches, one of them crashing into a fleet tug straining to pull a grounded LST off the beach. Out of ammunition and nearly out of fuel, Joe headed home. "Those Lily raids kept going on. The people replacing us up there hit another raid. The Japanese just kept sending bombers in all day and we just kept shooting them down."

Meanwhile, the ground support missions flown by Joe and the other Taffy pilots mirrored the relative speed and ease of the progress ashore. "I made several strafing runs four miles inland where a road and a bridge made a choke point. The Japanese weren't bringing in reinforcements and the ones who were there were bugging out. We also took out quite a few hard points where they would set up a machine gun nest or a mortar. There weren't very many of them. We'd get the word on where they were and just chew them up."

Sibuyan and Sulu Seas, Morning into Afternoon, October 24

Burt Bassett's TBM vectored northwest from *Gambier Bay* on morning antisubmarine patrol. As was more and more the case during these sweeps, Burt encountered no submarine activity. What he did encounter was the majesty of the carriers, battle line, and screening ships of Task Force 38. "It was the first time I ran into the big carriers. I was really impressed. There were actually two groups of carriers, along with battleships, cruisers, and destroyers. They were busy launching strikes against the Japanese fleet. I couldn't imagine they'd be so close to us. I thought, 'Jeez, with those guys around I'd never felt so safe.' "

What was prey to *Dace* and *Darter* the day before now became prey to Task Force 38 air groups, the beehive of ships and aircraft Burt had seen. *Dace* and *Darter*'s sitings were the clearest—though not the only—proof three Japanese surface forces were moving in on Leyte from the north and west. In response, the three task groups of TF 38 operating east of Luzon and northeast and east of Samar were pulled in toward the coast. The ships moved to guard San Bernardino Strait and the approaches to Leyte Gulf. Air groups prepared dawn searches to snoop west of Luzon and into the Sibuyan, Sulu, and Mindanao Seas.

During early air searches, U.S. planes spotted Kurita's ships as they angled around the southern coast of Mindoro Island and pointed north into the Sibuyan Sea. Four waves of fighters, dive bombers, and torpedo bombers dispatched from carriers *Cabot* and *Intrepid* attacked Kurita's force in Tablas Strait east of Mindoro through the late morning and early afternoon. *Musashi* and *Yamato*, Kurita's two massive battleships, drew most of the attackers' attention.

The first wave of attacks crippled cruiser *Myoko*, which dropped out of formation to limp back west to Brunei under destroyer escort. The second wave scored torpedo hits on both *Musashi* and *Yamato*; the sister battleships took the blows and steamed on, seemingly unimpeded. The third wave pummeled *Musashi* with eleven aerial bombs and eight more torpedo hits. The fourth left *Musashi* with yet another wound—the last in a toll of nineteen torpedo explosions. Her command facilities destroyed and slowed by damage to her port bow, *Musashi* at last dropped out and crawled north toward Manila, escorted by two destroyers and cruiser *Tone*.

Kurita's force emerged from these attacks with diminished but still considerable strength: four battleships, six heavy cruisers, two light cruisers, and ten destroyers continued north through Tablas Strait, turning east toward San Bernardino Strait. Because their speed was down to eighteen knots, Kurita now had no reasonable prospect of reaching Leyte at first light as originally planned. In mid-afternoon, fearing more air attacks, Kurita reversed course, moving, he hoped, outside the range of American planes until he could be covered by darkness.

As Kurita's force retreated temporarily west, his ships overtook *Musashi*—listing, bow down, and plowing its way slowly west. When Kurita's force once more turned east, the ships again passed *Musashi*—and saw her for the last time. As Kurita's ships disappeared over the horizon, the doomed *Musashi*, its bow at last completely submerged, listed more sharply and capsized so suddenly she took half of her crew to the bottom.

While Kurita's force absorbed the real pounding, Nishimura's smaller force was barely touched as it steamed up the eastern coast of Palawan Island and then turned east into the Sulu Sea, pointing toward Mindanao and the entrance to Surigao Strait. Planes from TF 38 carriers *Enterprise* and *Franklin* first sighted Nishimura's seven ships between Negros and Mindanao as the first wave of attacks on Kurita's ships began. Attacking aircraft scored minor hits on battleship *Fuso* and destroyer *Shigure*. Nishimura's ships escaped further damage, maintained speed, and steamed on without further attack as U.S. forces concentrated attention on Kurita's force. Still, their disposition and their intent were now clear. In the approaches and confines of the Strait, American units prepared to confront them.

Tacloban and Liloan Harbor, Leyte, Afternoon, October 24

After a long night of uneventful patrols, Ron 33's skippers had straggled drowsily into the midday briefing on tender *Oyster Bay*. But they broke from the briefing at a dead run. Boat 491's XO Terry Chambers, who'd stayed with the boat to get fuel, water, and chow, found himself swept up in newfound urgency: "Everybody was being frantically alerted about the Japanese coming through and where the boats were going to be positioned.

"At first our boat drew the 'messenger-hey-boy' duty; we had to stay behind to cope with emergencies, or lay smoke screen for the destroyers. Then somebody realized how wide Surigao Strait was; if the Japanese came up the middle they might not be spotted by the PTs scattered down either side of the strait. So at the last moment they decided to put three of us out in the middle to make sure nobody sneaked through."

⚓

Near Liloan Harbor on the northwest tip of Panaon Island, PT 127 had just returned from its own night patrol. "Squadron 7 had established a little base near Liloan," recalled Jake Hanley. "We'd gotten pretty brave since arriving. We hadn't seen any Japanese, so we began patrolling on the west side of Leyte towards Ormoc Bay. Some Filipinos tipped us off to a concrete block building filled with Japanese troops. We sat off the beach and blasted away at it with the forty millimeter. When we finally returned to Liloan, we were signaled to come in, refuel, and rearm. We had a big mission coming up that night. We joined up with the other boats and went out."

⚓

As the afternoon lengthened, 39 PTs loaded with extra ammunition, fuel, and additional people to handle small arms left Tacloban and Liloan Harbor. The boats deployed in thirteen three-boat sections in positions bordering Surigao Strait and its approaches: the eastern shores of Leyte and Panaon Island; the western shores of Dinagat Island and Mindanao; the shoal waters near Limasawa, Bohol, and Camiguin Islands in the Mindanao Sea.

The three late additions from Ron 33—section leader J. M. McElfresh's[5] 490 Boat, Harley Thronson's 491, and Bill Brown's 493—headed off to their mid-Strait stations. "Knowing what was coming," Bill Brown recalled, "we poked in a little extra horsepower." A section of Ron 7 boats, including the 127, went the furthest—a position in the middle of the Mindanao Sea just north of Camiguin Island. The boats cut south through a high chop, seas that only got rougher as night approached. Working the radar on the 127 Boat, Tom Tenner had simple instructions: "Spot anything and to try to figure out where it was, what speed, and what direction."

Philippine Sea, East of Luzon, Evening, October 24

Third Fleet commander Admiral William Halsey was the Navy's MacArthur. He was a fighting admiral well known to the American public, an icon of newspapers, radio, and movie newsreels. If the Navy's highest leadership (Nimitz in Hawaii, King in Washington) were faceless unknowns, Halsey could stand for the Navy's public image. Halsey took over after the first disastrous engagements in the waters of the Solomons: the Slot and Ironbottom Sound. He brought order, discipline, fighting spirit, and the glimmering prospect of victory in the days when U.S. forces were lucky just to hold on. Though he preferred to be called Bill by his peers, his nickname quickly became Bull. Halsey's impulsive and combustible personality was just part of the package.

But as America's fortunes in the war improved, Halsey's took a back seat to those of Admiral Raymond Spruance, a quiet and more reflective commander. Halsey and Spruance regularly swapped places in charge of America's Carrier Attack Forces in the Central and South Pacific—when Spruance was in charge they were called Task Force 58, under Halsey they were Task Force 38. Glory became a matter of timing. Spruance had the helm during the Midway victory while Halsey was confined to a Pearl Harbor hospital with a case of psoriasis. Spruance also got credit for the victories at Saipan and in the Philippine Sea, although some believed his studied caution (what critics dubbed the "Spruance Nuance") cost the United States still greater victories. Bull Halsey's actions would never taste of indecision. He was determined to make up ground in a fight that mattered.

By evening on October 24, Halsey knew Kurita's force had ended its westward jog, turned, and headed back toward San Bernardino Strait. At the same time, Ozawa's carrier force had been detected approaching the Philippines from the north; that threat was fresher and more inviting. Kurita's force had suffered blow after blow. Even if it continued through San Bernardino Strait and plunged south toward Leyte Gulf, Halsey estimated Admiral Kinkaid's forces should be ready with more than enough resources to destroy it.

The idea of keeping carrier and surface forces in place to block Kurita's thrust while waiting for Ozawa's arrival went against both Halsey's head and heart. Task Force 38 hadn't built its reputation waiting—it attacked. A final option—to leave his battle line behind to guard San Bernardino Strait and to attack Ozawa's undetermined strength without the air defense support of his battleships and cruisers—seemed an unacceptable risk. Halsey pounced on the opportunity (and took the Japanese bait). Ordering his three carrier task groups to consolidate, Halsey charged north to confront the Japanese carrier force, leaving San Bernardino Strait unguarded. And, because the intentions he signaled weren't entirely clear, Halsey gave the impression that San Bernardino still might be guarded.

As TF 38 steamed north, disquieting signs about Kurita's intentions continued. At nightfall, scouting flights from *Independence* placed the Japanese west of southern Luzon. An hour later they were spotted steaming between Bias and Masbate Islands just short of the western entrance to the Strait. A final course change pointed them directly toward San Bernardino Strait, where navigation lights that were usually darkened instead were lit.

Philippine Sea, East of Samar, Early Morning (Midwatch), October 25

Onboard *Gambier Bay*, Larry Epping had just begun midwatch on the bridge as officer of the deck. From midnight to 4 A.M. he was responsible for *Gambier Bay's* movements, a sobering weight for a twenty-three-year-old. At least his watch would be over before *Gambier Bay* rumbled to life for the morning launches.

Just below the bridge, in *Gambier's* radar room, Lou Rice also stood midwatch. "I was on the air search—the SK radar." Lou, a Third Class Radarman from Columbus, Ohio, was a three-year Navy veteran. His first ship was the *Henderson*,[6] a Marine troop transport that left Pearl Harbor just after midnight on December 7, 1941, and cleared the outer channel before the Japanese attack began. Lou joined *Gambier* during construction and wangled his way into radar training in San Diego before her commissioning. "Right around 2:30 A.M., maybe 2:45, I started getting these sharp pips. They were off at the end of the scope, but still very sharp. I called them in, and when I did I said 'They're acting like surface ships.' So they started plotting them next door in CIC."

The pips stayed visible on the scope and moved closer. After an hour or so the dead reckoning plot—a rectangle of Plexiglas on which radar target coordinates were recorded, connected, and tracked—showed them following an erratic but unmistakable track. "Someone said, 'Well, we better tell the Skipper we got some good pips coming on.' So the Skipper came to the bridge. I stayed on the radar and kept tracking. Then they got the recognition officer up. He thought they were ionized clouds. I remember the Skipper asking, 'Well, what does the radar operator say?' They kept calling into me, 'What do you say?' Finally I told them: 'I say they're surface ships.'"

⚓

Below decks, VC-10 pilots Burt Bassett, Jim Lischer, Joe McGraw, and Gene Seitz slept the sleep of the young. Although accommodations in *Gambier Bay*'s officer country might not have been as plush as those of a fleet carrier, they were much better than accommodations on the screening destroyers around them. Jim would be roused soon for predawn CAP. Burt would take his TBM up for midday ASP. Joe also would fly midday. "The early CAP was getting back at 10 A.M., and we were going out to relieve them. So we had the morning off."

Dick Roby tried to sleep, too. He had flown the lead for Gene's and his own division three mornings on predawn CAP. So he arranged a switch: He and Gene would be the day's ready pilots. But then at 2 A.M., Dick's sleep was interrupted by a call from the hangar deck. "I was technically the squadron ordinance officer, though it didn't mean much because the ship had its own ordinance officer. But I got a call we were about to load torpedoes. There'd been some surface action reported down south. So I went down to the hanger deck and watched while they charged the fuel flasks on the torpedoes. Then we got a message saying, 'don't load them.' We'd already loaded two, so we left them on the planes. We degassed those two planes and left them on the hangar deck."

The predawn order of launch would begin with depth-charge-loaded TBMs for antisubmarine patrol, followed by FM-2s for CAP, and finally more FM-2s for ground support. Jim Lischer's Wildcat was one of those, although on this morning he was to remain on deck in reserve, engine ticking over, wing guns loaded, ready to launch on a moment's notice if another plane had problems.

Leyte Gulf, North of Surigao Strait, Early Morning (Midwatch), October 25

Onboard *Monssen*, Mel Melvin stretched out his blanket topside under the turret of mount 54. *Monssen*'s crew had been alerted they'd likely be going in for a nighttime torpedo attack against a Japanese force approaching from the south and heading up Surigao Strait. Those not on watch should try to sleep. They'd be awakened when the time came.

Mel was now *Monssen*'s mount 54 gun captain, a prize job and a promotion from his 40-mm station. Mel had been in the Navy long enough and listened enough to know the risks and consequences of a destroyer going in close to launch torpedoes. "I knew the poor success of destroyer torpedo launches, especially in the Pacific." Torpedomen lied as baldly and as often as gunner's mates, but some of their stories about the problems with these fish rang true. The electromechanical components of their tubes often malfunctioned; the impulse charges used to launch them got corroded and wouldn't ignite. The torpedoes themselves had troubled histories: tracking poorly, broaching, falling short, hitting yet not exploding, and even turning to pursue the ship firing them. There was reason enough to worry but little to do about it. Mel rested his head on his kapok life jacket beneath the overhang of his mount and slept as he'd been told to.

⚓

The crew of *Monssen*'s squadron mate *Melvin* received the same news. Lieutenant Ed Hawk, *Melvin*'s meticulous, bespectacled medical officer, readied himself and his three pharmacist mates. The son of an Indiana physician who died when Ed was sixteen, Hawk graduated medical school in 1942 and joined the Navy following a brief civilian internship. He received his orders to the *Melvin* three months after serving stints as medical officer on slower and more vulnerable APAs. "I was glad to finally be aboard a ship that could defend itself and even fight back."

Most medical supplies, including sterile packs of instruments, dressings, splints, and slings were stored in a small trunk on the main deck next to the starboard bulkhead. Ed carried his own knapsack with dressings and other supplies. Scattered around the ship were rigid metal litters, Thomas splints, and medical kits containing dressings, slings, and other supplies that needed to be checked. Packets of morphine syrettes originally included in these kits were now carried by ship's officers. "The syrettes had a way of disappearing when they were left unguarded."

The wardroom, just forward of the ship's CIC, was *Melvin*'s primary dressing station and Ed's battle station. It was equipped with a spotlight suspended from the overhead, and a sink in the adjacent pantry that could be used for scrubbing up. A second dressing station was in the sick bay amidships and was manned by the lead pharmacist mate. A third dressing station was in the after head, where another pharmacist mate had his battle station equipped with supplies. The third pharmacist mate was assigned to one of the repair parties on the main deck.

⚓

On *Grant,* patrolling in the same waters, Ed Pfeifer left sleep to return to his battle station on the wing of the bridge. Ed was *Grant*'s torpedo officer; his gang operated *Grant*'s two quintuple torpedo mounts, both loaded and ready to go.

As he arrived on the darkened bridge, Ed checked in with Gun Boss Jerry Marsh, stationed one level up in the basket. It was Jerry who'd sent Ed down to get some sleep. "We'd been at battle stations since early evening and Jerry saw we needed to relieve the men in turns. So he set up his own little watch rotation for the gunnery and torpedo gangs."

Jerry was the plot room officer when *Grant* was at Saipan and took over as Gun Boss when his predecessor was transferred. "He was a great gunfire control officer." But it wasn't likely there'd be much use for his skills tonight. Tonight it was supposed to be torpedoes only: Ed's show.

As he stood on the bridge, Ed pondered what he and the torpedo officers on the other destroyers might face ahead in the darkness. "We'd practiced endless torpedo firing drills, some under incredibly bad conditions, but the torpedo gang had never fired at a real target—one that could fire back." Tonight could well be his night—their night. "I'd taken my turn deciphering incoming fleet messages and I'd been the one to receive and decode the message about what might be coming after midnight." At the time his eyes widened and his hands trembled; part excitement, part anticipation, and large part honest fear.

There actually was little preparation needed. The fish, fueled with compressed air, would be ready once the air was topped and heated by torpedo alcohol to improve their striking range. The Mark 15's magnetic exploder mechanism never worked effectively, so the device was deactivated and fish reset to fire on contact. *Grant*'s practice fires—staged at all times during the day and in all kinds of sea and wind conditions—were tedious but necessary. His men knew their jobs, Ed knew his.

"Earlier in the evening I overheard one of the fire control technicians talking about all the ships in the Strait ready to confront the Japanese. The tech had been on a destroyer sunk in the Solomons early in the war. He said, 'I wish we'd had all of this back then.' I thought, 'Well, tonight we do.'"

Depiction of torpedo attack by USS *Melvin* (DD-680)
during the action in Surigao Strait

USS *Samuel B. Roberts* (DE-413)

USS *Hoel* (DD-533)

USS *Gambier Bay* (CVE-73)

Elco-type PT (patrol torpedo) boat

USS *California* during the Japanese attack on Pearl Harbor

FM-2 fighter aircraft (also known as the Wildcat)

TBM (torpedo bomber) (also known as the Avenger)

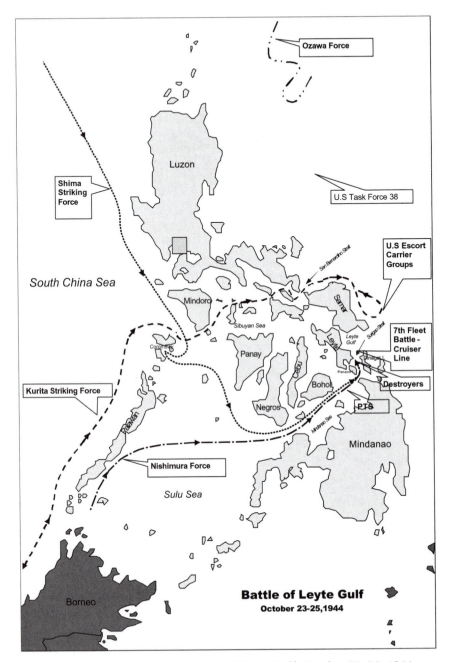

Labels on map:
- Ozawa Force
- Shima Striking Force
- Luzon
- U.S Task Force 38
- South China Sea
- U.S Escort Carrier Groups
- Mindoro
- San Bernardino Strait
- Samar
- Sibuyan Sea
- Leyte Gulf
- Surigao Strait
- Leyte
- 7th Fleet Battle - Cruiser Line
- Corregidor Bay
- Panay
- Dinagat I.
- Destroyers
- Cebu
- Panaon
- Kurita Striking Force
- Bohol
- Palawan
- Negros
- PTS
- Nishimura Force
- Mindanao Sea
- Mindanao
- Sulu Sea
- Borneo

Battle of Leyte Gulf
October 23-25, 1944

Summary of the actions in and around Leyte Gulf, October 23–25, 1944

Night in Surigao

Do not think of death as you use up every last bit of your physical and spiritual strength in what you do. Do not fear to die for the cause of everlasting justice. Do not stay alive in dishonor. Do not die in such a way as to leave a bad name behind you.

—Excerpt from Japan's *Imperial Rescript to Soldiers and Sailors*

STORM FRONT

Surigao Strait, Early Morning, October 25

At its widest point, Surigao Strait separates Leyte and Dinagat Islands by fourteen miles. The 490, 491, and 493 Boats sat midstream and waited. These would be confining waters for the big ships poised upstream, but to the sailors on the three small PTs it was like sitting in the middle of nowhere. As the hours dragged, 491's XO Terry Chambers felt both exposed and impatient. "The old military game of hurry up and wait. We eavesdropped on the VHF radio circuits—mostly ships' gossip and a confusing stream of sightings."

After midnight, clouds from an electrical storm brewing to the south covered what had been bright moonlight and moved over the boats. The clouds carried a squall and the crews prepared for a soaking. Just before the rain hit, the tips of the gun barrels and antennas buzzed with St. Elmo's fire; blue sparks and streamers of static electricity discharged into the heavy night air.

Terry remembered the Japanese ships coming in right behind the squall line. "I saw a lightning flash, and there they were in a column." Boat 491's skipper Harley Thronson's recollection had a different flavor. "The weather was miserable—really poor visibility. Suddenly we were in the middle of the Japanese formation. They turned on searchlights and opened fire."

Mindanao Sea, Afternoon and Evening, October 24

Transiting the Sulu Sea, Admiral Nishimura's seven ships approached Surigao Strait on schedule. Heavy cruiser *Mogami* with four destroyers led the column, followed by battleships *Fuso* and *Yamashiro*, Nishimura's flagship. Early that morning, American air strikes had scored a bomb hit on *Fuso*'s stern. The explosion destroyed a catapult plane and ignited a fire that crews had battled for nearly an hour. Destroyer *Shigure*'s forward gun mount was also hit and its crew killed. But now the fires on *Mogami* were extinguished, *Shigure*'s mount was repaired, and the ships crossed the Mindanao Sea and prepared to enter the Strait. Like Kurita, Nishimura was a seagoing admiral accustomed to the sacrifices and obligations of *Bushido*: his only son had been killed in the Philippines. And, like Kurita, Nishimura had no illusions about what lay ahead—absent a miracle, defeat, and destruction for his ships, near-certain death for him.

Second Striking Force, the orphan column of three Japanese cruisers and four destroyers commanded by Vice Admiral Kiyohude Shima, trailed thirty miles behind Nishimura's column. Although he was a principal player, Shima knew few details of the *Sho 1* plan. He had no precise instructions to communicate or coordinate with Nishimura, even though combining their forces would have doubled Japan's strike capacity in the Strait. It was a delicate matter of pride and seniority: Nishimura was more battle tested than Shima, but also less senior. This arrangement of following but not communicating or coordinating, although it made for odd tactics, avoided the awkward question of who should command if Nishimura and Shima did join up.

Shima's ships had sailed at daybreak from Coron Bay, a sheltered anchorage in the northern Palawan Islands. The tanker that was to have met them for fueling never showed, forcing Shima to redistribute his limited reserves and set off for Leyte with little fuel to spare. Second Striking Force's attack plan was to enter Surigao Strait as a single, separate column at sunrise on October 25. Shima's cruisers and destroyers would engage whatever remained in the wake of Nishimura's attack. If providence allowed, Second Striking Force would then sweep into Leyte Gulf to complete the destruction of the U.S. transports.

⚓

Aboard the U.S. combatants anchored in San Pedro Bay or patrolling Leyte Gulf, Seventh Fleet commanders still nursed painful memories of the disaster at Savo Island during the 1942 Guadalcanal campaign. U.S. and Australian warships assigned to protect the invasion transports had been overpowered at night by a nimbler Japanese force using better tactics, discipline, and weapons. Sleep-starved crews on the Allied ships had barely gotten off a shot, while the Japanese hurled salvo after salvo of 8-in. gunfire and launched deadly accurate spreads of long lance torpedoes. Three U.S. cruisers and one Australian cruiser were sunk in what sailors soon called Ironbottom Sound.

That night's carnage had forced the unprotected U.S. transports to flee, for a time depriving the Marines ashore of supplies and jeopardizing the Guadalcanal campaign. The Japanese navy had proven itself the master of night warfare. Two years later, planning for the night in Surigao was guided by a singular obsession: to avoid repeating Savo Island. The U.S. forces prepared to deal uncompromising destruction to the approaching Japanese.

⚓

The primary agent of that destruction was a parade of Seventh Fleet battleships shuttling slowly east and west north of Surigao Strait between Hingatungan Point on Leyte and a point north of Hibuson Island. Battle line ships consisted of *West Virginia, Tennessee, California, Maryland, Mississippi,* and *Pennsylvania.* All except *Mississippi* had been victims at Pearl Harbor three years before and had since been salvaged, patched, and returned to battle. By current standards all were old and slow, which explained their attachment to Seventh Fleet rather than Halsey's faster Third Fleet. Their speed was suited to the snail-pace invasion convoys and their guns, used primarily for shore bombardment, had all the firing reach and power necessary for this night's work.

During refitting, *West Virginia, Tennessee,* and *California* had each been equipped with the newest Mark 8 fire control radar (FCR), a replacement for the earlier Mark 3 FCR. Housed in fore and aft director stations designated Spot 1 and Spot 2, the Mark 8 FCR determined target range and direction more precisely than the Mark 3; it could detect very narrow targets (such as a ship headed bow on) and distinguish targets clustered close together. Using the Mark 8, crews could track surface targets as far away as thirty-two miles and begin firing at twenty-one miles. Most important, during night engagements, use of the newer system enabled accurate surface fire under complete radar control. Before the development of fire control radar, towering tripod masts and superior optics had given Japanese ships and crews the advantage in gunfire spotting and accuracy. But Japanese radar technology was only rudimentary.[1] Japanese ships risked being inescapably locked in U.S. crosshairs before they could calculate their own firing solutions.

In total, the six U.S. battleships' main batteries mounted sixty-four guns with either 16-in. or 14-in. muzzles. Despite this stunning firepower, there were limitations. Each battleship carried few rounds of the armor piercing (AP) ammunition needed to punch through the thick-armored skins of Japanese battleships. And after a week of shore bombardment, ships were even low on high capacity (HC) rounds used against unarmored targets. Gun crews were ordered to place remaining AP rounds closest to the gun breeches for initial salvos against the biggest Japanese ships, and to reserve their HC rounds for cruiser and destroyer targets.

Two and one-half miles south and parallel to the U.S. battle line were split lines of cruisers. *Phoenix*, *Boise*, and Australian *Shropshire* stood on the west side of Surigao Strait; *Louisville*, *Portland*, *Minneapolis*, *Denver*, and *Columbia* on the east side. The cruiser lines shuttled their own east–west circuits, shielding the battleship line and adding the offensive punch of their 6- and 8-in. gun batteries.

Cruiser *Nashville* had to be pulled from the plan. MacArthur was aboard *Nashville* and, sniffing the opportunity to witness a major sea battle firsthand, refused to budge. Because any harm to MacArthur outweighed any impact that *Nashville* could have in the coming fight, *Nashville* was tucked behind a screen of DEs and patrol craft protecting the transports in San Pedro Bay.

Battleship and cruiser lines traveled perpendicular to Surigao Strait's north–south channel. If things went as expected, the Japanese column would sail directly up the Strait, affording all the American big guns a clear line of fire along the cap of a "T." The northbound Japanese column would form the leg of that T (as had the Russians at Tsushima), limiting Japanese return fire to their forward guns. Once the T was capped, the American ships would command the northern entrance to the Gulf and be able to demolish the Japanese ships corseted in the narrow strait.

⚓

Twenty-eight U.S. destroyers were scattered through the Gulf, screening other ships, looking out for mines, and scouring island passages for submarines. When the Japanese entered the Strait, most DDs would be sent south to stab their flanks with surface torpedo strikes: six DesRon 24 DDs down the west side of the Strait, nine DesRon 56 DDs slashing down the east side.

Five DesRon 54 DDs became late additions to the mix. The ships were on submarine picket patrol and had been excluded from the original plan, but DesRon 54's commander Captain Jesse Coward coaxed an invitation for his ships to join. *McDermut* and *Monssen* were to attack down the west side of the Strait and three other DDs, including *Melvin*, down the east side. Added last, DesRon 54's DDs would go first, followed next by DesRon 24 and last by DesRon 56.

First to fight, though, would be the PTs. Boats stationed themselves—motors muffled down but running, crews at GQ stations—in thirteen sections of three boats each, flanking the Strait and its approaches. The two southernmost PT sections, whose six boats included Ron 12's PT 152 and Ron 7's PT 127, waited in the Mindanao Sea between Camiguin and Boho Islands. The northernmost sections hovered near Leyte's eastern shore just south of where the west side DDs would begin their strikes. All thirty-nine PT skippers had simple orders: report all contacts seen before attacking independently with torpedoes.

⚓

Onboard the battleships, cruisers, destroyers, and PTs, crews shook off the lethargy and boredom built up from days of tedious crossings, patrols, picket duty, and shore bombardment, using the afternoon and evening to get ready. Sailors serviced weapons, tied down loose items, secured hatches, restocked medical kits, and readied damage control and fire-fighting gear—all the routines essential to prepare the ship and to occupy the minds and hands of the edgy crews.

As night settled in, the Gulf, the Strait, and the Mindanao Sea approaches were crowded with U.S. combat vessels. Ships captains who might have stayed out of the action had instead clambered in. For those who had endured the humiliating low points of the war, there was a sense of at last being in the arena for the hour of exquisite revenge. But confining waters packed with attacking ships also created opportunities for confusion and lethal mistakes.

⚓

Battleship *California* went to GQ at 10:00 P.M. Turret 3's gun crew buttoned-up the mount, sat, and waited. Turret 3, the triple 14-in. gun mount called "after turret high," perched on the deck house aft of *California*'s superstructure. John Montgomery had worked and lived in Turret 3 since reporting to *California*, first as a handler in its lower powder handling room (where his bunk abutted one of the turret's magazines), then in upper handling, and finally in the gun house as center gun sight setter.

John had gained some weight since reporting to *California*, but he was still slender enough to routinely shimmy up the powder chamber with a putty knife and a rag soaked in castor oil to scrape off powder bag residue. His elevation from below decks to the gun house had been a practical necessity. "The charges were heavy. I could lift the bombarding bag, which was about seventy-two pounds. But I just couldn't lift the ninety-pound armor piercing charges, so they moved me up." Even for a small man like John, the gun house was confining. "The trainer and gunner had small bicycle seats, but I had nowhere I could really sit, just a little space near one of the hydraulic motors where I could crouch and brace my back against the bulkhead. We were there five to eight hours, just waiting and waiting. It got hot."

⚓

When destroyer *Grant*'s crew was first told about the coming night's attack, a ship's cook tracked down Emmett Crump. The cook, a boy from Tennessee, invited Emmett and a few other Southerners to sneak off to ship's galley to share a rare treat—bacon and tomato sandwiches made from the wardroom's supply of fresh tomatoes. "He didn't want them to go to waste and he figured it was even possible nobody would be around to enjoy them."

Despite the plans, the DDs continued regular afternoon and evening patrols. *Melvin* stalked the passage between Hibuson and the northern tip of Dinagat as if picket duty were the only thing in store for the ship and her crew. Still, her skipper Barry Atkins felt ready. The near disastrous attack by the Japanese Val two days before had jolted him with a bracing revelation. "I had never been on a Fletcher before. I was unfamiliar with their routines and before the attack, I'd been trying to do things the way the previous skipper Warner Edsall did. But when I called the officers into the wardroom to give them hell after the air attack, I suddenly realized this was my ship, not Warner Edsall's anymore. I really took hold at that moment. The XO once told me I was handling the ship like a damn PT, but that was okay with me. It was my ship."

⚓

The PT crews were keyed up. There'd been no call to use torpedoes off the beaches and jungles of New Guinea. Tonight, squaring off against big ships, the boats would have their chance.

Most boats carried extra riders: men from base force who had joined when the boats left New Guinea, plus the extras who managed to hitch a ride when action was brewing. One of 493's extras was a base force technician who'd come aboard to repair the radar and was still working as the boat left Tacloban. Another was a hospital corpsman named Bill Gaffney.[2] Gaffney was assigned to base force, but he had befriended 493's crew. "He was the type of kid you couldn't keep off patrol," recalled 493's skipper Bill Brown. "It was hard to explain why a boat would take a corpsman out on patrol, but Billy had to get into the action." On 493 and the other boats, crews waited through the night like platoons of foot soldiers expecting the Japanese to come over a hill, or cross no-man's-land.

⚓

Before dark a floatplane catapulted from *Mogami* to scout ahead of Nishimura's ships. The floatplane's pilot reports gave a poor, partial picture of what actually awaited. He spotted only a fraction of the battleships and cruisers in the U.S. battle line. He missed nearly all the destroyers and well over half the PTs—the cavalry and skirmishers lurking further south.

About this time, Nishimura realized his plan to rendezvous with Admiral Kurita at dawn on the 25th was out of the question. Air strikes had seriously delayed Kurita and would prevent his column from reaching the Gulf before late morning. Despite the unraveling plans, Nishimura's ships continued on course for the Strait. He radioed Kurita and Imperial Navy headquarters, projecting his own time of arrival in Leyte would be 4:00 A.M., a half-hour ahead of plan. At 11:15 P.M., while destroyer *Shigure* and the two battleships slowed near Bohol Island, cruiser *Mogami* and destroyers *Michishio, Asagumo,* and *Yamagumo* went ahead to reconnoiter.

SPARKS

Mindanao Sea, between Bohol and Camiguin Islands, 11:30 P.M., October 24–12:10 A.M., October 25

PTs 130, 131, and 152, three of six boats positioned furthest into the Mindanao Sea, were the first to spot the Japanese on radar. As the Japanese ships drew close, the three boats revved engines and dashed south. By 11:50 P.M., they actually saw the Japanese ships and began transmitting contact reports by radio. Within moments, lookouts on destroyer *Shigure* spotted the PTs. While *Fuso* and *Yamashiro* hung back, *Shigure* turned on searchlights, lofted illuminating star shells over the PTs, and advanced to confront them. Seconds later, 4.7-in. projectiles from *Shigure's* main batteries bracketed the PTs. The Battle of Surigao Strait began.

⚓

To Bob Clarkin on the 152 Boat, the next moments were a riotous blur. "The first thing I remembered was the boat hauling ass away. We hadn't fired torpedoes and we were caught in a searchlight. The noise was incredible." Bob heard an explosion forward. "Charlie Midgett, the guy on the bow thirty-seven-millimeter gun was down. He looked pretty bad to me. He probably died right away." Fires flared topside and below decks. "Some of the guys carried Charlie and a couple of wounded down to the skipper's cabin. The mattresses in crew's quarters were burning, so I went below, hauled them up, and tossed them over the side." By then, 152 was covered by screening smoke from the 130 Boat, but incoming rounds still howled and splashed around them. "The skipper signaled me to roll one of the stern depth charges." The charge exploded behind them. It was meant to fool the Japanese, but Bob doubted they'd even notice.

This was the first of a string of brief, unequal duels—a nuisance for the Japanese, chaos for the PT crews. Caught under destroyer star shells, searchlights, and gunfire, most boats had no time to line up a good torpedo shot. The 152 Boat—on fire, her bow splintered, one crewman dead and three others wounded—was the worst hit in the first duel. But Boat 130 also was pounded when its skipper Ian Malcolm[3] slowed to lay covering smoke for 152. "We took a hit on our port forward torpedo. It shaved off most of the warhead's TNT and ripped up twelve feet of deck before it left through the bow. The fish's detonator cap was hanging by a wire. I dove for it, but one of the gunner's mates got there first, tossed the detonator cap to me, and I batted it over the side." The concussion silenced 130's radio gear. Unable to communicate what he'd seen, Malcolm nursed the 130 southeast to link up with the three PTs waiting near Camiguin Island.

⚓

In 127's chart house, Tom Tenner picked up something on his radar screen. "I saw some blips and called them out. The skipper wanted to know more, but it was hard to judge course and speed; sometimes the radar picked them up sometimes it missed them, depending on how high the waves were. It seemed there were about eight ships: two large blips, one medium, and the rest smaller. We finally estimated their speed at twenty to twenty-two knots.

"Just then Boat 130 came over. They'd been shot up and lost their radio, but their skipper was able to tell us what he'd seen." Sitting topside as pointer on the forty-mm, Don Bujold heard Jack Cady's greeting to Ian Malcolm. "The boat captains had these Rudy Valle-type megaphones. I remember Jack Cady shouting across to Malcolm: 'Mal, are you scared?' And Malcolm shouted back: 'Hell, no, I'm terrified!' "

When the 130 Boat arrived, 127's radioman Jake Hanley left his top-side GQ station and went below. "We moved bow to bow with the 130, and Malcolm came aboard. We crowded into the chart room. Ian was pretty excited, but Cady was a man who could calm anyone down. Cady took down Malcolm's information; I got the code book out and converted the information into coded groups of four or five letters to transmit by voice on the radio. I had to repeat the code groups over and over before I got an acknowledgment. I could tell the Japanese were trying to scramble the signal, but I finally got a confirmation."

It was the 130's information and 127's transmission, received just after midnight, that first alerted the battleship, cruiser, and destroyer lines ex- actly what was coming and when to expect it. Meanwhile, Nishimura radioed Kurita: "Advancing as scheduled while destroying enemy torpedo boats."

Northern Mindanao Sea, Near Limasawa Island, 11:50 P.M., October 24–1:30 A.M., October 25

Three PT sections hovering near Limasawa Island spotted *Mogami* and the three destroyers as they curved north and prepared to rendezvous with *Yamashiro, Fuso,* and *Shigure.* The PTs (Ron 12's 146, 151, and 190 Boats) gave chase and fired torpedoes at *Mogami.* All the torpedoes missed and the boats sped away untouched under star shells, searchlights, and intense gunfire from destroyer *Yamagumo.* When 151's port engine briefly failed, its crew dropped depth charges, hoping, as had the 152's crew, to delay and confuse the Japanese.

At 1:00 A.M., Nishimura's two groups of ships—each of which had brushed aside a torpedo boat attack—reunited near Limasawa Island. When the ships reached the entrance of the Strait thirty minutes later, Nishimura again broke radio silence; this time he signaled both Kurita (whose ships were by now beyond San Bernardino Strait and in the Philippine Sea) and Shima (still thirty or so miles astern of Nishimura) his intention to enter the narrows between Panaon and Mindanao and continue fifty miles north into the Gulf.

Other than the irritating scrapes with the torpedo boats, Nishimura reported no more news about his enemy's situation. The Japanese must have felt that whatever lay ahead was best opposed in darkness, where their weapons and nighttime tactics gave them the edge. Two destroyers, *Asagumo* and *Michishio,* now led the battle formation. One mile astern steamed Nishimura's flagship *Yamashiro,* flanked by destroyers—*Yamagumo* to starboard and *Shigure* to port. Last in line, abreast and spaced six hundred yards apart, were *Fuso* and *Mogami.*

Surigao Strait, between Panaon and Sumilon Islands, 1:30 A.M.–2:15 A.M., October 25

The PTs could no longer depend on stealth or surprise. The Japanese had already swatted six boats and slipped by three more. Nishimura's seven ships now approached the choke point between Panaon and Mindanao, where fifteen more PTs waited—six boats in two sections near Panaon, nine boats in three sections on the opposite shore. The Japanese column took the shortest tack between their rendezvous near Limasawa Island and the Strait, maneuvering close to Panaon's southern tip as they changed heading from northeast to nearly due north. The PTs closest to Panaon, among them Ron 12's 194 Boat, stood in the way.

The 194's scrape with Kurita's ships was another brief and chaotic encounter. Andy Gavel, one of 194's torpedomen, stood near the cockpit on the boat's port side. "We made a run and I just managed to drop a torpedo over the port side. The guys on the thirty-seven-millimeter were firing on one of the Japanese ships. Then, as we swerved, the star shells lit us up like daylight. Next thing I knew they got us with a five-incher in the stern. Harold Jenkins, the pointer on the aft forty-millimeter, got hit. He was a cop from Philly, the oldest guy on the boat, thirty-six, I think. The shell also knocked out two of our engines, so we only had one left. We began putting out smoke. It seemed like they were peppering us with everything; quite a few people got shrapnel, but not me. With only one engine, we just had to wait it out. We couldn't do anything more."

⚓

For the next boats upstream it was more of the same. Three boats waiting close to the southern tip of Panaon chased after the Japanese column as it nosed into Surigao Strait. The boats snapped at the giant's heels with the same results: more missed torpedo shots and futile bursts of small caliber gunfire; more star shells, more blinding searchlights, and more incoming volleys of large caliber gunfire.

Across the Strait, two sections of PTs hovering near the northwest tip of Mindanao missed the action entirely. But a third section—boats from Ron 36, one of them J. P. Wolfe's 524 Boat "Bet Me"—picked up the scent, rumbled out from the cover of Sumilon Island, and attacked from the southeast. As the Ron 36 boats (PTs 523, 526, and 524) closed to within a mile of the Japanese column, the Japanese ships were backlit by their own star shells fired to illuminate the PTs on the opposite shore. The three boats formed abreast and steered west to begin torpedo runs. From his station at the port side torpedo rack, Walter Kundis could hear Wolfe's excited drawl on his headphones. "The skipper kept shouting 'Let's get in closer, let's get in closer!' We were only about a thousand yards from them. I was waiting to pull the lever and kept thinking 'Jesus Christ, we'll be able to tie up to them pretty soon.' "

Ron 36's boats were still unnoticed when Walt finally got Wolfe's command to fire. "I pulled the release lever. As the torpedo dropped, the boat dipped and I lost my balance." Walt began to topple. Once he hit the water he'd be on his own—none of the boats would dare stop. Just then Bob Wingfield, another torpedoman, grabbed Walt by the belt, broke his fall, and hauled him back in.

All of the Ron 36 torpedoes missed; the boats turned and fled in column at top speed, shielding their escape with smoke from 526. Unscathed, they found shelter in a cove behind Sumilon. But Walt heard an unsettling radio transmission from further up the Strait, from what he thought was the 493:

"On the headset I heard somebody screaming. 'Don't shoot, we're a PT boat!' They must have thought PT boats were shooting at them."

⚓

The 490, 491, and 493 boats faced head-to-head what boats just downstream had attacked from astern and on the flanks. The 491 immediately took withering fire. "Somehow, we'd gotten inside their destroyer screen," Terry Chambers remembered. "We were facing big ships and all we could do was aim our guns at the lights and the ships' bridges—like sticking our fingers in their eyes. We'd knock one light out and another went on."

On 493, Ted Gurzynski hunkered down behind the portside .50s, waiting for Bill Brown to release the guns. "The Japanese broke out searchlights and star shells. They found us—lights so bright you thought you were on stage—and started to fire at us. By then we were firing, too."

Standing in 493's cockpit, Bill Brown concentrated on torpedoes and guns and left boat driving to his XO Nick Carter.[4] "Nick was a good boat handler, so he had the wheel. I just tried to keep line of sight with the people pulling the lanyards to release the torpedoes."

Harley Thronson took 491 into its torpedo run. "For awhile we were moving in tandem with Bill Brown's 493. John McElfresh's 490 Boat was up ahead somewhere, but we really couldn't see him. I was able to get two torpedoes away. I don't know if we got a hit or not. An incoming shot blasted out the spotlight behind the cockpit, just missing Terry's head. We turned to get out of there. The Japanese ships were so close we could have bumped into one of them on the way out."

Meanwhile, Bill Brown released 493's torpedoes. "We ended up firing three torpedoes—a piece of shrapnel got imbedded in the hull and jammed the fourth fish in the rack. I ordered Nick to turn hard left, open throttles, and get out. I ran aft to turn on the smoke generator." The searchlight and star shell illumination made Bill feel like he was in a jailbreak: "I could even read the dials on my watch."

"We were running for hell," recalled Ted Gurzynski. All the guns that could bear—including Ted's .50s—continued blasting at the searchlights. A shower of 4.7-in. rounds continued splashing around them until 493 got hit once—and then twice more. "The first shell went right through, just below the deck but above the engines, just missing the gas tanks. The next knocked out the generator and went through the bottom of the boat on the starboard side." Boat 493 began to flood.

The third round was a deadly one, recalled Bill Brown: "It hit just aft of the chart house and got most of us. It hurled Nick and me out of the cockpit and up against the ready room canopy." Ted Gurzynski saw that Billy Gaffney, the corpsman, had been thrown into the well of the boat. "Billy was standing right there at the rack when the shell hit. He was killed instantly, blown right out of his shoes. Just the way he stood there, that's the way those shoes were. They didn't even turn over." Anthony Tatarek,[5] 493's cook, stationed at the forward 20-mm, suffered an agonizing gut wound. Moaning forlornly, he died within minutes.

Nine others on 493 were wounded or burned, including Bill Brown, who had flash burns, and Ted Gurzynski, whose hands were salted with bits of shrapnel. The 493's charthouse was wiped away, but its lone occupant, radioman Bill Sekerak,[6] had survived—spared when loss of power to the radios sent him aft to check the boat's generator. Tiny Al Brunelle, sitting miraculously untouched in the flooded engine compartment, was Sekerak's inadvertent savior: When water started coming in, Al cut the circuit breakers. Al also managed to slow the flooding by stuffing his kapok life jacket into the hole in the bottom of 493's hull. "I used my head instead of my body."

When Bill Brown finally signaled him to stop firing the .50s, Ted Gurcynski leaped from the gun tub. "The guns were red hot like Roman candles." Guns and engines silenced, 493's smoldering shell circled and drifted west toward Panaon. Bill Brown ducked into the engine compartment to inspect the damage. He marveled that Nick Carter still had the boat under control. "Nick was quite a sailor. We approached some rocky shoals as we got closer, but he got us through. But then finally we hit the rocks—bonk.

"The bow just hit bottom and 493 settled right there, bow up and stern down, maybe one hundred yards from shore. Everybody got back on the guns. We didn't know what was there." After a few minutes of waiting and peering into the darkness, one man jumped over the side and started wading to shore. "Somebody went first to see if anything was there while we covered him. We were ready to go down fighting. One by one we got off and waded to shore." Finally, the bodies of Billy Gaffney and Anthony Tatarek were carried to the beach.

⚓

By 2:15 A.M., Nishimura's ships had dueled or evaded 27 PT boats. The boats had fired over thirty torpedoes, all off target. Three crewmen—Midgett on 152, Gaffney and Tatarek on 493—had been killed, twenty others wounded. One boat—493—was aground; the others had raced or limped successfully to shelter along the shores and islands of the Strait. PT crews tended their wounded, caught their breaths, gulped water, and smoked cigarettes. The Japanese ships had lost a few searchlights and any pretense of taking the Americans by surprise.

Ten miles up the Strait, one final section of PTs drew a bead on Nishimura ships. But DesRon 54's commander Captain Jesse Coward warned the boats off. The destroyers were ready to go in.

LIGHTNING

Surigao Strait, between Leyte and Dinagat Islands, 2:30 A.M.–3:30 A.M.

At 2:30 A.M., DesRon 54's five DDs, began advancing south in two columns: *McDermut* and *Monssen* on the west side of the Strait close to Leyte's eastern shore, flagship *Remey*, *McGowan*, and *Melvin* on the east, the ships traveling five hundred yards apart.

Melvin's CO Barry Atkins had to race his ship into position. "We were still patrolling the narrows between Hibuson and Dinagat. We were pretty far east, while *Remey* and *McGowan* were running between Leyte and Hibuson. So, when word came to attack, I had to hurry just to catch up with the others as they went down the Strait." Ray Dupler, *Melvin*'s Chief Yeoman and Barry's phone talker on the bridge, felt equal parts "ready to go" and "ready to run." "As we went in I kept looking around, thinking, 'If anything happens, which direction do I swim? Which island has the fewest Japanese?'" *Melvin*'s CIC officer Brit Turner knew the details of the PT boats' sightings and realized what was coming: "My birthday was the next day. I was twenty-two and I was wondering if I was going to see twenty-three." On the fantail, John Ruddick, a twenty-one-year-old snipe from West Texas assigned to the after repair party, waited with the simple confidence that seemed to mark his life: "That was a peculiar thing about me, I guess. I'd never been in a situation where I thought I wasn't going to make it. I figured if *Melvin* went down but its mast was poking up, I'd be the one holding it up."

Just before *Monssen* began its run down the west side, its CO C. K. Bergin[7] flipped on the intercom to speak to his crew. For those like Mel Melvin, who'd never stood watches on the bridge and knew the captain only by story and mimicry from those who did, it was like hearing the disembodied voice of God. The voice told them the Japanese were close. *Monssen* was about to make its torpedo run. He knew that each of them would do their duty. He would do his. He prayed that God ("I knew he meant the one that outranked him") would be with them all. Ahead, on *McDermut*'s bridge, CO C. B. Jennings ordered up none of the small speed changes that infuriated the snipes and earned him the name "Jingle Bells" Jennings. Instead, *McDermut* plowed steadily through the dark, first at twenty knots and then at twenty-five. Below, on the main deck, starboard side, Motor Machinist Mate Dick Ralstin huddled with the rest of forward repair—a damage control party of deck and engineering rates.

The temperature topside was eighty degrees; bridge, torpedo, and gun crews on the 40s and 20s caught the breeze stirred by the ships' movement. Crews at interior battle stations got no relief behind dogged portholes and watertight doors, in the confines of CIC, radar, and gun plot rooms, in the swelter of engineering spaces, standing, sitting, or waiting in darkness or under the spectral glow of red battle lamps.

While the U.S. ships steadily accelerated, the Japanese redeployed forces into battle formation. Destroyers *Asagumo*, *Michishio*, *Shigure*, and *Yamagumo* moved to the van, trailed by battleships *Yamashiro* and *Fuso* and cruiser *Mogami* at one-kilometer intervals. Neither side had yet found the other on radar. The Japanese ships traveled north at twenty-five knots. The two short southbound columns of five American DDs and the longer northbound formation of seven Japanese DDs, battleships, and cruiser converged at a combined speed of forty-five knots, quickly ratcheting up to fifty-five knots—a land speed exceeding sixty miles per hour. They were like darkened, barreling trains converging onto the same set of tracks.

⚓

DesRon 54's skippers had been cautioned to hold their gun batteries during the approach—another hard lesson at the expense of the ships buried in Ironbottom Sound. Muzzle flashes only revealed the hunter; 5-in. 38 projectiles could hardly dent battleship armor. Gun bosses like Bill Robie on *Melvin* and gun captains like Mel Melvin on *Monnsen* sat as spectators in the hatches of directors and mounts.

At 2:40, steaming on the east side of the Strait astern of *Remey* and ahead of *Melvin*, *McGowan* first picked up the Japanese on its surface radar eighteen miles away. *Melvin*'s radar operators picked up the contacts two minutes later. At 2:50, division commander Jesse Coward on *Remey* ordered the three east-side destroyers left to course 150 degrees to give all three DDs a clear firing angle.

At 2:57, Coward ordered turns further left to 120 degrees and assigned targets to west- and east-side columns. All five DDs would target the three big ships at the end of the Japanese formation. *Remey* would fire at the first of the three—it turned out to be *Yamashiro*. *McGowan* and *Melvin* had the next—*Fuso*. On the west side *McDermut* and *Monnsen* got the third—*Mogami*. At 2:58 Coward ordered all the columns to increase speed to thirty knots, turn, and fire torpedoes when ready.

Just then a searchlight swept over the east side column. Standing in front of *Melvin*'s pilothouse, skipper Barry Atkins wasn't concerned about the light. "The range was over ten thousand yards, and I knew from PT attacks that searchlights aren't very effective beyond five thousand yards." What did concern him was the target distance. "We were still out of range. You have to go in as close as you can, and when they open up it's time for you to launch. When Coward ordered us to fire, I thought to myself: 'What the hell is he doing? If it was up to me I'd wait.' But then I thought: 'Well, Jesse's the boss.' If I was boss and somebody didn't do what I wanted done,

I'd throw him the hell out of my squadron. So I got ready to fire—though I did hold off a little bit to get us just within range."

Each of the east-side ships pivoted to starboard, a piece of choreography that unmasked the torpedo launchers and took the ships out of column. When torpedo launches began, *Remey*, the closest in column on the east side, was about four-and-a-half miles northeast of *Yamashiro*; *Melvin*, last in column, was about six miles northeast of *Fuso*, but nudging closer.

The DDs' CICs adjoined the ships' radar rooms—two small spaces separated by a curtain. On one side of the curtain, radar operators picked out the ranges and bearings of assigned targets from clusters of blips on SG radar screens and called them out to plotters on the other side. Plotters marked the positions on plotting boards, building a trail across time to establish target courses and speeds.

The full array of target data (bearings, ranges, courses, and speeds) was called up from CIC to the bridge where torpedo officers and fire control technicians dialed it into the Mark 27 torpedo directors. These steel boxes, faced with panels of backlit displays and brass control knobs for dialing in target data, calculated and fed target bearings to indicator dials at the torpedo mounts. The directors' electromechanical logic had to account for all the vessels in motion: the firing ship, the target ship, and the torpedo itself. It was a precise calculation, but it was also like passing firing instructions to a blind marksman.

Crews at the mounts had to keep pace with changing angles between hunter and target, cranking the tube barrels to bearings that "matched pointers." Crews also had to set speed, depth, gyro angle (the torpedo's basic course setting), and spread (the angles of divergence between torpedoes as they left the mount). At these distances, the Mark 15s traveled a little faster than 33 knots—intermediate speed. For the big targets approaching through the Strait, the torpedoes were set to run deep—twenty-two feet below the surface. Successful trips—fish set and held to the right course (not to where the target was, but to where it would be), speed and depth, a prey that hadn't outguessed the hunter—would take anywhere from eight to ten minutes.

Torpedo officers turned firing keys—one for each torpedo—sending electronic signals to the tubes. At the tubes the signals ignited black powder impulse charges that jerked the torpedoes forward. As the torpedoes began to move, tripping latches started torpedo engines and gyros. On the rush through the barrels, the torpedoes rode slotted rails that ensured they would jump rather than fall into the water.

At 3:01 A.M. torpedoes began leaping from *Remey*, *McGowan*, and *Melvin*. Within seventy-five seconds, twenty-seven fish were on their way. Clear of the launch tubes and under their own power, the torpedoes became self-contained vessels—TNT-capped twenty-four-foot-long engines of alcohol and compressed air storage flasks, combustion chambers, valves, nozzles, turbines, reduction gears, driving propellers, and guiding rudders. During their journeys, the Mark 15 torpedoes hungrily consumed internal reservoirs of air and alcohol. In mid-section combustion chambers, compressed air and fuel mixed, burned, and expelled streams of superheated gas to spin torpedo turbines, reduction gears, and propeller shafts. In torpedo warheads, exploder mechanisms began arming as torpedoes gained distance from launching ships. Within a minute of launch, mechanisms were set to trip warheads whenever the torpedoes hit solid objects. Close would not be good enough.

When working right, torpedo machinery also attended to instructions dialed in before launch. Lead ballast, mounted in the nose, kept torpedoes from rolling. Two internal control mechanisms—one for depth, one for steering—worked to keep torpedoes true to settings. Sensors and detectors (gyroscopes for steering, diaphragms and pendulums for depth) spotted variations and sent correcting orders to steering and depth engines. Engines nudged vertical rudders to counter drift, horizontal rudders to correct depth.

⚓

From his GQ station in *Melvin*'s wardroom, Medical Officer Ed Hawk heard the activity in CIC just off the adjoining passageway. "I picked up someone's voice saying, 'Seven is gone, eight is gone, nine is gone, ten is gone.' Then 'Let's get the hell out of here!'" Ed couldn't resist the temptation to go out on deck. "Jim Woods[8] was on deck with his midships repair party. As we stood there, a star shell burst above the mast, a salvo splashed the water off the port beam, *Melvin* heeled over turning north, and smoke started to pour from the stacks." From his station in the gunfire director, Bill Campbell could see the same star shell flashes. "Most of them fell short, but some went off far enough behind us to silhouette all three ships."

The three DDs fled northeast on courses to take them between Hibuson and Dinagat Islands. Japanese gunfire reached out for them. To fire torpedoes, Barry Atkins had brought *Melvin* incrementally closer to the Japanese than either *Remey* or *McGowan*. Now he swung her hardest to port, pulling *Melvin* to the inside of the retreat track. "Barry K kept us zigzagging all the way out," recalled Ray Dupler. "We made our smoke screen and funnel smoke, and the turns really spread out the smoke—first to one side and then the other. As we moved to the next leg, the Japanese shells went by, heading for where we'd just been."

All three ships ran out of column, a good thing: an orderly formation would have presented Japanese radars with a big combined contact—a "knuckle" that would have made gunfire targeting much easier. As it was, the Japanese shells fell short and wide. To John Ruddick on *Melvin*'s fantail, the Japanese shells sounded like "West Texas freight trains going over a wooden bridge." To Barry Atkins, the shell splashes felt like depth charges going off. "On New Guinea, I'd taken close-in fire like this from Japanese destroyers. I told the bridge crew not to worry—they won't hit us. But I had no reason to think they wouldn't."

⚓

Coming down the west side of the Strait, *McDermut* and *Monssen* maneuvered east of the six DesRon 24 DDs waiting, like horses at a starting gate, to go in next. *McDermut* and *Monssen* went to twenty-five knots and turned slightly west on a course that hugged Leyte's eastern shoreline. Surface radars picked up the Japanese ships bearing fifteen miles southeast. As *McDermut* and *Monssen* closed, the Japanese fired star shells and caught *McDermut* in a searchlight beam.

When *McDermut* and *Monssen* swung left to get into firing position, the Japanese opened fire on *Monssen*. *Monssen*'s CO swung her even further left and even closer to the Japanese, this time to make sure her torpedo mounts weren't masked by *McDermut*. A chorus of anxious groans went up from crew watching from the weather decks. "We were awfully close as it was," recalled Mel Melvin. "Getting even closer didn't seem like such a good idea. A lot of us were saying under of breath 'Turn right, dammit, turn right.'"

Both ships finally swung south, fired torpedoes, and continued careening to starboard as they retreated northwest. *McDermut* and *Monssen* cranked up speed, sent up covering smoke from stacks and smoke generators, and zigzagged frantically. Spotlights and gunfire chased them; shell splashes washed over the after mounts. The smoke generator on *Monssen*'s stern caught fire. Quickly, mattresses from the crew's after berthing space were heaved up and tossed on to smother the flames.

DesRon 54's piece of the battle was over in less than twenty minutes. Its skippers and crews had only to wait for the results of the torpedo shots. "After about six or seven minutes of being straddled by Japanese gunfire it became annoying," recalled *Melvin*'s skipper Barry Atkins. "Finally I asked CIC, 'When the hell do our torpedoes arrive?' They told me two more minutes."

From his perch on the *Melvin*'s director basket, Bill Campbell could still see the Japanese ships astern. "*Melvin*'s fantail fishtailed and vibrated like it was going to fall off. Then there was a huge explosion." Across the Strait, soaked in seawater and watching from the top hatch of *Monssen*'s mount 5, Mel Melvin witnessed the same explosion. "One of the Japanese ship's forward mounts popped straight up in the air like a big hand had picked it up and thrown it away." The eruption turned out to be *Fuso*, the next-to-last ship in the Japanese column.

Fuso was struck amidships by one torpedo, the first impact in an accelerating chain. Inside the torpedo's warhead, an exploder mechanism—a condenser discharging electricity through a simple switch—ignited a detonator charge. The detonator then exploded a booster charge, in turn triggering the main charge. Exploding under water, virtually all the force of the torpedo warhead's eight hundred pounds of TNT transferred to *Fuso*'s armor. The force breached *Fuso*'s hull and ruptured fuel tanks, igniting fires that spread to an ammunition magazine. The magazine explosion—the final cataclysm—split *Fuso* in two. *Fuso*'s severed torso and trunk drifted on the surface, disgorging dead, wounded, and dazed Japanese sailors, most destined for the bottom of the Strait.

Fuso's destruction had been the work of a torpedo from *Melvin*.[9] *Remey*'s torpedoes, targeted for battleship *Yamashiro* and set for *Yamashiro*'s range, were mistakenly aimed at destroyer *Yamagumo* and missed both ships. *McGowan*'s, aimed correctly at *Fuso,* but set with *Yamashiro*'s range, also missed. Firing from across the Strait, *Monssen* and *McDermut* had better results. *Monssen* scored a hit on *Yamashiro*, whereas *McDermut*'s torpedoes, intended for cruiser *Mogami,* instead tracked north of the big ships to hit at least three Japanese destroyers. One destroyer, *Yamagumo,* soon exploded and sank, while the bow of a second, *Asagumo,* was blown off. Bowless *Asagumo* and *Michishio,* the third destroyer, both slowed.

In the jaws of DesRon 54's swift pincer, despite misjudgments and many more misses than hits, torpedoes from the five DDs had destroyed, crippled, or slowed five of Nishimura's seven ships. All DesRon 54's temporary ships and temporary sailors had emerged untouched.

⚓

Even as the first chain of explosions continued, the next DD contingent prepared to go in. The ships—five American and one Australian destroyer assigned to DesRon 24—churned down the Strait in two staggered sections. *Hutchins, Daly,* and *Bache* went first, hugging close to Leyte's eastern shoreline as had *McDermut* and *Monssen.* Their skippers intended to loop south of the Japanese force, blocking any seaward escape. The second section, Australian destroyer *Arunta* leading *Killen* and *Beale,* began its run further north and only a bit further east in the Strait.

As the DesRon 24 ships neared their launch points, the explosion of destroyer *Yamagumo* bathed the Strait in bright light and geysers of sparks, exploding munitions, mangled bodies, and debris. *Arunta, Killen,* and *Beale* fired torpedoes first, a combined spread of fourteen fish aimed at a dwindling choice of targets: destroyer *Shigure,* cruiser *Mogami,* and battleship *Yamashiro.* Only one of the torpedoes hit, a fish from *Killen* that hammered a second blow against *Yamashiro.*

Once *Hutchins, Daly,* and *Bache* reached the southern limit of their run, just east of Leyte's Amagusan Point, they turned sharply to port, headed north, acquired targets, and fired fifteen torpedoes, but none found a target. The three DDs completed a full loop, swung east and finally north, trading gunfire with cruiser *Mogami,* now retreating south. *Hutchins* launched a final spread of five torpedoes, aiming at bowless *Asagumo,* instead hitting *Michishio,* which immediately exploded and sank. As they left the turmoil, the three DDs also overtook the wounded battleship *Yamashiro,* still heading north and by now taking fire from the lines of U.S. cruisers and battleships.

THUNDER

Leyte Gulf, East of Higatungan Point and North of Hibuson Island, 2:30 A.M.–3:10 A.M.

The column of battle line ships paraded through smooth seas brushed by a light southeast wind, under clear dark skies interrupted by occasional squalls. The serene steel majesty above decks hid human exhaustion within. The long wait and oppressive heat sapped energy from battle line gun crews who'd had been at GQ since well before midnight. Above decks, buttoned up in the thickly armored lozenge-shaped gun houses or entombed in hot, airless, watertight spaces below decks many were beyond misery. Four levels down in *West Virginia,* Marvin Childress, an eighteen-year old Missourian, was one of twenty men waiting it out in the after powder magazine. "We were down about as far as you could go. We went in early and stayed a long time at GQ. They'd shut off all the hatches and we'd pretty much used up the little cooler of water we had down there. One man wore earphones, but there wasn't much information coming our way." Few had a sense of the history that was unfolding above them.

At 3:04 (three minutes after DesRon 54's torpedo launches, five minutes before the first torpedo hits), the Japanese ships began showing as blips at the edges of SG radar screens in *West Virginia*'s plot room, estimated distance forty-four thousand yards. At 3:05, *West Virginia,* last in the battle line on the westbound leg, countermarched east and became first in line. At 3:10, main battery plot reported that Spot 2, *West Virginia*'s aft Mark 8 FCR, had picked up the targets first seen on the SG radar. As the minutes passed, Spot 2 never relinquished its aiming lock on the remaining Japanese ships.

Surigao Strait, near Hibuson Island, 3:30 A.M.–4:00 A.M.

DesRon 54 and 24 DDs had already launched nearly eighty torpedoes. Surigao Strait was crisscrossed with their wakes, with the maneuvering U.S.

DDs and the dismembered, sinking, crippled, or struggling remnants of Nishimura's column. Japanese dead as well as wounded and shipless survivors crowded the waters.

But the destroyers weren't quite finished. Even before *Hutchins*, *Daly*, and *Bache* launched their last torpedoes, DesRon 56's nine ships, positioned north of the eastern line of U.S. cruisers, went in. Their skippers planned to envelop and choke the remains of the Japanese force, now effectively reduced to northbound battleship *Yamishiro* and three retreating ships: cruiser *Mogami*, bowless destroyer *Asagumo*, and untouched destroyer *Shigure*.

DesRon 56 separated into three sections of three ships each, Section one, destroyers *Newcomb*, *Richard P. Leary*, and *Albert W. Grant*, took the middle of the Strait, approaching the Japanese head on. Section two, *Robinson*, *Halford*, and *Bryant*, approached to the east, along a line west of Hibuson Island to keep them east of the Japanese. Section three, destroyers *Bennion*, *Leutze*, and *Heywood L. Edwards*, headed south on a line further west, steering to stay clear of DesRon 24's escape route while keeping to the west of the Japanese.

Bob Read was a quartermaster stationed in *Leary*'s pilothouse. "It was calm weather and a night black like pitch except for the wake from *Newcomb* ahead of us." Bob Durand, another quartermaster, had the wheel. "I was feeling scared as hell. I'd been scared before and since, but never as bad. You couldn't run or hide, and you couldn't dig a hole in the deck. I just kept my mind on following the *Newcomb*."

Leyte Gulf, East of Higatungan Point and North of Hibuson Island, 3:30 A.M.–4:30 A.M.

Some battleships and cruisers had firing solutions as early as 3:30 A.M., but held fire as DesRon 24's six DDs retreated and DesRon 56's nine DDs attacked. The battleship column was by then on its eastbound leg, traveling at fifteen knots, ships spaced at one-thousand-yard intervals. *West Virginia* led, followed by *Maryland*, *Mississippi*, *Tennessee*, *California*, and *Pennsylvania*. The eastern line of cruisers steamed sixty-five hundred yards south of the battle line, also due east, but, at ten knots and five-hundred-yard intervals, more slowly and more closely together. Cruiser *Louisville* was in the van, followed by *Portland*, *Minneapolis*, *Denver*, and *Columbia*.

The big ships could wait only so long for the DDs: their armor piercing (AP) rounds needed distance—and the trajectory and acceleration that came with distance—to be effective. The battleships had permission to begin firing when targets closed to twenty-six thousand yards. At 3:51, the cruisers opened up with targets at fifteen thousand six hundred yards. During the next eighteen minutes, 6- and 8-in. guns on the three west-side cruisers and five east-side cruisers would unleash an orgy of gunfire—more than one thousand rounds from the west side, more than three thousand from the east. Most early salvos targeted battleship *Yamashiro* before firing shifted to cruiser *Mogami* and destroyer *Shiguri*. Some rounds would go disastrously astray.

Battle line fire was more deliberate. *West Virginia*'s 16-in. guns fired the first battleship rounds at 3:53 at the Japanese twenty-two thousand eight hundred yards distant. Two minutes later, *Tennessee*'s and *California*'s 14-in. guns opened up. As the first six-gun salvos thundered, the battle line pulled ahead of the eastern cruiser line. But at 3:55, just as *Tennessee* and *California* opened fire, the battleships turned right simultaneously to course one hundred twenty degrees; the course change brought the six ships parallel, all heading southeast. Four minutes into the turn *Maryland*'s big guns joined the barrage. *Maryland*'s gunners aimed using *West Virginia*'s shell splashes because *Maryland*'s FCR could not calculate a firing solution. Then, beginning at 4:02, all six battleships countermarched, returning to column on course two hundred seventy. Last became first in line, and first last: *Pennsylvania, California, Tennessee, Mississippi, Maryland,* and *West Virginia.*

In the battleships' main batteries—the 16-in. guns on *Pennsylvania, Mississippi, Maryland,* and *West Virginia*, the 14-in. guns on *California* and *Tennessee*—gun house, handling room, and magazine crews worked the vertical assembly lines that produced salvos. On *West Virginia*, Marvin Childress and the others in the after powder magazine jumped to work. "We brought the bags out—both AP and bombardment—and passed them down to the turret ring. Then we shoved the bags up the chute. The gun room grabbed them and we kept passing them until they told us to stop."

In the gun houses, projectiles arrived before powder bags and were pushed and seated in gun breeches by chain-driven ramming pistons. Powder bags followed and the ramming piston returned to pack them against the projectiles. When the rams withdrew, breechblocks lifted, closed, and latched. Gun captains stepped off loading platforms and pushed "ready" switches.

Had the battle line guns been in local control, gun house crewmembers like John Montgomery would have trained, sighted and fired the guns. As it was, the crews could only brace themselves as firing keys were squeezed in gun plot rooms. Each three-gun salvo actually was a stuttered sequence— simultaneous firing would only throw off trajectories. Topside, the eruption of noise, smoke, and flaming gas from the gun muzzles was volcanic. Inside the gun houses, the noise was muffled: a "whoosh"—an immense whisper— followed by the lunging hydraulic recoil of tree trunk–size barrels and breeches. Four levels down, Marvin and the magazine crew heard very little. "We could feel a little vibration, that's about all. But we knew it was something big."

⚓

Battleship *Yamashiro* was the U.S. battle and cruiser lines' most conspicuous target. When firing began, *Yamashiro* was headed nearly due north,
but as the U.S. battleships turned southeast and then west, *Yamashiro* also
turned west and then finally south. She was retreating. It was like a carnival
shooting gallery in which the targets were shooting first. As *West Virginia*,
then *California* and *Tennessee* and finally *Maryland* opened fire, the
American battleships stood within an arc ten degrees east of *Yamashiro*'s
bow to about five degrees west. Head on at first, *Yamashiro* showed a
narrow target profile. Then her westbound course expanded the target until
Yamashiro's target surfaces—her bridge, funnels, and mainmast—were
beam-on. As *Yamashiro* fled south, the American battle line stood thirty
degrees abaft *Yamashiro*'s starboard beam.

⚓

On their climb up and their plunge down, the big projectiles rumbled with a
distinctive freight train clatter. But near the top of their trajectories, arcing
over DesRon 56's advancing ships, the projectiles glowed like constellations
of red-hot coals.

DesRon 56's section two and section three ships had launched torpedoes quickly but unsuccessfully at *Yamishiro* and *Shigure,* while the two
Japanese ships were still northbound. Section two's ships were chased by
Japanese salvo splashes but escaped untouched as they turned to port and
retreated close in to Hibuson Island. Section three's destroyers, also untouched, turned to starboard and fled west to the shelter of Leyte.

On *Grant*'s bridge, torpedo officer Ed Pfeifer shuttled between the
Mark 27 directors on either bridge wing as the angle on *Grant*'s target
shifted—it turned out to be *Yamashiro* turning from north to west. Three
operators from the torpedo gang followed Ed. "Whenever I changed directors, Ed Carlson stayed behind on the other to maintain target and speed
settings." Aft, on the torpedo mounts, crews scrambled to match pointers:
one man trained the mount while the other tweaked gyro, speed, and depth
settings.

It was 4:00 A.M. before *Newcomb, Leary,* and *Grant* were ready to fire
torpedoes. Standing at *Leary*'s helm, Quartermaster Bob Durand was
suddenly busy: "As we closed, the target turned ninety degrees to port. I
brought the helm over to head us southwest. The torpedoes were set to go
off to starboard, but we'd changed the angle of the attack, so they had to be
reset for the port side. Just as we fired, somebody hollered, 'torpedoes to
port!' and I got a 'full right rudder!' from the skipper. I spun the wheel over
against the stops. Two torpedoes went up the port side, close aboard. Then

someone hollered, 'Jesus Christ, torpedoes to starboard!' I expected the next command, so I swung the wheel hard to port and those fish missed us close aboard our starboard side."

At *Grant*'s torpedo mounts, crews laboring to match pointers were also changing speed settings. As target range decreased, the torpedoes could burn more fuel over a shorter distance—settings were ratcheted from slow to intermediate and finally to fast. On *Grant*'s bridge, Ed Pfeifer adjusted his firing solution. "Jerry Marsh promised to tell me if the target was a battleship, cruiser, or destroyer. This meant changing the torpedoes' depth setting—shallow for a cruiser or destroyer, deep for a battleship. But when it came time to fire, all Jerry kept saying was 'Ed, it's a big son of a bitch!' To be safe, I left the depth at shallow." Ed began turning the five firing keys for the after mount's tubes. The first key turned and the first fish was gone. But the second key broke in Ed's hand; he ordered the after crew to fire the remaining four torpedoes by hand.

Newcomb, *Leary*, and *Grant* fired thirteen torpedoes in total. After *Leary*'s maneuvers to evade incoming torpedoes, all three DD's headed west to parallel the course of the upstream battle line and prepared to turn northeast to escape—*Newcomb* still leading, followed by *Leary* and *Grant*. The ships rode under the arcs of projectiles from both sides. Their after 5-in. guns began firing at the Japanese ships. On *Leary*'s bridge, Torpedo Officer Lieutenant E. F. Harrington and Quartermaster Bob Read were timing the torpedo runs. "It was plenty noisy now. You could see the flashes from their guns and from ours. Someone's shell flew right between the two stacks. A terrible sound, like a locomotive." Bob Durand recalled, "Lieutenant Harrington yelled 'Now!' With that there were two heavy explosions downrange." Someone's torpedoes, most likely *Leary*'s, had hit *Yamashiro*.

Newcomb, *Leary*, and *Grant* turned northeast. *Newcomb* and *Leary* were in the clear, but *Grant*'s luck ran out: during her turn she was rocked by salvos from both sides. *Grant* slowed and absorbed blow after blow—6-in. rounds from the U.S. cruisers, 4.7-in. rounds from the Japanese. Bob Durand remembered the moment: "Somebody cussed out: 'the *Grant*'s been hit.' She stayed in column for awhile and then she fell out."

DELUGE

Leyte Gulf, West of Hibuson Island, 4:00 A.M.–5:00 A.M.

With *Grant* under fire, Ed Pfeifer ordered the forward torpedo mount crew to jettison torpedoes. "Suddenly there was a huge explosion on the main deck, about thirty feet below and behind me. Bodies flew across the bridge." Someone fell across Ed's sound-powered phone line, sending him sprawling to the deck. His back flashed with pain. "When I got to my feet, I saw that Ed Carlson was down and not moving on the opposite wing."

Grant's after 5-in. mounts had been firing under director control during escape. Ralph Natali, a second class gunner's mate, was mount 5's pointer. "I heard Marvin Jones, the mount captain, shout 'Standby!' Then there was a big thump and the mount's hydraulics went out." A gust of shrapnel swept through the gun house and Ralph felt a buzz of heat spread across his back.

Grant was dead in the water after being hit nearly twenty times, most often, it turned out, by rounds from U.S. cruisers. The explosion in mount 5 had also torn through the crew's after berthing compartment. A gash at the waterline flooded *Grant's* forward engine compartment, storerooms, and berthing compartments. A hit to one of the forward 40-mm gun mounts exploded nearby ammunition and ignited raging fires. Explosions amidships killed medical officer C. A. Mathieu, five radiomen, and nearly all of a repair party. Part of *Grant's* superstructure was flattened and its radar stanchions toppled. An explosion in the scullery killed the Tennessee cook who had invited Emmett Crump to feast on bacon and tomato sandwiches. Lights, telecommunications, radars, radios, and steering were gone.

Grant's CO, T. A. Nisewaner, ordered Ed to the engineering spaces to find out if the ship could get underway. Hits to the engineering spaces could be like gut wounds—a watertight door might conceal fatal internal damage. When he got below, Ed found a hive of activity and a chief who promised that they'd soon be getting up steam. Ed scrambled back to the bridge, reported the news, and began to help with the wounded. Ed Carlson was dead; one of the phone operators was still alive but badly wounded.

Alerted to the destruction on *Grant,* the battleships and cruisers paused their fire. Emmett Crump and the rest of mount 3's gun crew stumbled out, shaken and confused. Fires interrupted the darkness and lit up the surrounding carnage. Up forward, Emmett could see that most of *Grant's* masts and radar stanchions were either toppled or standing in disarray. "I had no idea what had happened or what I should do." Finally, a corpsman showed Emmett and the others how to administer the morphine syrettes and sent them off to comb the ship for injured.

Ralph Natali reached the after crews' quarters, where he ran into Bill Swain, a pharmacist mate first class and the only surviving member of *Grant's* medical department. Ralph helped Bill treat the wounded. The most seriously injured seemed to be from the boiler spaces. Several men had been parboiled by steam. "As we undressed one, sheets of skin and muscle peeled away along with his clothes. Another man crawled in with his leg broken and his foot barely attached by muscle and tendon." When Swain left the after head, Ralph followed him through the ship as Swain tried to deal with what seemed an unending stream of wounded.

Back on the bridge a signalman picked up a battery-powered signaling device. In the dark pre-dawn he stood out on one of the bridge wings, flashing recognition signals at an approaching ship. It was a dangerous moment of truth—every gun still afloat in the Strait was likely to be aiming and ready to fire at any spark of light that showed. The men on *Grant's* bridge had no way of knowing whether U.S. ships or Japanese ships were approaching. Grant's signal was answered by a signal of recognition. The approaching ships turned out to be destroyers *Newcomb* and *Richard P. Leary*, sent back to lend a hand.

REMNANTS

Surigao Strait, 3:40 A.M.–5:00 A.M.

The guns in the Strait went silent at 4:10 A.M. Ten minutes later, southbound battleship *Yamashiro,* ablaze from bow to stern, capsized and sank, taking Admiral Nishimura and all but a handful of her crew down with her. Badly damaged cruiser *Mogami* and destroyer *Shigure* retreated. The U.S. battle and cruiser lines, heeding the threat of the torpedoes that had nearly struck *Leary,* temporarily pulled north and west. At 4:19, when U.S. battleship and cruiser guns were released to resume fire, there were no targets in range.

At 3:40, Admiral Shima's ships had finally entered the Strait. Shima's flagship *Nachi* led, followed by cruisers *Ashigara* and four destroyers. Earlier, as the column passed between Panoan and Mindanao Islands, it was attacked by PTs and cruiser *Abukuma* took a torpedo hit on its port side amidships. *Abukuma* slowed, dropped out of formation, and had to be left behind unescorted.

At 4:10 Shima's ships sailed past the two severed, burning remnants of *Fuso.* At 4:20, with destroyers now in the lead, cruisers *Nachi* and *Ashigara* pivoted to starboard and launched torpedoes at phantom targets off to the northeast. As *Nachi* continued east, it approached the southbound, slowly moving cruiser *Mogami.* Thinking *Mogami* to be dead in the water, the column turned to starboard, intending to pass *Mogami.* Instead, *Mogami's* bow knifed into *Nachi's* port quarter. With alarms blaring and water flooding its steering compartments, *Nachi* slowed to eighteen knots.

Maneuvers of indecision followed. *Nachi* briefly turned south to assess damage, and then once again north. Shima judged the events around him— the carnage of the Japanese ships, the absence of radar contacts, and the eerie silence following a clamor of explosions. He collected his forces, communicated briefly with Japanese commanders in Manila, and headed south. As morning approached, there was one more turn to the north and

then a final retreat. Shima's ships headed south, accompanied by the remnants of Nishimura's force: destroyers *Shiguri* and *Asagumo* and crippled
cruiser *Mogami*. Behind in the waters of Surigao Strait were the carcasses of
four Japanese warships: battleships *Fuso* and *Yamashiro*, and destroyers
Yamagumo and *Michishio*. Dawn was still two hours away.

Morning off Samar

DERBY BASE

Philippine Sea, East of Samar Island, 12:35 A.M.–5:30 A.M., October 25

Just after midnight, the 22 ships in Admiral Kurita's First Striking Force emerged from San Bernardino Strait in one long column under bright moonlight and scattered clouds. They formed a broad front that sailed east until 3:00 A.M., and then southeast to parallel the coast of Samar. The ships encountered dark clouds, wind, and squalls but no opposition: Halsey's Third Fleet carriers, battleships, cruisers, and destroyers were on their way north to intercept Ozawa's decoy force.

Halsey had eyes and appetite for Japan's carriers. He knew the Japanese surface ships had been mauled by air and submarine attack as they approached from the west and he believed the force had been severely crippled. The Japanese might even have turned back, but if they hadn't, Halsey was confident Seventh Fleet ships and planes should be able to finish them off. Yet, when Halsey reported Third Fleet's intentions, task forces commanders in Leyte Gulf and off Samar read the situation differently. They assumed Halsey would take his three carrier groups and leave a rearguard of battleships and cruisers to block San Bernardino Strait.

In the predawn hours there was still time to detect or rethink unfolding events. Night reconnaissance flights launched from Third Fleet carrier *Independence* searching west toward San Bernardino reported that the normally darkened navigation beacons in the Strait were now lit, but their crews never spotted Kurita's ships. Three night-flying "Black Cat" seaplanes launched from Leyte Gulf also flew out to reconnoiter. Two planes searched the wrong sector, while the third searched the right sector at the wrong time; none spotted anything suspicious.

As they pushed north, some of Halsey's Third Fleet skippers couldn't shake the suspicion they were somehow being lured into a trap. But messages conveying these concerns never got through the protective ring of staff officers guarding Halsey's sleep. Further south in Surigao Strait, as guns cooled and pulses slowed, Seventh Fleet's Admiral Kinkaid sought confirmation that Halsey forces still guarded San Bernardino Strait Kinkaid's query went out a little after 4:00 A.M., but it was three hours before Halsey replie.

⚓

At 5:00 A.M., Kurita received a message with ominous but inconclusive news about the fate of Admiral Nishimura's and Admiral Shima's forces in the south. Off Samar there was still no sign of opposing submarines or surface ships. But, as the sky lightened in the east and the possibility of air attack again became real, the Japanese ships began maneuvering into a circular air defense formation—destroyers on the outside, cruisers and battleships on the inside.

Suddenly, battleship *Yamato's* radar picked up aerial contacts. Within moments, lookouts in the ship's top hampers spotted a fast closing American plane and a line of masts to the southeast. Reports of full-size carriers, destroyers, cruisers, and even battleships flooded Strike Japanese communication nets. Eyes and imaginations exaggerated the size of the threat, but so did inexperience. In this war it was rare for opposing ships to see each other before, during, or after an engagement. Lookouts were accustomed to crowded skies and empty seas. But here unmistakably was a thicket of ships' masts and superstructures rising on the horizon.

The timing was difficult. Most of Kurita's ships were still on their way to stations in an air defense formation when a bigger threat loomed on the surface. He could only assume that what was ahead would be big—and, at long last, decisive. If, indeed, there were carriers, it was crucial that his ships cut off their passage to windward before the Americans could launch planes.

5:30 A.M.–7:00 A.M.

Just before dawn, Taffy 3's escort carriers moved inshore, turned northeast into the wind, and launched routine morning missions. Fighters flew off into squall-laden clouds to cover ships in Leyte Gulf and provide CAP for Taffy 3; torpedo planes scattered to patrol for submarines. The thirteen Taffy 3 ships were arranged in a wide circle formation: Seven task force escorts—DDs *Hoel, Heermann,* and *Johnston,* DEs *Butler, Dennis, Raymond,* and *Roberts*—ringed the outer three-mile diameter. CVEs

Fanshaw Bay, Gambier Bay, Kalinin Bay, Kitkun Bay, St. Lo, and *White Plains* formed the mile-wide inner core.

Like numerals on a clock face gliding across a tabletop, ship positions depended on formation heading. While the Taffy 3 ships steamed northeast to launch CAP and ASP, screening escorts *Hoel* and *Heermann* took the lead, while *Johnston* and *Roberts* trailed. All four would be on the wings when the formation turned east or west.

Gambier Bay's LSO Bill McClendon remembered an uneventful first-light launch. "I was up at four A.M. for launches at six: catapult torpedo planes first, fighters on deck run next. Then down to the ready room to get coffee." Following launch, carriers and screening DDs and DEs turned southwest. This put *Johnston* and *Roberts* in the lead, *Dennis, Butler*, and *Raymond* on the wings, *Hoel* and *Heermann* astern. Most Taffy 3 ships secured from GQ and set Condition 3, leaving a third of ships' companies at watch stations manning a third of ships' armament. The rest of the crews went to breakfast.

VC-65's Tom Van Brunt flew one of four TBMs launched from *St. Lo*. "It turned into a messy morning aloft: rain, low clouds, spots of real poor visibility. My friend Bill Brooks took the northwest quadrant and I took the northeast. We hadn't been airborne more than fifteen minutes when Bill came on the net using our call sign. 'Derby Base, Derby Base, contact, contact. I have the Japanese navy in sight.' There was a pause and then a skeptical voice came back. 'How do you know they're Japanese?' Bill's response was slow, exasperated: 'I can see the biggest damn red meatball flag flying from the biggest pagoda mast I ever saw! They're shooting at me!' "

⚓

What Admiral Kurita faced was more a matter of fate than glory. What might have seemed an opportunity as momentous as Tsushima was tempered by exhaustion and loss. For days, Kurita's ships and crews had run a gauntlet of air and submarine attacks. Japanese anti-aircraft fire had been ineffective. The Americans had filled the skies with aircraft, whereas the Japanese had only a few floatplanes intended for scouting and spotting mounted on their biggest ships. Kurita himself had barely escaped drowning when his flagship *Atago* was torpedoed from under him.

Whatever his feelings, Kurita abandoned his defensive formation. Not waiting to better organize his ships—forming battle lines to concentrate firepower, sending cruisers and destroyers out ahead to launch torpedoes—Kurita immediately ordered "General Attack." This command freed his captains to attack independently, each choosing his own target and setting his own angle of approach. It was permission for chaos. Lead elements, driving at flank speed, anxious to strike, belched random long-range salvos.

Most of Kurita's ships lacked effective fire-control radar for gunnery spotting. Instead, they depended on colored dyes released by projectiles as they hit the water—a different color for each ship's guns—to evaluate and correct accuracy.

⚓

When dawn GQ secured, Holly Crawforth was in *St. Lo*'s Radio 2, a cramped complex of communication and radar gear on the gallery level adjacent to the forward hanger deck. Holly practically lived in Radio 2. "I was the only radio tech assigned to K division. They woke me up so many times to go fix or tune something, I decided it was easier to just sleep there."

Holly heard rumbling outside. "I thought it might be one of the gallery-level twenty millimeters firing at incoming aircraft. Then I heard one of the radiomen say Japanese ships were behind us and headed our way. I thought he was joking, but when I went next door to radar I found out he wasn't." An operator showed Holly the blips painting on the SG radar. "That has to be Halsey," I said. "But the operator told me it couldn't be." No ships were responding to IFF—a transmitter/receiver that pulsed encoded electronic signals to detect the "friend or foe" identity of an approaching contact.

⚓

Aloft, Tom Van Brunt continued tracing his patrol quadrant. "Every time I came back on the south leg I could see that Japanese fleet firing. Then we got word for all planes to attack the Japanese ships—expend all ammunition no matter what it was. All I had were three depth bombs with hydrostatic fuses."

FLYING BOXCARS

7:00 A.M.–7:10 A.M.

Kurita's ships bore down on the U.S. forces in a ragged frenzy. Furthest east, six heavy cruisers—roughly organized in three columns of two cruisers each—raced to outflank the Americans and choke their escape east. Battleships *Yamato*, *Nagato*, *Kongo*, and *Haruna* followed close behind, while furthest west and nearest the coast of Samar, a column of two light cruisers and twelve destroyers trailed.

On most of the American ships there were few clues of the danger closing in. *Gambier Bay*'s Lou Rice, the radarman who had picked up the Japanese ships as radar contacts nearly four hours earlier, was still on watch, though he'd moved from radar to plot. Lou's conviction the contacts were ships not clouds had been vindicated, but it hardly mattered now. "I remember the skipper saying 'It's the first time I ever saw ionized clouds firing nine-gun salvos.'"

Crews on some U.S. ships thought that what had been spotted on the horizon was the backwash from the night action in Surigao—the broken remains of the Japanese force escaping north. Dudley Moylan, *Roberts'* ASW officer had been awake most of the night. "The battle in the Strait was going on and we could hear some of it over our TBS.[1] We were all pretty excited. I don't think I even thought about going to bed until about four." *Roberts'* XO Bob Roberts even made an announcement inviting the crew to take a look. Many, including Moylan and *Roberts'* communications officer Tom Stevenson, still wearing his bedroom slippers, came topside to gawk.

Mel Harden, seventeen, a deck division seaman standing watch in *Roberts'* forward 5-in. mount, was waiting to be relieved for chow. "I was looking out the side hatch and saw puffs of flak over some masts off to the northwest. We thought it might be a Japanese snooper pestering one of the other escort groups." But as the target—a distant speck—flew closer, Mel and the others could see the plane was American. "That told me the masts must be Japanese ships. We could see flashes from their guns, followed by booms and then colored splashes out on the surface." Just like that *Roberts'* crew was called back to GQ. The forward mount crew climbed inside the gun house and buttoned up.

Aboard destroyer *Hoel*, Sam Lucas witnessed the same puffs of flak and the same indistinguishable aircraft speck. Sam, a young seaman from Covina, California, and new to *Hoel's* torpedo gang, was stationed on *Hoel's* fantail to operate the depth charge racks and smoke generator. Like Mel Harden, Sam was waiting hungrily for his breakfast relief. "I had no idea what to make of it and I didn't hear anything about it on my headphones." But then Sam noticed something that made him forget the idea of breakfast altogether. "They looked like flying boxcars—a few of them tumbling end over end in the air and heading our way. They were huge. Even with the headphones covering my ears I could hear them—'Whop! Whop! Whop!'—before they hit the water." GQ sounded and a torpedoman showed up to take Sam's headphones. "As I took off the phones, I heard the skipper on the net saying 'Small Boys, form up on me.'"

⚓

Word of the Japanese attack spread through Taffy 3 ships by plain language announcements over TBS circuits. Aboard *Johnston*, Bobby Chastain, an eighteen-year-old seaman from landlocked Kansas, was the first to reach the number-four mount. Still dopey from standing midwatch and dawn GQ, he couldn't figure out why they were called back to battle stations. By the time Chastain had settled himself at the trainer's station, Bob Hollenbaugh, mount 4's gun captain, had arrived. "Bob told me we'd be firing under director control, so I began training the mount to match pointer readings from plot. Then I heard the mount's squawk box: 'Japanese fleet fifteen miles astern.'"

Below decks on *Hoel*, Glenn Parkin paused for a moment near his locker before heading for his GQ station in mount 2. He had been through this before. "I just knew we were going to catch hell. I took two packs of cigarettes and some matches from my locker. I crunched in the corners of the packs and matches and stuffed them into two condoms I carried in my wallet. Then I tied the packages to my shirt pockets."

Aboard *St. Lo*, curiosity had driven Holly Crawforth to the flight deck, only a few steps up from the gallery level. Standing underneath *St. Lo*'s island, he could see ships on the horizon. Flight deck crews were bustling among the few planes still left from the dawn launch. *St. Lo* was turning into the wind to launch. Fear eclipsed curiosity and Holly ran back to Radio 2.

END RUNS

7:10 A.M.–8:40 A.M.

Carrier launches were rushed and frantic. The six CVEs turned just easterly enough to get lifting winds across their bows. The new heading delayed retreat but at least brought them no closer to the Japanese. Pilots and flight deck crews disregarded details of armament and fuel loads to get every flyable aircraft aloft.

On *Gambier Bay*, Joe McGraw and Leo Zeola,[2] another VC-10 fighter pilot, were in the coffee locker when they heard the squawk box alert. They hustled to the ready room where Vereen Bell, the squadron's air intelligence officer, told them to get to their planes immediately. Joe grabbed his helmet and sprinted out. As he ran past the ready board he saw, scrawled across it in huge block letters, "TASK FORCE 20 MILES NORTH & CLOSING!"

"When I got to the flight deck the last of the planes were already turning over. Dawn CAP and ASP were out, so there were only about a half dozen TBMs and maybe eight or ten FM-2s. I raced towards an empty Wildcat on the stern port quarter. It turned out Leo was heading for the same plane and we both arrived at the same time. I climbed up the starboard wing while Leo was on the port wing, which had steps and handholds to help the pilot. It slowed Leo down and I got to the cockpit just ahead of him." Leo would be riding this one out onboard *Gambier Bay*.

Jim Lischer ran for his standby Wildcat. "I heard explosions astern. They were so loud and close I ducked under the Wildcat's wing. Behind us *Kalinin Bay* was surrounded with shell splashes." Jim's plane captain, a boy even younger than he was, helped him into the cockpit. "The plane captain shouted, 'Good luck!' and I shouted back, 'Good luck to you! I think you're going to need it more than me.' I never saw that boy again."

Bill McClendon was busy getting planes airborne. "We'd be in and out of the wind. We launched whatever we could." Gene Seitz's Wildcat was the first plane in line. "I was assigned to fly the ready plane on the catapult. I ran out, jumped in the cockpit, and started up. Once off the deck I made a right turn and looked back. The ship was straddled by columns of water. Some guy on the radio was saying 'I repeat, 4 battleships, 8 cruisers, 12 destroyers bearing 360.'"

Burt Bassett's TBM took off loaded for submarine patrol. "It had bombs with hydrostatic fuses. Not much good against a ship on the surface. Few of the other planes were even loaded. While I turned it up on the catapult I saw a huge splash off to port, close in, maybe one hundred yards away." Bill had to dead launch one TBM. "The pilot Hank Pyzdrowski[3] had climbed in, got it manned, and turned it up, but we were out of the wind. We couldn't launch him, even from the catapult. Hank was pissed off and shaking his fist at me, but he and his crew finally got out and we shot it off the catapult into the water."

⚓

By then Tom Van Brunt was lining up his TBM on a cruiser that seemed isolated from the other Japanese ships. "I decided my best chance with the depth bombs was to drop them right alongside. I told my crew we'd be getting on top of a cloud and then dive through it. We had to come in steep. We didn't have any fighter escort; by then they were off on their own trying to strafe with their peashooters.

"I climbed and dived, but when I got through the cloud I realized I'd come in too shallow. I had to climb again and make a steeper dive, this time without dive flaps to slow me. When I finally dropped the depth bombs and began to pull up I almost blacked out. The TBM's redline was 320 knots and I was nearly at 400—it was a really rugged plane. My gunner John South[4] and my radioman Lester Frederickson[5] told me two of the bombs straddled the cruiser. They saw explosions but couldn't give any damage assessment. I got on my horse to go look for some place to get more ammunition."

Tom Van Brunt's target, the heavy cruiser *Suzuya*, was damaged, slowed, and began taking on water. *Suzuya* never returned to the battle and sank early in the afternoon.

⚓

Larry Epping saw order and outward calm on *Gambier Bay*'s bridge. "We were getting reports of colored shell splashes astern—splashes of four or five different colors, always landing closer." Nearby, Verner Carlsen, *Gambier Bay*'s chaplain, clutched an intercom microphone. "My job was to be a play-by-play announcer, giving the crew below decks an account of what was happening topside. It was difficult not to create panic with the shells coming in. I had to balance what I said with what I saw." Verner's nightly prayer for the crew called for a similar difficult balance. "I could never bring myself to pray for victory or deliverance from harm—and the skipper never asked me to. I could only pray for the strength to face whatever lay ahead for us with resolve." Meanwhile, Charlie Heinl, a seaman from Ohio assigned as an ammunition passer on one of the deck-level 20-mm, was questioning his own resolve: "I was on the port side catwalk and I stood out and watched a little bit. When the shells started coming in I decided if I was going to get killed I didn't want to see it. So I stepped back in the ammo locker."

On the flight deck, Joe McGraw waited for his turn to launch. "I got in a few prayers watching Bill McClendon go through the usual launch routine for the planes on deck run—motioning them forward to the island, signaling the pilot to throttle up, then sending them off. It was just taking too long. When Smokey Bennett,[6] the pilot in front of me, took off, I saw an incoming shell hit the forward edge of the flight deck. Deck timbers flew up as Smokey's tail went by, but I wasn't sure Bill saw this.

"Then Bill was signaling me to taxi up. Instead, I wound up the engine where the plane stood, raised my arm and waved frantically for Bill to stand aside. I pointed my nose toward the starboard quarter and gunned across the flight deck. As I did, *Gambier Bay* began turning starboard away from the wind and the flight deck pitched to port. I was climbing uphill just to get off deck."

Airborne at last, Joe reached down to retract his landing gear; it took twenty-eight turns of a hand crank to lock the gear in place. "I made four turns when a salvo splashed the water just ahead of me." The impact sent up telephone pole-size geysers of water. "I knew hitting one of the geysers would be like running into a tree. So I let go of the crank and grabbed the stick. I was still at full throttle, but didn't have enough air speed to turn, so I put on right rudder." Joe's Wildcat skidded untouched to the right of the water spouts.

⚓

With Taffy 3 eastbound, destroyer *Hoel* was positioned on the formation's exposed northwest flank. All the ships had been ordered to make covering smoke. *Hoel*'s stern was a hive of activity; men piled into the 4 and 5 mounts and onto the open 40- and 20-mm gun tubs. One of them was Larry Morris, a loader on one of the twin 40s perched above and between the number-three and number-four guns.

Below on the fantail, Sam Lucas had two jobs. First, turn on *Hoel*'s smoke generator—a cluster of four large cylinders connected to a valve and dispensing nozzle. Turning the valve caused the tanks' chemicals to combine and the nozzle to belch a stream of white smoke. Next, secure the depth charges—big six-hundred-pounders in two racks, one on either side of the smoke generator. "It felt like the noise was going to swallow me. The ship must have already moved to flank speed—the fantail was shaking like it was going to come loose. I could see other ships beside us, like we were in a race." *Hoel*'s 5-in. guns began firing. Sam still heard the "Whop! Whop! Whop!" of incoming rounds from the Japanese big guns. He tried to pay attention to the job at hand—wiring the depth charges on safe to keep them from exploding if the ship went down.

Hoel and *Heermann* turned northwest to confront the Japanese ships, while *Johnston*, Taffy 3's other DD, raced from the far side of the formation to join them. The maneuver brought *Johnson* closest to the Japanese and her two forward 5-in. guns, mounts 1 and 2, fired first. Mount 4's gun captain Bob Hollenbaugh recalled: "The skipper got on the squawk box telling us we'd be going pretty close to the Japanese. I looked out my hatch and I could see their masts. Then we closed up and began firing in automatic."

Zigzagging, with speed up to twenty-five knots, *Johnston* targeted cruiser *Kumano*, the lead cruiser of a column trying to cut off the CVEs. *Johnston*'s oblique angle of attack exposed the ship to return salvos from four Japanese cruisers. As splashes straddled *Johnston*, her gun batteries stepped up to rapid fire and torpedo crews got ready to launch. Meanwhile, *Hoel* charged battleship *Kongo*. *Hoel*'s forward 5-in. guns opened at fourteen thousand yards and *Kongo* returned fire. On *Hoel*'s fantail Sam Lucas finished securing the depth charges and scurried to shelter.

⚓

Rather than climbing high and circling to build formations, Taffy 3's plane crews picked up teams at low altitude and roared north in makeshift echelons. VC-10's CO Ed Huxtable flew lead in a pickup team of Avengers and Wildcats. Burt Bassett flew on Huxtable's wing. "I ended up behind the skipper during launch. It was only time in the war I ever flew on his wing. There were three or four other aircraft, a couple on my wing, a couple on his."

All of them headed back across *Gambier Bay*'s path, flying under low clouds to go after the Japanese ships. Joe McGraw was still climbing and headed in the opposite direction as Huxtable's group swept by. He had to push his Wildcat into a quick dive to avoid colliding. "I finished cranking my landing gear in place and whipped around to take up an escort position on the port side of Ed's formation."

"The skipper didn't waste any time," recalled Jim Lischer. Huxtable led the formation just above the base of the cloud deck and then pointed them directly in. Burt Bassett strained to see the targets ahead. "We wound up at fifteen hundred, maybe two thousand feet. Scuddy clouds in and out. I just couldn't see the ships at all. But Hux saw them well enough to bring us close. He gave his signal, so I peeled off and made my run. But I got hit before I ever got ready. My tail section was shot and I was losing control. I thought the controls were severed. I dropped my bomb purely by instinct and tried to climb."

In the meantime Huxtable radioed, "Fighters in to strafe." As Joe McGraw peeled away, he saw Japanese destroyers below him and off to the west making a starboard end run on the U.S. ships. In front and below were a cruiser and what looked like two battleships. "My wingman and I lined up first on the cruiser. We pushed over and strafed the bridge and the AA mounts around it. As we went by we jinked up, down, and sideways to avoid the flak. It was pretty light and disorganized on the first run." Joe next approached the bigger of the battleships—probably battleship *Yamato*—to make a strafing run on its bridge. Gene Seitz, teamed with a Wildcat pilot from *Kalinin Bay,* also swooped in on a battleship. "I aimed for the bridge and flew through a lot of AA. After I pulled out, it was still coming after me. I remember looking back and yelling indignantly, 'Don't shoot at me, Goddamn it, I've already made my pass!' "

While Joe and his wingman continued to harass the big ships, Dick Roby, Gene Seitz, and two other FM-2 pilots worked over two of the Japanese destroyers little more than ten miles away from Taffy 3's ships. "We came in above a thin cloud layer. We could see them, but they couldn't see us and they had no fire control radar. We fell on them in a sixty-degree dive, almost vertical, and pulled out at three hundred feet. Every round in our wing guns was armor piercing and we aimed amidships, trying to get boilers and engine equipment. You could see the hits and the damage and they turned around."

Coming out of these first runs, the flock of Taffy 3 planes assembled at the back of the Japanese formation. Huxtable checked in with them, asking who still had ordnance. Then the group formed up, turned and went back in, this time from astern.

⚓

When *Johnston* had nosed to within ten thousand yards of cruiser *Kumano,* her crew began launching torpedoes—five each from the two mounts at three-second intervals, each torpedo set at slow speed, shallow depth, and tight, one-degree spreads. *Johnston* then turned to port and retreated into the cover of her own smoke. No one on *Johnston* was able to see the torpedoes hit, but some of the crew reported three distant underwater explosions about eight minutes later. In fact, *Kumano* was holed by several of *Johnston's* torpedoes and damaged by gunfire as well. *Kumano* slowed and dropped out of the action to fight fires and control damage.

Johnston began taking hits during her retreat, fourteen-inch projectiles from the battleships, six-inch from the cruisers. "After the torpedo attack we made a sharp turn," recalled Bob Hollenbaugh. "Hauling ass, I mean we were going! I was down on the deck of the gun house trying to clear some powder cans out of the chute when all of a sudden I heard this big 'Thump.' It was a shell hitting on the port side, just forward of mount four. It pierced the deck, apparently hit the reduction gear, and knocked out one of our engines. The stern just came up out of the water and slammed back down. I lost communication with the director. I heard Bobby Chastain, the trainer, and Sam Moody,[7] the pointer, saying, 'Boats, we got no power.'"

The armor piercing shells penetrated *Johnston's* thin skin without exploding. Their impact, however, rocked *Johnston*, killing and wounding crew, including three officers on the bridge, knocking out the after engine room, and disabling *Johnston's* gyro compass, steering engine, and surface search radar. Seaman Bill Mercer, stationed at one of the forward 40-mm mounts, recalled the impacts: "It seemed to almost lift us out of the water. I thought, 'Damn, was that a torpedo?'" Bill was standing under the wing of the bridge just forward of the Captain's gig. "Someone yelled from the bridge, 'Stand-by below.' A body was being lowered to the main deck. As the body was even with me it seemed to stop and I could see that the head was completely gone."

Power was out in mounts 3, 4, and 5. *Johnston* slowed and seemed poised for obliteration until a fierce squall dropped around her like a curtain. During ten minutes of soaking grace, Johnston's crew ministered to wounded, shored up damage, and restored what power they could.

Johnston emerged from the squall with speed up to seventeen knots. Power and hydraulics had returned to mount 5, but 3 and 4 were still out. Bob Hollenbaugh tried to gather his wits. "I jumped up on the gun captain's platform and looked out the hatch. There was a twin forty millimeter right between mount three and four. Walt Howard[8] was on the handlebar director used for the forties. I shouted, 'You got communication with the gun director?' He shouted back, 'Yeah!' So I screamed, 'Ask him if we can fire in local control. We have no power.' Three or four seconds later Walt hollered down, 'Permission granted!'"

Up forward, Bill Mercer was working close to the number-two gun. "The mount had so many shell casings piled up around it that the gun couldn't swing. J. B. Strickland[9] and I began throwing the brass over the side. Then the mount took a direct hit. Glenn Heriford,[10] one of the gun crew, was blown out the starboard-side hatch. I carried Herf to the bulkhead under the bridge wing. One of his legs was practically blown off. I started carrying Herf to the wardroom, but when I got to the main deck, two other men carried him the rest of the way. I never saw Herf again."

Evans took *Johnston* back on the attack, first challenging a Japanese destroyer and then the cruisers with 5-in. gunfire. Screening ships then got orders to attack with torpedoes. Destroyers *Hoel* and *Heermann* formed up to go in. *Johnston*, its torpedoes expended, joined the line to provide supporting gunfire.

⚓

Hoel took its first hit during this torpedo run. A shell ripped through the ship's gunfire control director just above the bridge and knocked out the ship's voice communications. Glenn Parkin, the sight setter in mount 2, needed readings from the director radar to set accurate target range and deflection. "After the first hits knocked out our radar, my readings were useless. Both training and elevation switched to manual. For the rest of the fight I traded off with the trainer whenever sweat blocked his vision."

Nine thousand yards from battleship *Kongo*, *Hoel*'s torpedo crews fired a spread from the forward mount. *Heermann* followed *Hoel* and launched all her torpedoes—seven at cruiser *Haguro* less than nine thousand yards away and three at battleship *Haruna*, point-blank at four thousand yards. Both destroyers then reversed course to starboard and fled southeast.

Samuel B. Roberts had taken cover in the same blinding squall that enveloped *Johnston*. When *Hoel* and *Heermann* peeled off to begin their runs, Tom Stevenson, stationed in *Roberts'* combat information center, heard skipper Bob Copeland on the net. "The captain asked if this meant the 'small small boys' too. He got a quick 'negative' and some vague instruction about forming up with the other DEs. I think he just figured the DEs weren't showing up."[11] Copeland ordered the helm swung left and *Roberts* fell in astern of *Hoel* and *Heermann*.

Roberts' low profile, the feature that made the ship so stable in a churning sea, helped conceal her as she bore in on heavy cruiser *Chokai*. Tom Stevenson watched the column's blips on surface radar. "I could see *Hoel, Heermann*, and *Johnston*. We were slower and got further behind." The column was under fire and a shell aimed at *Johnston* severed one of the wires on *Roberts'* main mast. The wire fell across the torpedo mount, injuring *Roberts'* chief torpedoman as he tried to set torpedo speed, depth, and launch angle.

Roberts reached and passed the intended launch point and the torpedoes still weren't ready. In CIC, Tom Stevenson watched XO Bob Roberts quickly recalculate torpedo settings and pass them by voice to the crew at the tubes. "By then we were closer than anybody, maybe four thousand yards." And *Roberts* was moving fast. Sonarman Vince Goodrich's CIC GQ station was near the pitometer, *Roberts'* speed gauge. "The repeater jumped to twenty-eight knots and hung there." When *Roberts'* torpedo crew finally launched the fish, they seemed like good shots, running hot and straight. Tom Stevenson stared at the crowd of contacts on the surface search radar. "It looked like we made a great shot."

⚓

During a retreat through covering smoke, *Heermann* pushed her speed to nearly thirty-five knots, quickly outrunning crippled *Johnston* but nearly ramming *Fanshaw Bay*. After *Heermann* backed to avoid *Fanshaw Bay*, *Johnston* came limping out of the smoke and nearly collided with *Heermann*'s bow. After escaping these two collisions, *Heermann* took her first hit and first casualties—a shell to the bridge that killed four, including the helmsman. As *Heermann* ran astern of the carriers to screen them with smoke, her hull absorbed more blows. Eventually flooding brought *Heermann* so far down by the bow that her anchors plowed a furrow through the water and slowed the ship to twenty-five knots.

Meanwhile, *Johnston* was firing a flurry of 5-in. rounds at battleship *Kongo*, now less than seven thousand yards away on *Johnston*'s port side, and also at a cruiser whose gunfire had bracketed *Gambier Bay*. *Kongo* returned 14-in. salvos but missed. Bob Hollenbaugh had *Johnston*'s mount 4 firing in local control. "Bobby Chastain cranked it by hand. It was geared down, but it took a hell of a lot to move it. Bobby was a little kid and he tired awful easy, so guys would trade off with him. Moody stayed in the pointer chair and I had glasses. It wasn't difficult to find targets—there were cruisers everywhere. I could line us up okay—the range was the trouble. Walt Howard on the handlebar director gave us some ranges, which helped a little." Mount 4 fired slowly. "The shots lacked the distance and punch they might have had if the mount was at full power."

Evans next plunged *Johnston* at another Japanese column—a light cruiser and four following destroyers—closing on the starboard flank of the escort carriers. *Johnston* fired at the column while absorbing hits that slowed her to fifteen knots. Evans was still on *Johnston*'s bridge, but he was surrounded by dead and wounded. He had lost his shirt and two fingers from his left hand.

⚓

Roberts skipper Bob Copeland pressed to join the screen between the Japanese ships and Taffy 3's CVEs. As *Roberts* pulled away from its torpedo run, Copeland released the 5-in. guns to fire at an enemy cruiser in hot pursuit. To fire astern, the forward mount had to train close in to *Roberts'* forward superstructure. Bill Wilson, a gunner's mate stationed at one of the 20-mm mounts just below the bridge, dove and hugged the deck face down to escape the blast effect.

George Carbon was *Roberts'* forward mount trainer. "We were shooting at one of the heavy cruisers, firing maybe every five seconds. They tried to control us from the bridge, but the mount was jerking around so fast the shellman and powderman couldn't stand up. Finally they let us go into manual control. My targets kept changing. The gun captain was standing above and right behind me. He would pick out the targets and kick me in the right or left shoulder to turn. I was really frustrated trying to get something in the sights. We were laying down a lot of smoke."

Mel Harden stood behind George, grabbing hot shell casings as they ejected from the breech and heaving them through the mount's rear hatch to the main deck. Caught up in the frantic rhythm of the gun crew's work, trying to avoid getting scorched by hot brass, Mel quickly lost all track of which direction *Roberts* was headed. "We were firing, but I had no idea how we were doing."

Astern, the cruiser *Roberts* had fired on erupted in steam and smoke. *Roberts* stood clear of the near collision between *Johnston* and *Heermann* and got into screening position on the flank of the escort carriers. As Japanese cruisers closed in on her port beam, *Roberts'* two 5-in. mounts opened up to port. The Japanese cruisers' 8-in. mounts returned fire, aiming for both *Roberts* and *Gambier Bay*.

⚓

After their desperate launches, Taffy 3's six CVEs had steered southeast and then southwest trying to escape. Despite the frantic efforts of Taffy 3's diving aircraft, and the torpedoes and gunfire of the DDs and DEs, the slow CVEs were being relentlessly boxed in by Japanese cruisers to the east, Japanese battleships astern, and Japanese destroyers to the west. *White Plains, Fanshaw Bay*, and *Kitkun Bay* were furthest from the Japanese, *St. Lo, Kalinin Bay*, and *Gambier Bay* closest.

From the battle's opening moments, things went badly for *Kalinin Bay* and *Gambier Bay*. The morning wind continued to blow from the northeast, so neither could be hidden by smoke, and both stood clear and ever closer in the gun sights of the Japanese. At 7:50 A.M., just as she completed launching aircraft, *Kalinin Bay* was the first CVE to be hit—by a cruiser shell, the first of fourteen more. The initial blow to *Gambier Bay*—a direct hit on the flight deck—came twenty minutes later. Lou Rice recalled: "I was still in CIC. There was a shudder and a fantastic explosion. When I stepped out I saw a guy running back over the after elevator. He went right off the ship when the after elevator blew up." From that moment on, the mauling of *Gambier Bay* never let up.

LAST DOGS

8:30 A.M.–10:00 A.M.

As *Hoel* raced southeast, she was hit twice more, this time astern. "An explosion just aft of my forty millimeter buckled the deck," Larry Morris recalled. "There was steam everywhere. The other loader on the mount, a guy named Ingram,[12] just flat out disappeared—I never saw him again." Explosions knocked out *Hoel's* after fireroom and port engine and silenced mounts 3, 4, and 5. *Hoel's* rudder jammed hard right and the ship circled northwest towards battleship *Kongo*.

On *Hoel's* fantail, Sam Lucas lay flat, head down behind the shield of a 20-mm mount. The smoke generator cylinders had been damaged and the generator nozzle sprayed wildly. "Chemicals were flying across the deck— guys took cover to avoid the spray as much as the shrapnel." Mount 4's barrel had been sheared off. When its crew tried to fire manually, the round backfired and the gun exploded. "Each time we changed course, four's gun house banged back and forth between the port and starboard stops. I didn't expect to get out. I knew we'd be staying until the last dog."

Propelled by one engine and now guided by muscle power from after steering, *Hoel* turned to attack a heavy cruiser column lead by *Haguro*. *Hoel's* torpedo officer climbed the after quintuple mount as it lined up for a shot. Entering the speed, depth, and angle settings by hand, he fired *Hoel's* second and last spread of torpedoes. The fish churned off toward *Haguro's* starboard bow five thousand yards away.

Boxed in, with *Kongo* on the port beam and cruisers on the starboard quarter, *Hoel* tried to escape southeast. For a few minutes *Hoel* fishtailed and "chased" salvos, heading to the spot of the last splash, expecting the next would fall elsewhere. But then *Hoel's* remaining engine was knocked out and the forward magazine caught fire. *Hoel* slowed and continued to take hits and casualties. Sam Lucas prayed. "I was lying in blood. I looked astern and saw a Japanese floatplane come in to strafe us. You could hear machine guns all around. Mount five's trainer and gun captain were running up forward. The mount captain got hit. We tried to help him, but he was gone."

At 8:40 A.M., with *Hoel* listing twenty degrees and dead in the water, abandon ship was ordered. *Hoel* had been rocked by forty direct hits, two thirds of her crew was dead, and nearly all the living were wounded. The order, passed by word of mouth, most often reached men only when they'd been driven from battle stations by dead equipment, smoke, steam, or fire.

Up forward, mount 2 kept firing until smoke cascading up from the handling room forced its crew to flee. Outside the gun house, Glenn Parkin saw a deck covered with bodies. "Carl Krupp,[13] one of the gunner's mates, had his leg blown off. Four of us tied a line under Carl's arm and tried to lower him over the side. We were still taking large caliber shells. One came through that killed Carl and wounded most of us. I got shrapnel in both my legs."

Before abandoning ship, Glenn made a desperate search for his friend Phil Akerman.[14] "I went aft on the starboard side to the torpedo locker where I knew Phil was stationed. There were dead and wounded everywhere and I couldn't get through. Phil was probably one of bodies piled on the deck. I finally decided to get the hell off the ship."

A thousand yards is close range at sea, where the horizon and the earth's curvature define long distance. In *Hoel*'s final minutes of existence, Japanese cruisers stood that close, tearing her apart with 8-in. salvos fired on flat trajectory.

Larry Morris stayed near the crippled after 40-mm for a few minutes, but then climbed down to the main deck and made his way forward along the port side to the bow. "When I heard abandon ship I realized I was in a pretty elevated location and knew I ought to get back aft before jumping. But by then a quick jump into water made more sense and I went over the side." Sam Lucas left from the fantail. "The stern was pretty low in the water. I just stepped over the side. Cruisers were pouring shells into us."

Glenn Parkin had moved forward from amidships and found a life jacket near mount 1. "I looked at the horizon and thought 'God, what a long swim to San Francisco.' I threw the life jacket into the water and jumped in after it. I swam a little bit and then stopped to look back at *Hoel*. She started to roll and sink stern first. The bow was riding high and the Japanese were still hitting her with heavy shells. Then she went under."

⚓

Roberts passed *Hoel*, dead in the water, stern awash, its crew scrambling to escape. There was no thought of stopping. *Roberts* was still untouched. Splashes from battleship rounds walked like the steps of giants up her wake. Lou Gould, one of *Roberts*' sonarmen, came up for a moment to watch from the bridge. "I saw three huge splashes one hundred yards off the port quarter. I didn't want to see any more and ducked back into sonar." Hoping to dodge the next salvo, Copeland ordered a quick all back full. When splashes landed ahead, Copeland quickly ordered all ahead flank. *Roberts* accelerated, but her luck had ended: she was rocked by 8-in. rounds from a Japanese cruiser.

Roberts' forward 5-in. mount had fired so many rounds astern that powder casings piled up on the bow blocked its turning path. Mel Harden had to clear shell casings from the gun house by heaving them out the mount's starboard door. "Once I took a look out the door when the gun was trained to port. Everything forward—lifeline, anchors, capstan, anchor brake hatch covers—was completely gone."

A Japanese cruiser stood so close off to port that its guns had to be raised for loading and then lowered to fire at *Roberts'* flat profile. An incoming round sliced through the magazine compartment beneath the forward mount. The handling room crew passed up what ammunition they could—they'd fired all but twenty rounds—and then closed off the magazine hatch. When the big shells hit, George Carbon could feel the whole ship shudder. "I don't remember being scared, just really frustrated trying to get something in the sights because of all the smoke. Then a shell hit the mount and broke the sight all to pieces. I had nothing to aim through anymore."

One armor-piercing round punched a hole through *Roberts'* hull near the waterline, crippling the forward fire room and dropping her speed to seventeen knots. The explosion drove Tom Stevenson out of CIC: "Number one fireroom was right under us. All of a sudden our lights went out and steam and asbestos came up through the vents. We all ran out to the starboard side. Down on the main deck there were all these bodies. I thought, 'there's nothing I can do down there.'" Along with many others, Tom made his way to the bridge. "It got so crowded that Copeland was pleading with people to leave. I went aft to the starboard signal deck. As I did, we took a hit on the after end of the deck housing. It knocked everybody down. The flag bags next to me caught fire."

Dick Rohde and *Roberts'* Chief Radioman Tullio Serafini had left the darkened communications room next to CIC and were heading forward when the big blow came. "The blast toppled us both," Dick recalled. Dick struggled to his feet. Serafini's shirtless torso was covered in blood. "I thought to myself, 'How can he be standing there?'" Then Dick saw his own wound, a gash of blood, flesh, and exposed muscle on his left leg. "I told myself, 'I am not going to look at it again.'"

The damage from this biggest blow, two 14-in. shells from one of the battleships, was catastrophic. It ripped a thirty-foot gash in *Roberts'* port side near the waterline. From his station up forward, Bill Wilson could see the result. "Debris and steam exploded out the port side." *Roberts'* after engine room was destroyed and her fuel tanks ruptured. Most crew below decks had been killed. A slick of black fuel oil surrounded *Roberts.*

All power and communications were lost. Fires erupted on the fantail. The ship's compressed air system, used to clear hot explosive gasses and powder from the gun breeches, also failed. A round in the after mount breech cooked off. The resulting explosion killed or fatally wounded everyone in the mount's crew except for Sam Blue,[15] the fuse setter, who was blown clear of the shattered gun house and into the water. *Robert's* after deckhouse had been atomized, along with the anti-aircraft mount on top. All the ship astern of the stack was a mass of twisted metal.

In the forward mount, George Carbon was dazed by the hit that shattered the gun sight. "I came to, looked around, and nobody was there except the mount captain and me. We got out and went over to the starboard side. The ship was stopped and we saw a torpedo coming at us. It went right underneath the ship." Dudley Moylan saw the same thing from the bridge: "The skipper said 'Standby for tor...' but by then it was already underneath us. We went to the other side where we saw it reappear and just keep going."

Copeland ordered abandon ship a little after 9:00 A.M. Dudley Moylan went to free the flotation net on the starboard side of the open bridge and throw it into the water. "I was unraveling the lines when one of the signalmen came up to me, shook my hand, and said he hoped I'd make it. It surprised me. I was just trying to get the lines untangled and not thinking about what it meant."

Tom Stevenson, who was responsible for destroying most of the ship's secret equipment and documents, found his way down from the signal bridge to the darkened radio room. "First I found the secret coding wheels. They were metal, so I just threw them overboard. We also had some electronic countermeasures equipment. I was supposed to use a small grenade to blow the machine up, but I was worried I'd be blown up along with it. But then someone came along and fired into it with a Thompson submachine gun. It was lucky he didn't kill us along with the machine.

"Next I had to go below to a safe that held all the secret operations plans and codebooks. I persuaded one of the signalmen to go with me. The documents were in weighted bags. We passed them up through a scuttle, and we could only take so many at a time. After throwing the first load over the side, I said, 'We have to go back.' The guy wasn't about to, so I made the second trip alone. I got the last bags and left the ship's payroll behind."

By the time Tom returned to the main deck, most of the crew was already off the ship. Tom tossed the last bags over the side, but one bag bobbed to the surface. "The skipper was standing right there, and told me I ought to do something about that bag." So Tom dropped over the side and swam after it.

Dudley Moylan had also made his way to the main deck. "Staubach,[16] the chief electricians mate, was there in bad shape. I stayed with him for a while, but couldn't do much. I stepped into the water and got behind some people sitting in one of the rafts. I told them to get the raft away from the ship so it wouldn't get pulled back."

Dick Rohde clambered down a ladder to the portside rail of the main deck where he stopped to remove his shoes. "I seemed to be alone. There was burning oil on the water. I'd been taught in basic training to get below the oil and swim away, so that's what I tried to do, but I realized I could only kick with one leg. My left leg just dragged."

Dick's life belt was shredded and useless. All he could see was a Japanese ship, very close, still firing at the ship. Near *Roberts'* stern Dick saw a smoking hole in the side and tried to stay clear. "I came across a small kapok life jacket bobbing on the surface. It belonged to the ship's mascot, a small black dog named Sammy. There was no Sammy, just his life jacket. I grabbed it, tucked it under one arm, and it gave me some buoyancy."

When Mel Harden left the forward mount he was only a few feet from his abandon ship station—the raft on the starboard side forward. Someone had tried to push the raft over the side, but it still leaned against *Roberts'* hull. "I climbed down the cargo net with another guy and we pulled it the rest of the way into the water." The raft drifted toward the stern and the men followed. "As we got aft, I could see that the forty-millimeter mount on the deckhouse was gone. The after five-inch was still there but the gun house was all mangled."

George Carbon hurried down the starboard side until he was amidships. "I could see depth charges burning and I thought, 'Those things are going to go off.' A guy was sitting on the deck leaning against the bulkhead. He'd had his leg blown off. He was dying right there; his eyes were already glazing over. He said, 'Look what they did to me.' I couldn't do anything for him but I told him, 'I'm going to go get you some help.' I didn't know what else to say." Meanwhile, shipmates were urging George to get off the ship. " 'Hey Offie—my nickname—hurry up and jump. But I didn't really have to jump in, just step over the side. Then they were yelling 'Hurry up and swim!' I was swimming as fast as I could. The water was full of diesel oil and I had it all over me. I got to the net and I hung on. Just then the ship started to go down. The bow came straight up." It was 9:35 A.M.

⚓

Traveling on the unscreened eastern wing of the formation, *Gambier Bay* had been taking a merciless pounding all the while. Ensign Fred Mallgrave, in charge of the after engine room, had been listening to Verner Carlson's account when he got a desperate call from the forward engine room "They'd been hit and the room had started flooding. The engine was out of commission, they were about to abandon the space, and wanted me to start the bilge pump."

Then, "Wham. Here came a shell into our area and water right in after it. The shell pierced boiler number three's casing and went into the generating tubes. I told the crew to kill the fire and secure the boiler. When that was done it was 'Let's get out of here!' I sent everybody out and then I went up the ladder, all the way to the hanger deck. The power was off but the emergency battery circuit kept the overhead lamps on and we didn't have any steam line breaks. We were on the run, but I don't remember being panicked."

Tony Potochniak had left his duty station in a compartment just back of the after elevator and fled to the port catwalk moments before the first shell hit. "I had a premonition, grabbed my life jacket, and got out." The explosion that ripped *Gambier Bay*'s flight deck also destroyed Tony's compartment. "I went down the catwalk to the parachute loft where they repacked the aircrew parachutes. It was one of the first-aid stations and it was filling up with wounded. I was helping the flight surgeon (it was Burt Basselt's friend Wayne Stewart) when a shell came down through the flight deck. I saw a burst of flame. Shrapnel caught the doc right in the back of the neck and killed him right away—he just fell across the guy he was working on."

During the shelling, Bill McClendon crouched by *Gambier Bay*'s island. "I was trying to keep steel between me and them. I saw the nose cap of one incoming shell come bouncing across the flight deck. As I just stood there and watched, my chief ran over and kicked it over the side. I could see us slowing down and then stop in the water. It finally struck me to get the hell off."

Above, on *Gambier Bay*'s bridge, Chaplain Verner Carlsen realized that the ship was not going to make it. "My squawk box commentary for the crew was drifting into prayer." Even the prayers were breaking off in mid-sentence whenever Verner felt a sudden jolt or heard another explosion. "Finally someone told me I might just as well hang up the mike—the line was dead."

By 8:50 A.M. the ship was drifting without power and listing increasingly to port. A hit to the forward part of the hangar deck had connected with one of the torpedo-loaded TBMs; the explosion obliterated the forward elevator. As the other surviving Taffy 3 ships left them behind, *Gambier Bay*'s crew was ordered to abandon ship. By then Verner had already left the bridge and gone down to the flight deck to attend the casualties. "When I heard the abandon ship command, I jumped down to the catwalk, ran along it to pass the word and help get some of the wounded into the water." When he felt he'd done all he could, Verner climbed the catwalk railing and jumped.

Bill McClendon grabbed a rope dangling down the starboard side. "I started climbing down hand over hand with Hank Pyzdrowski right above me. I got about halfway down when Hank slipped. He knocked me off and we both fell maybe twenty feet. I had water in my helmet. I was stunned but still conscious, clearheaded enough to know I needed to get as far from the ship as I could. So I started swimming."

Larry Epping also found his way to a knotted rope. "There was a sailor climbing down ahead of me who panicked and froze. I gave his head a kick with my foot and we both got moving again." Once in the water, Larry swam away from drifting hulk to get outside the vortex he thought might take him down. "Out ahead I saw floating rafts. One of them got hit by a shell meant for the ship."

The wounded had been evacuated from the parachute locker by the time Tony Potochniak made his own escape over the port side. "I was near the bow and the ship was listing hard to port. Guys were in such a hurry to get off they weren't cutting the life rafts. It was hard to do—they were held by heavy-gauge wire—but I had a ten-inch bayonet with me and cut two of them loose. I started going down a rope but I dropped. By the time I reached the water, the rafts were full.

"I came across a guy named Butch, a ship's photographer. His mouth was locked wide open from shock. He had a life jacket on and I took him in tow. The waves were big. We swam around to the starboard side as the ship rolled way over. She slid into the water, and as she did I noticed one of her screws was missing. She went flight deck down—very quick."

⚓

As *Gambier Bay* plunged, a column of Japanese cruisers and destroyers fired torpedoes at the next closest carriers, *Kalinin Bay* and *St. Lo.* Launched at long range, the torpedoes slowed and broached the water short of their targets. One was exploded by gunfire from a TBM pilot, another by gunfire from *St. Lo*'s single 5-in. mount.

The Japanese ships then turned their full attention to *Johnston.* Gunfire from destroyers to starboard and cruisers to port crippled *Johnston*'s remaining engine room and fireroom. Communications circuits failed. *Johnston*'s gunfire director and plotting computer lost power as did the gun mounts.

A topside ready-locker used to store 40-mm ammunition was hit, and onboard shell explosions compounded the damage of incoming rounds. Fire on *Johnston*'s bridge forced Evans to escape aft. He resumed control by yelling orders down to after steering, where men tugging chain falls turned the rudder. It was an indelible tableau: *Johnston*'s hatless, shirtless, wounded skipper Ernest Evans standing in the center of the maelstrom, shouting and motioning with his arms—a bareback rider, a symphony conductor.

But *Johnston* was struggling inside a tightening circle of Japanese destroyers, powerless to move and nearly defenseless against broadside heavy caliber gunfire. Evans finally ordered *Johnston*'s depth charges set on safe and, at 9:45, ordered abandon ship. *Johnston*'s survivors began jumping off.

By now only Bob Hollenbaugh's mount 4 was still firing—to the last under manual control. "The ship was dead in the water. I looked on the port side. I saw guys in the water and thought: 'Those guys are ours.' I told the gun crew 'Let's get out of here.' I didn't have to tell them twice."

Bobby Chastain exited mount 4 through the port side hatch, jumped onto a floater net rack and into the water. He'd left his lifebelt hanging on his bunk below decks. Even without it Bob was glad to be jumping clear of the dread that had weighed on him since the call to GQ. Compared to the hell that *Johnston* had become, the vast ocean seemed like a welcome place.

Bill Mercer wasn't so sure. "I was standing amidships port side. A round had come in and killed some guys behind, and another came in so close I remember touching my face to see if I'd gotten a flash burn. I slid down the bulkhead and sat down on deck by the galley. We were dead in the water and two officers came up the port side from the fantail telling everyone to abandon ship. Several guys already had jumped, but I didn't go. I was afraid the ship might get underway again and leave me behind. But then I saw Captain Evans telling men to abandon ship. I went over the side and swam off the port quarter as fast as I could.

Johnston's survivors—later estimated at 200 out of a crew of 327—scrambled to rafts and floater nets. Within fifteen minutes, *Johnston* rolled to starboard and sank bow down. Treading water fifty yards from *Johnston*'s fantail, Bobby Chastain could see the ship's twin screws as the stern heaved up. "The ship went down like it had been shoved down a chute."

CROSSWINDS

8:30 A.M.–1:00 P.M.

Low on fuel, Tom Van Brunt looked for a place to land. "I went back to *St. Lo,* but they were under fire and I couldn't land. So I headed south to Taffy Two and eventually landed on *Marcus Island*. I went down to the ready room and found five other TBM pilots from different carriers who'd landed before me. The air officer announced they were arming our planes with torpedoes and we'd be heading out on a strike with fighter cover. He asked which of us was senior and it turned out I was. So I was going to be leading the strike."

As he waited first on the catapult, Tom sensed a problem. "The wind wasn't right. *Marcus Island*'s skipper didn't want to get any closer to the Japanese ships, so we were going to take off crosswind. We each had a two-thousand-pound torpedo and a full tank of gas, and I don't think any of us knew whether we were going to make it. I'd be the first one to try." Taking off in a crosswind was the thing Tom worried about most ever since his first training hops in Yellow Perils. "I had the engine revved up real high when I left the catapult. We were a long time just barely staying above the water. I kept the throttle wide open and finally we started to climb. Lester, my radioman, came on the line: 'Sir, we're leaving a wake. We need an outboard motor.'"

Lester's words, coming from a boy who was usually so quiet, broke the spell that was hanging over Tom. "I'd been praying so hard since I learned I'd lead the strike. His joke was a real tension reliever."

⚓

VC-10 aircraft kept attacking the Japanese ships as long as they could. For the first runs, the pilots reformed and covered each other in runs alternatively from ahead and astern. But with each sweep the flak became more intense, planes had to separate, and few had ordnance to expend or fuel to burn. It turned into a chaotic free-for-all.

Dick Roby couldn't see any other aircraft when he came up after his second run. "I floated around for a few minutes in the general direction where I thought Japanese were. Finally I joined up with the squadron leader from *Kitkun Bay*. We came at the Japanese from the north, and from then on it was every man for himself. I lost track of how many runs I made. We lined up with any torpedo bomber that had a bomb bay open and went on in ahead. The Japanese were shooting everything at us. I'd probably already shot up half my ammunition on those first two runs."

Joe McGraw also ran interference for the TBMs. "If the Japanese crews expected to be strafed, they'd keep their heads down. Most of the TBMs were out of ordnance and I only fired short bursts. The best we could do was draw antiaircraft fire away from the fresh planes filtering in from the south. At first they came in ones and twos, very disorganized, but then there were more and more."

New planes—some from ashore but most from Taffy 2's CVEs—began showing up in squadron strength. The VC-10 planes briefly mingled to support them until, after being aloft for nearly three hours, they had to find places to land. Some VC-10 pilots already knew they wouldn't be returning to *Gambier Bay*. Joe McGraw had seen her get hit. Others, like Gene Seitz, had heard it officially: "We got a radio call from the CIC officer on *Gambier Bay:* 'We're going down. Your nearest field is Tacloban on Leyte. God bless you.' "

On his way to Tacloban, Dick Roby came across two TBMs from *Fanshaw Bay* escorting a *Gambier Bay* FM-2. "The fighter pilot they were escorting was Dillard, one of my wingmen.[17] Dillard's hatch had been blown off by a near miss and the kid was punchier than a three-dollar bill. He'd suffered a concussion, lost his helmet, and his face was a mess. They turned him over to me and I brought him on to Tacloban." Dillard lined up for a landing, but when he touched down, his plane hit a soft spot in the sand and flipped. "It tore up the airplane, but somehow he got out ok. They had to pull his airplane out of the way before I could land."

When Gene Seitz made his approach, he could see Tacloban's runway was barely operational. "The airstrip was covered with maybe three hundred yards of Marston matting[18] and the rest was just earth." A lot of planes had landed ahead of Gene. Some—like Dillard's—had crashed or gotten stuck in the mud and had to be pushed to the side. "As soon as we touched down they came around with a gas truck and started filling our tanks. Then a second truck came running down the flight line loaded with two-hundred-fifty-pound bombs. A guy on the back of the truck would kick one off in front of each airplane." Some Japanese fighters came in to strafe Tacloban. "We watched them like spectators until we realized they were trying to get us." Once the VC-10 aircraft were fueled and armed, they lined up for launch. Dick Roby's plane lost power and had to be pulled off the line, but Gene Seitz and three other FM-2 pilots got airborne. "They headed us out to the carriers. When we got back we could see four of them with no escorts, and all trailing oil."

⚓

Joe McGraw had flown west toward Tacloban but then changed his mind. "I had about thirty gallons of fuel and knew the other escort carrier groups were not far south. If I landed at Tacloban I might not be able to go back." Joe soon found Taffy 2. "They'd set up a perfect system: three of the six carriers were launching planes while the other three recovered planes. I got in the traffic pattern for *Manila Bay*, the nearest recovering carrier. When I landed and got to *Manila Bay*'s ready room, VC-80's CO asked me: 'Your plane still up?' I told him it was, so they rearmed and refueled me. I became a VC-80 section leader for another strike."

On this strike, flak from the Japanese ships was heavier and more organized. But with more planes coming in all the time, Joe's section only had to stay over the Japanese for an hour and a half. "As I pulled out from my last strafing run and jinked over the water to escape the flak, I heard a big 'CRACK' over my shoulder." Flying the Wildcat there was always a wall of engine noise, so a sound like that told Joe something was close. "I gave the plane full left rudder and pulled the stick back into my belly." The Wildcat went up and left in a turn that Joe prayed would take him out of the line of fire. "I got clear and rolled over to see what had exploded so close. I saw this huge white phosphorescent cloud shooting out huge balls of fire. It was a phosphorus round lobbed up by one of the battleships. When I finally landed on *Manila Bay* I saw the tail section was peppered with what looked like birdshot." It was now afternoon, but Joe's day was far from over. His plane went below for rearming and refueling. He'd been scheduled for a CAP launch.

⚓

It took a long time for Tom Van Brunt and the four other TBM pilots launched from *Marcus Island* to reach cruising altitude: "When we finally got altitude we tried to join up with the fighters, but we couldn't see them anywhere or raise them on the radio. So we headed towards the Japanese fleet without them. As we got closer we could actually see the Japanese turn and begin to head away. We picked out a line of four ships. The last and biggest was a *Kongo* class battleship, so I radioed the others we'd attack that one."

It was a moment very near the end of the morning's battle off Samar. Four U.S. ships—carrier *Gambier Bay*, destroyers *Hoel* and *Johnston*, destroyer escort *Roberts*—had been sunk. Four Japanese ships—heavy cruisers *Kumano, Chikuma, Chokai,* and *Suzuya* (Tom Van Brunt's early morning victim)—were sunk, about to sink, or out of action. On the surface of the Sea of Samar thousands of ship survivors floated amid patches of oil and debris, clinging to each other and to the hope of rescue. Miraculously, nine Taffy 3 ships were still afloat, still running for their lives—and most were destined to survive. Mysteriously, the Japanese were disengaging.

Tom Van Brunt lined up for his run. Navy torpedo pilots had been taught to start high, dive steep, and come in fast, taking advantage of the dropping resilience of their "pickle-barrel" torpedoes. "As we got ready to dive, my gunner, John South, came on the line. 'Sir, here comes the best goddamn torpedo plane in the United States Navy! Let's make it count!' Now *that* was a pep talk! So we started down.

"Lester was calling off the altitude—we were coming in fast at three hundred feet off the deck. I finally dropped the fish maybe eleven hundred feet from the ship's starboard side—too close to even try evasive action." Tom flew the TBM directly over the battleship. "As I did I felt the left rudder go completely limp. I kept low on the deck and got as far away as I could before I started to climb. I found I was able to climb and I could turn with right rudder."

Tom flew back to where he could see the Japanese ships. "The ship we targeted had fallen out of line and had a slick on its starboard side. I couldn't swear that I hit it, but one of my wingmen reported that I had. I started back to see if any of the carriers were taking planes aboard."

EXIT

9:10 A.M.–12:36 P.M.

Admiral Kurita's order was a recall, not a retreat. Early in the fight, his flagship *Yamato* had turned north to avoid the torpedo spreads fired by *Hoel* and *Heermann.* Torpedo wakes had bracketed *Yamato*'s port and starboard sides. Avoiding them took a precious ten minutes, during which Kurita didn't dare turn. He ended up well north, out of sight of the battle and confused about its progress. Kurita knew that drenching squalls, obscuring smoke, and maneuvers to avoid U.S. air attacks and surface torpedo attacks had widely dispersed his ships. (He did not know that most Japanese battleships and cruisers had pulled to within arms reach of the U.S. carriers and escorts.) At 9:10 A.M., Kurita ordered his forces back north toward *Yamato*—to re-form, assess damage, and reconsider the prospects for attacking transports in Leyte Gulf. The Japanese ships disengaged, the Taffy 3 ships continued to flee south, and Kurita's opportunity slipped away.

During the next hours, Admiral Kurita was pinned by indecision. The Japanese heard a string of plain language transmissions from the Americans—Taffy 3's desperate calls for help; Admiral Kinkaid's instructions to Admirals Oldendorf, McCain, and Thomas Sprague to send ships and aircraft; Kinkaid's appeals to Halsey's absent battle group. The traffic convinced Kurita that massive forces were bearing in from beyond the northern, eastern, and southern horizons.

First Striking Force continued north until 10:55 A.M. and then turned west. Just before noon Kurita's ships again turned south and kept that course for half an hour. It seemed they had regained their resolve. But by 12:36 P.M. they were again headed north, intent on escaping through San Bernardino Strait.

DIVINE WINDS

Everyone talks about fighting to the last man, but only the Japanese actually do it.

—British Field Marshall William Slim, Supreme Allied Commander Southeast India

WINGS STRAIGHT AS A SWORD

Surigao Strait, Sunrise, October 25

In company with two other PTs, Squadron 7's 127 Boat skimmed the Mindanao Sea heading back to Tacloban. "The sun was just barely up," recalled Don Bujold. "At one point we got shot at by a Japanese cruiser. It was wounded—its topside was a real mess. We ducked in behind a couple of small islands to get out of the way, and when we got going again, we saw things floating in the water. At first we thought they were coconuts, but finally saw they were the heads of Japanese sailors. When we passed close to a few stragglers separated from the main group, I remember Dudley Johnson saying in that Texas drawl of his, 'I bet there's an admiral in there somewhere who's been busted to a seaman deuce by now.'

"When we got back to Tacloban and reached the tender, some Japanese planes flew over. Boy, they went by fast! They came in low and the gun crews on the tender opened up with all they had, but the planes didn't stop. They just kept going out to sea."

Off Samar, 7:35 A.M. to 12 noon, October 25

Just a few hours earlier, Holly Crawforth was convinced *St. Lo* was doomed. "I even got an order from the bridge to set up the radio transmitters on five hundred kilocycles—the frequency for distress signals."

Then, as suddenly as it began, the fight was over. Holly heard one of the radar operators say, "They're turning around!" Target ranges being passed from radar to *St. Lo's* 5-in. gun kept opening out. It was nearing 11:00 A.M. After being swallowed by fear for hours, Holly was ecstatic. *St. Lo* had escaped untouched, although word began to seep through that other Taffy 3 ships hadn't been so lucky.

Instructions came to secure from GQ and return to condition One Easy. Without ceremony or more explanation, *St. Lo* eased back to normal routine. "I sent my two strikers down to chow and when they came back I went down." Holly was still at chow when the galley loudspeaker piped the dreadfully familiar GQ gong. "I heard a few quick thumps of twenty-millimeter gunfire—and then this chain of crashes and explosions."

⚓

At dawn, six Japanese "Zeke" fighter-bombers had taken off from Cebu and flown eastward. At 7:35 A.M., the aircraft, some carrying 250-kilogram bombs, approached Taffy 1's twelve ships steaming northeast of Mindanao. The group's four carriers, *Petrof Bay, Sangamon, Santee,* and *Suwannee,* were preparing to launch aircraft to support Taffy 3's fight further north.

The Japanese planes approached the ships at mast level, trying to elude radar. Suddenly they climbed to several thousand feet and just as suddenly plunged. Instead of taking evasive action, the Zekes dived directly for the ships. One crashed through a flight deck elevator on *Santee,* killing sixteen and opening a gaping fifteen-by-thirty-foot hole. The pilot of a second plane aimed at *Petrof Bay* and a third at *Sangamon;* each plane was deflected by anti-aircraft fire before it could reach the ships. *Sangamon*'s attacker was hit by a 5-in. shell from carrier *Suwanee,* whose gunfire also destroyed a second Zeke and crippled a third. This last plane managed to slice through *Suwanee*'s flight deck forward of the after elevator. Stunned and terrified by the experience, carrier crews rallied to contain fires and keep the ships operational.

Toward midday, four more Japanese planes made a run at Taffy 1's carriers. One plane was hit by 5-in. gunfire and exploded in mid-air. A second, enveloped in smoke, turned and fled. A third looped into the clouds and came straight down to hit the water twenty feet from *Petrof Bay*'s bow, exploding and drenching the ship in gasoline. The final plane spiraled toward *Petrof Bay*'s flight deck, but crashed into the water astern. *Petrof's* crew, which had been called to GQ during the earlier attack, remained on full alert for the next four days.

⚓

A later account captured the nightmarish quality of these first kamikaze attacks: "The Japanese aircraft emerged from the clouds and began to dive . . . approaching . . . slowly and deliberately, . . . maneuvering just enough not to be hit too soon. . . All those who watched . . . felt their mouths go dry. In less than a minute he would . . . crash his machine on the deck . . . All the batteries were firing: the 5-inch guns, the 40 millimeters and 20 millimeters, even the rifles. The Japanese aircraft dived through a rain of steel. It had been hit in several places and seemed to be trailing a banner of flame and smoke, but it came on, clearly visible, hardly moving, the line of its wings as straight as a sword."[1]

At almost every turn in the war, American soldiers and sailors had individual brushes with Japanese fanaticism and fatalism—and with their own tendency to underestimate it. Once, after sinking a Japanese barge during a night operation off Leyte, PT 127's crew rescued a Japanese crewman. Tom Tenner got the job of hauling in the prisoner. "I threw the guy a line and told him to climb up. He was small and soaking wet—if he weighed one hundred pounds that was a lot. He spoke a little English and told us the war was lost as far as he was concerned. We gave him a life jacket to wear and another for a pillow, put him on top of the cabin and headed back. Then somebody said, 'We better search him.' We found he still had four hand grenades strapped to him. It showed what a bunch of bozos we were."

The war in the Pacific was filled with such encounters, many of them deadly, but this was different. For the first time, Americans were experiencing combat suicide orchestrated as a systematic weapon. Intending it as an experiment, the Japanese had created an attack unit comprised of twenty-six fighter aircraft, half of them piloted by suicide pilots, the other half assigned to fend off American interceptors as the "body crashers" aimed at the carriers. As the first contingent of body crashers lunged for *Santee, Petrof Bay,* and *Suwannee,* nine more took off from Mabalacat and zoomed east toward Taffy 3's beleaguered formation. At 10:25 A.M., they made contact with Taffy 3's four surviving CVEs just as crews began standing down from GQ.

One Zeke dived at *Kitkun Bay;* its wing struck only a glancing blow to *Kitkun Bay*'s superstructure, but its bomb exploded, causing severe damage. Moments later, *Kalinin Bay* was also badly damaged by a plane crashing its deck. Two Zekes were shot down and two more were driven off by gunfire from *Fanshaw Bay* and *White Plains*. But then a final plane crashed into *St. Lo*'s forward flight deck elevator, knifing all the way through to the hanger deck. Plane, pilot, bomb, and aviation fuels exploded, igniting *St. Lo*'s ready storage of ammunition, bombs, torpedoes, and fuel.

⚓

Minutes before, Tom Van Brunt had nursed his TBM back to the *St. Lo* and found she was at last recovering aircraft. "I radioed our LSO: 'Do you think you can bring me in on a right hand turn? I haven't got any left rudder.' He said he could as long as I had good control, but I had to wait until everybody else got aboard."

Tom circled at fifteen hundred feet, watching his buddies land. "All of a sudden the wing of a Japanese plane fluttered right in front of me. The plane had been shot down by flak. I didn't see the wing and almost hit it." Then he saw a second plane career toward *St. Lo* and watched as it, too, was shot out of the air. What Tom didn't see—and what *St. Lo* gunners missed as well—was a third Japanese plane approaching astern. "He came right up the wake, pulled up, nosed over, and crashed into the flight deck. It was a huge explosion and you could see people right away jumping over the side."

⚓

Larry Collins, twenty-nine, one of *St. Lo*'s communications officers, was in the wardroom when the GQ alarm sounded. "My GQ station was near the fantail, and I usually got there through the hanger deck. But I guess the Lord steered me another way. I went up the same ladder, but instead of getting off at the hanger deck, I kept climbing to the gallery level. The Japanese plane hit while I was still climbing. I turned and ran forward. Explosions started coming one after another—maybe a half dozen of them, and each time the ship would shudder."

Larry joined lots of others who had jammed on *St. Lo*'s forecastle. "I'd been there less than five minutes when an officer appeared on the flight deck above where I stood. 'Captain orders abandon ship,' he called down to us. One man near me heard that, stood on the rail, and jumped into the water, windmilling his arms and legs, shouting 'Oh boy! Thirty days' leave!' all the way down.

"Pretty soon I got up on the rail with a few others and we all jumped. I was still wearing my helmet, and when I hit the water I bit my tongue—the only wound I ever got. We swam hard as we could away to windward. Finally, when I couldn't swim any more, I turned on my back and inflated my life belt. Some of us gathered together as best we could, shared flotation gear, and waited. *St. Lo* was drifting downwind and still exploding. Her whole port side flew up in the air and pretty soon she was gone. We weren't in the water too long—within a couple of hours a destroyer picked us up."

⚓

When he heard the explosions, Holly Crawforth ran to a forward ladder leading to the hanger deck. Someone cautioned him, "Don't go up." "I started to turn back but I just had to see." Holly glimpsed smoke and fire sweeping across the deck and a huge hole in the flight deck just behind the after elevator. He ducked back below, and took a roundabout series of passageways back to Radio 2.

Radio 2 was dark, but the strikers were still there. "I told them to get the hell out. We went over to Radar, which had a door opening onto the catwalk." The door was jammed but they quickly unhinged it, tumbled out, and ran forward along the starboard catwalk, away from the smoke and fire. Holly inhaled the acrid scent of exploded ordnance. After emerging unscratched from the morning's ordeal, it was hard to believe they'd finally been hit.

When he got forward, Holly saw sailors evacuating the wounded—putting life jackets on them, looping lines around their torsos, and lowering them to the water. "But the process was just too slow. Finally all we could do was put jackets on them and drop them over the side."

Holly got to a knotted line hanging from one of the forward gun tubs. "I didn't get very far on the line—maybe ten feet. The man above me lost his grip and peeled the rest of us off as he fell." Holly hit the water hard and plunged so deep he wondered if he would make it up.

When he finally surfaced, Holly tried to use his life belt but it was torn: the CO_2 to inflate it just bubbled out. Holly ditched the belt and began swimming. As he looked around he could see St. Lo's stern drifting in his direction. He stroked as fast as he could to get clear, but he noticed his right shoulder hurt.

"I came across a sailor with two kapok life jackets. Instead of wearing them, he had them laid out, one under his head and one under his legs, just like it was a day at the beach. He gave me one of the jackets. It had the name Harry Tobin on it. I didn't know who Harry Tobin was or what had happened to him."

Holly's right shoulder really hurt now. "I'd caught some shrapnel but didn't know where or how. My arm went numb and I finally grabbed it with my left hand, tucked it in my belt and just swam with the other. I let the current carry me to the top of the waves and then I'd stroke like hell going down."

Holly encountered a cripple named Elmer. "He said 'I can't see out of one eye.' It turned out a piece of shrapnel had gone up his nose and come out through his eye. I told him to grab my belt and I'd pull him along.' He paddled with his free hand I paddled with my good hand."

Holly and Elmer were rescued by Dennis, which had left her escort station and slowed to pick up survivors. Cargo nets were draped over Dennis' sides for survivors who were able to climb. "For a few minutes I had trouble convincing the people on deck that Elmer and I needed help. Finally some guys climbed down to carry us up. There must have been hundreds of survivors on Dennis' main deck."

Holly took Elmer down to the ship's mess where a sick bay had been hastily improvised. St. Lo's flight surgeon, who had already been plucked from the water, was working with Dennis' pharmacist mate to treat the wounded. After finding Elmer a place to sit, Holly went back topside.

"*Dennis* had taken some hits that morning. She was down by the bow and her forward pumps weren't working. Her CO came on the loudspeaker asking for volunteers to go forward and help bail. We were all so tired that none of us budged. Pretty soon the CO was back on the loudspeaker: 'If you survivors don't want to go down with another ship you'll give us a hand bailing up forward.' That was all we had to hear." With his left arm draped uselessly at his side, Holly joined the bucket line.

AGROUND

Panaon Island, 2:00 A.M.–6:00 A.M., October 25

PT 493's crew, armed with submachine guns, carbines, and pistols, set up a small defense perimeter on a stretch of beach separated from Panaon Island by a narrow channel. They did what they could to patch wounds, and sat to wait out the night. The wounded were bleeding or limping or both, but most could get about. The tip of third officer Dick Hamilton's nose had been sheared off by one of the explosions. It was a wound no one envied—he looked like he had a clown's nose—but it was not life-threatening.

During the first hours ashore, 493's skipper Bill Brown and a few others made a tentative foray across the channel into the island's jungle. He knew the crew couldn't stay for long on the narrow spit of land—at some point they might have to try getting back by land. "I was carrying a carbine, but when I stepped off the reef I was in water over my head and lost it." When the small scouting party reached the far bank, they climbed up and worked their way inland until they came across a hut. "Whoever was there had shoved off. They were probably as afraid of us as we were of them. We thought they might have been Japanese, but they could have been from Brooklyn for all we knew. One of our guys, a tall kid, nearly hung himself on some sort of communications line that was strung through the trees. We cut the line and hightailed it back."

Meanwhile, the men waiting on the beach saw huge explosion and tracer rounds arcing like meteors off to the north. "It seemed like it was mostly going from us to them," recalled Gunner's Mate Ted Gurzynski. When morning light reached across the Strait, they saw the remnants of *Carole Baby*, poking nose-up, just off the beach. The boat was finished, held up only because her stern was wedged into the bottom and air was trapped in her nose.

Ted and the rest of the men turned their efforts to rescue. "Somebody had sense enough to grab an American flag when we left the boat. We spread it out on shore so that ships coming to look for us would see it." Some men fanned out along the beach looking for ships or aircraft, ready to wave, ready to swim—or duck and run if they had to. What they spotted first was the enemy—the hulks of several Japanese ships limping south.

⚓

On the 491 Boat, then cruising near the shoreline of Panaon Island, CO Harley Thronson and XO Terry Chambers spotted the same Japanese ships. "After the night action we lost contact with the 490 and 493 boats," Terry recalled. "We lay off the beach to watch the rest of the battle. Japanese ships were blowing up right in front of us.

"About 4:00 A.M. things settled down and after a couple of hours Harley figured we ought to get back out on station. As we went into the Strait, we saw what turned out to be *Mogami*. She had fires on her stern and another ship alongside. We spotted her before she saw us and we decided to sneak up and fire our last two torpedoes at her." With Terry at the wheel and Harley cueing the torpedoes, 491 made its run. "It was broad daylight by then," Harley remembered. "We took on the heavy cruiser. The Japanese finally saw us coming and started shooting the hell out of us."

From their beachhead, 493's crew could see the action unfold. Bill Brown couldn't believe his eyes. "The boat was going against that damn rascal in daylight. I thought its skipper must be out of his mind, but then again we were all probably stupid enough to try the same thing."

Harley gave the signal to launch torpedoes. "We were probably too far away." As the fish made their runs, Terry saw the Japanese ships turn to starboard. "The torpedoes went down the side of them. By then we were running away and eight-inch shells were splashing all around us. Fortunately, they were still firing armor-piercing rounds. One column of water hit the top of my helmet and jammed it down on my head. We chased shell splashes to avoid being hit. At one point Harley told me to turn hard right. He had his eye on one splash, but I saw a different one and turned left instead. If I hadn't made that mistake we'd have been blown out of the water."

"We were under fire for maybe five minutes," recalled Harley. "It was a miracle we escaped. We headed for a point of land just to the north and ducked in there. Then Terry and our quartermaster Al McCready spotted some people ashore. Some guy was waving a white shirt. Sure enough, there were people and the wreck of a PT in the water with only its bull nose showing."

Ted Gurzynski watched 491 approach. "They had every gun trained on us. They thought it could have been a Japanese set up, but then they recognized the guys."

The 491 nosed close to shore. The 493's surviving crew and the bodies of Gaffney and Tatarek were taken aboard. A line was attached to *Carole Baby* and, as the tide shifted, the 493 Boat came off the bottom. Despite his wound, Dick Hamilton volunteered to go back onboard to demolish the boat's code machine. Then 491 towed 493 further out into the Strait where it went right to the bottom.

The 493's survivors watched *Carole Baby* go down and then huddled on 491's deck for the trip back to Tacloban.

ADRIFT

Off Samar, Afternoon, October 25 through the Afternoon, October 26

Eight ships—five American, three Japanese—were down in the waters roughly thirty miles east of Samar. North to south, the ships had sunk across a thirty-mile span of four thousand fathoms-deep ocean. The northernmost and last sinking had been the Japanese heavy cruiser *Suzuya*, just after 1:00 P.M. The southernmost and last American ship to go was *St. Lo* at 11:25 A.M.

Scattered between these unmarked boundaries were the debris-strewn graves and struggling survivors of six other ships: U.S. destroyers *Hoel* and *Johnston*, destroyer escort *Samuel B. Roberts,* and escort carrier *Gambier Bay;* and Japanese heavy cruisers *Chikuma* and *Chokai.* Perhaps five thousand men had either abandoned or gone down with their ships. Those fortunate enough to jump clear were alive but in shock. Many suffered from grievous, untreated wounds. They were helpless witnesses to the chaos of a battle raging all around them. Fleeing south, with the Japanese in hot pursuit, skippers on the surviving U.S. ships had not dared turn or even slow to assist. As the chase finally eased, some of the Japanese ships paused to rescue their own sailors—just as, several hours later, American destroyers would quickly scoop up *St. Lo*'s survivors. Meanwhile, survivors of *Hoel, Gambier Bay, Roberts,* and *Johnston* had simply been left behind.

⚓

As the first shock of plunging into the ocean wore off, *Hoel* survivors began swimming to the rafts and flotation nets cut loose from the ship. There were barely 100 of them, from a crew of 350. The stronger, uninjured swimmers coaxed or hauled some of the wounded with them. Glenn Parkin and his friend Bill Murray[2] found their way to one of *Hoel*'s floater nets— rectangular webs of canvas interspersed with cork floats—and hung on. "Bill told me 'I'd give my soul in Hell for a cigarette.' When he said that, I remembered I had cigarettes and matches stuffed in my shirt pockets. They were still dry when I took them out of the condoms, but the water had swollen my fingers and I had a hard time lighting them. We finally got them started but the first drags made us sick."

Japanese ships glided through a swath of *Hoel* debris. Larry Morris, still swimming alone, treaded water and tried to keep a low profile. "The

Japanese had to see me and the others. I figured they'd shoot at us just like we'd sometimes done when we caught them in the water going from island to island. But they came right through us and didn't fire a shot."

Glen Parkin recalled it differently. "We thought they were going to run us down. We heard small-arms fire, and dove under the net as deep as we could. We saw one big ship, then another, and then the biggest ship I'd ever seen, maybe seventy-five yards away." It was *Yamato*.

"As the Japanese went by, one of our aircraft came in to make a strafing run. We were so close we could hear the bullets hit the wood decks. The Japanese were shooting back with about every gun they had, but the fighter was back in the clouds within a few seconds. Then the Japanese ships scattered—all we could see was smoke from their funnels."

Larry Morris and Sam Lucas joined a group of survivors clinging to a raft and a floater net. "There were forty-two when we started out," Larry recalled. "We didn't have any food or medical supplies. We did start out with a keg of water, but I'll be damned if we didn't manage to lose it during the first night."

Many in Larry's group had terrible injuries. "One big guy, a shipfitter named Tiny Hienritz,[3] had a piece of shrapnel about the size of a coffee saucer lodged in his side. Tiny never complained during all the time we were in the water, and he managed to survive." Others didn't. "During the next two days twelve or thirteen died. Each time, an officer in the group went through a brief ritual. If the guy had a life jacket we'd take it and then push him off."

Glen Parkin's group was also without supplies until a small piece of good fortune floated by. "We loss track of the time, but it was probably late afternoon. Someone spotted an object floating a couple hundred feet away. Charlie Sampson[4] and I swam out to retrieve it. It was a large crate of potatoes."

As night came, the wind strengthened and the waves got higher. Glen could sometimes see lights when the net took its riders to the crest of a big wave. "The lights seemed close, but we didn't know who they belonged to. Erling Husvik[5] and I took turns holding each other's head out of the water so we could catch a little sleep. It was a hell of a night—with more to come." By daybreak three in the group were dead. "We wondered who would be next. During the night we also lost the potatoes—we had nothing to lash the crate to the net."

As the day lengthened, sharks circled under the bright afternoon sun. To Glen it seemed there were hundreds. "They would swim along the floater net so close we could grab their dorsal fins. Someone even tried to stick a knife in the back of one. Before it was over, we lost two men to sharks." Frustrated and desperate, one man left the net and swam after them, holding a knife in his mouth. "That was the last we saw of him, though we could see the turbulence around the shark—and blood."

⚓

While *Gambier Bay* remained afloat and without power, it drifted in the
current and was pushed by the northeasterly wind. As it sank, *Gambier
Bay*'s hull listed steeply to port. For men abandoning ship to starboard, it
was either a long descent by rope or a perilous jump. On the port side it was
easier—barely a few feet from the flight deck to the water's surface. But
once overboard, these survivors had to get away quickly as *Gambier Bay*'s
roll to port accelerated. Survivors downwind and downstream also risked
being pulled under when the ship went down.

Over eight hundred crew and VC-10 squadron personnel escaped
Gambier Bay alive, most leaving without a thought to what they wore or
carried. Like many others, Chaplain Verner Carlsen still wore his GQ
helmet when he dropped from *Gambier Bay*'s flight deck. "The chinstrap
wrenched my neck when I hit the water."

Many wore some sort of flotation device, although lots of the inflatable
belts and vests had been shredded by shrapnel or scrapes against sharp
obstacles. Explosions to *Gambier Bay*'s flight deck had sent huge, splintered
wood beams into the water. Some men clung to these or to the wood chocks
used to hold aircraft wheels in place.

Even before the ship plunged, the survivors began to gather in groups.
Natural collection points were the ship's rafts—buoyant oblong donuts,
belted by ropes, with an inner lattice of planking and ropes that allowed
water to pass through. There were not nearly enough rafts and in many, as
Bill McClendon recalled, "the interior ropes and planking were rotted."
Rafts were supplemented by floater nets, and there were even a handful of
inflatable aviator life rafts.

As the groups assembled—some contained as few as 10 or 15 men, one
grew to nearly 150—certain routines played out. Strong swimmers made
it to rafts on their own, bringing wounded, and then swimming out to get
more. The wounded were lifted or heaved into the porous shelter of the raft
interiors, while the rest clung to ropes or climbed the floats on the nets,
riding them like saddles. Some rafts and nets were joined together. Leaders
emerged in the larger groups—usually senior ship or air group officers—to
take responsibility for herding stragglers, doling out meager supplies,
keeping up spirits, restraining acts of desperation, and casting loose the
dead. During the next two tortuous days, these groups formed, grew,
reconfigured, and dispersed in a constantly shifting mosaic of despair and
stoicism, delirium and composure, death and survival.

The mosaic's biggest portion began as a group of twenty to thirty
survivors riding or clinging to one of the rafts. Among the shifting roster of
occupants—as others joined and rafts and nets were linked—were *Gambier
Bay*'s Chaplain Verner Carlsen, Seaman Charlie Heinl, VC-10's LSO Bill

McClendon, Ensign Fred Mallgrave from engineering, Aircraft Machinist Mate Tony Potochniak, and Radarman Lou Rice.

Verner Carlsen was among the first to arrive. As the raft filled with wounded, he stayed outside, hooking his arm through a rope to keep anchored. "A sailor next to me asked me why I was still wearing my glasses. I told him I was nearsighted. He let me know the lenses were gone." Bill McClendon also arrived early and grabbed an outside rope. "With my Mae West inflated I didn't need extra buoyancy, so I was holding on just to keep with the group. We had a one-man aviator life raft and we ended up putting a young enlisted man with a badly damaged foot inside. We didn't want him sitting in the water attracting sharks."

Radarman Lou Rice arrived clinging to an aircraft chock. "One of the CIC officers and I tried to swim with the chock, but we had a hard time getting anywhere. Finally we had to drift aft and swim past the fantail. When we arrived, they were tying rafts and floater nets together. I got up on one of the cork floats. The ship was going down. We expected aviation depth charges to explode, so a lot of us were bracing."

There were few explosions, but there was the brief menace of a passing Japanese cruiser. "We were underneath one ship," Lou recalled. "I looked up. One of the Japanese gunners had cocked a machine gun and was going to start to spraying, but another guy—an officer I think—knocked him away from the gun. The officer saluted us as they went by. I couldn't believe it." Meanwhile, others saw shipboard photographers eagerly snapping photographs and taking home movies like cruise boat tourists.

There was some food stowed on the raft—cans of Spam and a handful of malted milk tablets—but no fresh water. The keg bungs had popped loose when the rafts hit the water and the kegs had filled with salt water. The day grew hot. Bill McClendon tied a white handkerchief over his forehead to block the sun while others, like Charlie Heinl, improvised similar protection. "I took my knife and cut off about six or eight inches of my trousers to cover my forehead." Through the day and into the evening, more survivors joined—some from rafts, and some still clinging to pieces of planking. A group joining near nightfall included *Gambier Bay*'s CO. According to one survivor's recollection, what started as one raft increased to a sprawl of three floater nets, seven rafts, and two aviator rafts.

Early on the first day, Chaplain Carlsen led the men in reciting the Lord's Prayer. He beseeched they not be strafed, and be protected from perils above and below the surface. Verner was the chaplain—responsible for ministering the spiritual needs of the men in the raft and in the water with him. But he also had to attend to his own survival—and his doubts about whether he would make it. "I allowed myself one spiritual anchor. When we passed through Pearl Harbor, I learned my first child—a daughter—had been born. My wife and my baby were waiting for me in Sydney, Montana, and I kept assuring myself that I would be seeing them soon."

All along, the men noticed sharks. Their fins kept breaking the water's surface and the men tried to keep them away by splashing water. "They were small hammerhead sharks, more nuisance than harm," Fred Mallgrave recalled. Others, though, remembered the sharks as more lethal, eventually taking several men outside the rafts and on the floater nets. "The sharks got one guy an elbow's length away from me," Charlie Heinl remembered. "To this day I don't know who he was." During the first hours several in the rafts also succumbed to wounds or burns, and several more would die either that night or the next day. There was little doubt the sharks feasted on the dead as they were released to the sea.

By nightfall, the cool water had become cold, the surface air even colder. "If you were still able to pee, you'd pee and try to huddle in it," recalled Lou Rice. Bill McClendon teamed with Buzz Borries[6] to lash one of the raft oars to the underside of the raft. The oar's blade made a levered seat, counterbalanced by the weight of the men inside the raft. "We took turns: one sitting on the oar blade, the other straddling his legs and holding on. It kept us warm and prevented us from drifting away."

On the second day Charlie Heinl got a kapok life jacket from another survivor who had two. "The kapok kept me afloat with my head out of the water and I managed to fall asleep. Some of us were beginning to hallucinate. A couple of times I thought I was on the ship's bridge. Another guy was going to take one of the wounded to a hospital. Some men said they were going to one of the islands. Some just disappeared."

"As darkness fell," recalled Fred Mallgrave, "we surrounded the cork nets with life rafts to protect the wounded from sharks. We saw a Japanese twin-engine bomber and Very pistol[7] flares from the other survivor groups. In the meantime, most of the men were going slightly 'haywire.'"

⚓

Even after *Roberts'* survivors jumped ship, the smoking hulk still drew Japanese fire. The men in the water were anxious for *Roberts* to sink, and, when it finally did, some, like Seaman Bill Wilson, saluted.

When Tom Stevenson reached the water, he thought he had it made. "It was a strange thing to be thinking, but I was in my element. I'd competed in swimming—I'd even been offered a swimming scholarship at Columbia." Tom and a few other strong swimmers hauled wounded to a raft and helped shepherd others to the floater net. "We swam over to a group holding on to piece of the ship's maintenance scaffolding. We tried to persuade them to join us. They wouldn't budge, but we did move one badly injured man to the raft. The guys on the scaffolding never made it." Tom still had one of the security bags left to be sunk. "I collected sheath knives from some of the men (extra weights they were glad to lose) and loaded them in the bag until it was heavy enough to sink."

Before Lou Gould jumped overboard, a shipmate had pressed some ammunition clips into his hands. "The guy was taking a Thompson submachine gun with him and wanted me to carry extra ammunition. Once I got in the water, I realized I couldn't hold the clips and inflate my belt at the same time, so I ditched the clips. We joined up at the floater net, and I apologized to him for not bringing the clips. 'That's ok,' he said. 'I lost the gun.'"

When three Japanese ships steamed in their direction, Tom sprinted away from the floater net. "If the Japanese were going to kill or capture us, I thought, they'd head for the groups around the rafts and floater nets instead of a single swimmer." Mel Harden recalled the CO telling them to stay low and not move. The ships came close, but just glided by. Tom Stevenson glimpsed crewmembers on one ship standing on deck, some dressed in white coveralls. Some saluted or waved. One figure even hoisted a newsreel camera to his shoulder. When the Japanese were gone, Tom returned to the floater net. Except for the nets, the rafts, and their occupants, the sea seemed to him suddenly vast, empty, and quiet.

⚓

It became a tale of two ordeals for the *Roberts*' survivors. Those who abandoned ship on the starboard side from amidships forward formed the larger of two groups. During the hours ahead, the sailors in this group—among them CO Bob Copeland, XO Bob Roberts, George Carbon, Lou Gould, Mel Harden, Dudley Moylan, and Tom Stevenson—seemed to be bolstered during most of the ordeal by generous reserves of leadership, teamwork, and humanity. Meanwhile, a smaller group, survivors who, like Dick Rohde, Vince Goodrich, and Bill Wilson, escaped from the port side and from astern, seemed to be shadowed by meanness and rancor.

"Somehow I got into a raft," Dick Rohde recalled. "A pharmacist's mate took off my dungarees and put sulfa powder on my leg." Then, even though he was wounded, Dick was sent off to the floater nets. "I wondered how the sulfa powder was going to help my wound if I was in the water and why I couldn't stay on the raft. The guys there seemed in better shape than I was." Finally, Dick returned to the raft and tried to climb in. "I'll never forget it. One of the guys just knocked me back out. I was too weak to do anything about it, so I just went back to the floater net."

Dick's group soon encountered sharks. "We started to argue about what to do. Some guys wanted to use the yellow dye marker in our emergency kit to frighten them. Others shouted we needed to keep it if we wanted to be spotted. Some guys kicked their feet to keep the sharks away. Others screamed that this would just bring them closer." Vince Goodrich was one of those who kicked—he was glad to be wearing shoes. "I remembered what my boot camp instructor told me: If you kept your shoes and got ashore you'd have shoes. When I had to kick one of the sharks away, I was glad I'd kept them on. I wasn't ready to die."

⚓

Roberts' second and larger group of survivors clung to a raft and a floater net. The group parceled raft medical supplies into several brass powder casings collected from the water. They began rationing out food—some water and small supplies of Spam, hard tack, and malted milk tablets. Before nightfall they drifted through a few welcome showers, but they also drifted into a vast slick of thick, acrid oil.

The oil clung to everything and got into the men's ears and eyes; everyone was coated in black. "At first we used gauze to wipe the oil out of our eyes," recalled Mel Harden. Later the group snared a crate marked with Japanese symbols—it turned out to be filled with pungent raw onions. "Nobody could eat them, but they were the only things not covered in oil," Dudley Moylan recalled. "So you could get at a clean layer of onion and wipe your face off."

Tom Stevenson was exhausted from the first hours' efforts. The air was cold and the oily water barely warmer. "My life belt helped me stay afloat, but I didn't have a shirt, and the belt was chafing my back and chest. If I'd had a kapok vest, the collar would have supported my neck." Like others in the group, Dudley Moylan resigned himself to a night without rescue: "George Carbon and I were at the edge of net. I would half encircle him so that he could rest. And then he would do the same for me." During the first night the group lost two or three people.

⚓

"We saw our first shark about three P.M. on the first afternoon," the *Johnston*'s Bill Mercer recalled. "It was a pretty big one about one hundred yards from us, but coming closer. It swam along my side of the raft, and rolled as if it was going to hit someone. We pushed down on the shark to keep from being bitten. And it worked—the shark didn't hit anyone and it seemed to scare him away. We had more shark attacks after dark, and this time several guys got bitten: one on both thighs, one in the back, one on his arm and shoulder, and one in the kidneys. Two of them died."

Two badly injured men—both with severe burns and both blind—had been placed inside a life raft with another injured man to care for them. During the night, both burn victims also died, within ten minutes of each other. "It was a long night. From time to time, someone would scream out and someone would yell, 'Shark!' and the rest of us would start kicking and splashing frantically, trying to scare the shark away. As far as I know, it worked. It was very tiring, kicking and splashing all night but we did it."

The second day brought clear skies, bright sun, and the lure of landfall to the west. At sunup two men set off for shore; at noon, six more including, Bill Mercer, followed. "We took a four-by-four timber and headed off. Late in the afternoon we caught up with the first two guys; they'd come across a life raft from the *Johnston*. It had contained a forty-millimeter shell filled with rations, but one of the guys managed to lose it over the side. We thought we could probably make landfall during the night, so we split up our money and our knives and planned what we'd do when we hit the beach. But then the current turned and carried us back out to sea. The night seemed much longer than the first one, because we were starting to think and talk crazy. Sometime after dark I removed my kapok. When I let go of the jacket in the water, it sank—I realized I had been keeping it afloat."

ALOFT

Afternoon, October 25, through the Morning, October 26

With *St. Lo* gone, Tom Van Brunt had to find an alternative place to land. "I finally decided to go to Leyte. Tacloban had a steel mat runway, but so many Navy planes had already landed some were being pushed into the ocean to make room. I knew there was another field thirty miles south at Dulag—a grass airstrip that we had bombed a couple of days before. It was supposed to be nonoperational, but it seemed the only other choice."

Tom approached the strip at Dulag by making a right hand turn. "I'll be darned if they didn't start shooting at me from the ground—small-arms fire. But we got on the ground okay, pulled into the woods, and got out of the plane to inspect the damage." It was just as well they'd not been able to land on *St. Lo*. "The cable to the left rudder was completely gone and the elevator cable only had three strands out of sixteen. The main thing, though, was I'd lost my tail hook."

One witness to Tom's shaky landing turned out to be Tom's friend Burt Bassett. "I was standing there beside the runway with some other guys watching these planes come in. I saw a TBM come in and the pilot was barely able to control the plane. He was zigzagging back and forth, but he finally landed in one piece and got out with his crew. When I approached the plane, I was dumbfounded to see Tom Van Brunt from the University of Florida. I didn't even know he was in the Navy. And he had been stationed right nearby on the *St. Lo*."

⚓

In mid-afternoon Joe McGraw made his third launch of the day—his second from *Manila Bay* as part of VC-80. This time he led a section in a four-plane

CAP orbiting Taffy 2 at ten thousand feet, ready either to fly north or to intercept Japanese air raids coming in over Mindanao.

"We got vectored to intercept a small raid of Japanese aircraft coming in from the south and climbed to twelve thousand feet along the way. When we got there, Japanese planes were popping out from a line of storm clouds below us. I counted eighteen Vals—six echelons of three with twelve Zero escorts behind and above. I thought, 'If they're calling this a small raid, we are in big trouble.'"

Although there were only four of them, the VC-60 planes were in a perfect position to make a run. "The Japanese didn't see us, the Vals were busy tightening up their formation, and the Zeros were still pretty disorganized. All we had to do was turn and dive."

The CAP division leader jumped the lead Val in an echelon and his wingman dove on that Val's inboard wingman. Joe and his wingman followed, targeting the next echelon in the same way. "We were on them quick, hitting the Vals' engines and wing roots." All four Vals went down in flames.

"The rest of the Vals wobbled. They were confused—a few even unloaded their bombs. But the lead Zero finally spotted us and pushed over to attack, followed by the others. I spotted them and called 'Zeros coming down.'" The four Wildcats pulled up into the attackers, climbing hard and tight to keep the Zeros from getting on their tails. "The lead Zero went nose to nose with our division leader and smoked his engine with cannon fire— a true marksman's shot." The division leader's Wildcat spiraled down.

The rest of Wildcats wove untouched through the scrum of Zeros. Joe corkscrewed his airplane, leaving his wingman behind as he climbed. None of the Zeros could line him up for a shot. "I topped out of the climb and rolled over on my back to look down. The Zero lead was just pulling up from the dive that splashed our division leader. His wingman was a little up and behind." Joe was again in a perfect attack position. "I continued my roll until I lined up the wingman. I gave him a long burst. His fuel exploded and he was gone."

The pilot in the lead Zero must have been enraged. It was clear from the shot that splashed the CAP leader the pilot was a virtuoso. But he'd also managed to lose four Vals under his protection and now his own wingman.

The Zero turned on Joe. "The pilot jerked the Zero up on its nose, whipped the plane around, and got it heading straight at me, firing his cannon. It was the greatest turn in a fighter that I'd ever seen—or would ever see again." Joe's reflexes took over. "I rolled left and knife-edged him." The Zero's cannon fire passed close but clean by Joe's tail.

"We passed within feet of each other and I could see row after row of victory markings on the fuselage near the canopy. The pilot was an old hand." The Zero slammed into another hard turn and Joe did too. "I got into the tightest turn I'd ever made."

Joe surprised both himself and the Japanese pilot. "I got around as quickly as the Zero. I lined him up for a quick shot and got a burst into his engine." The two planes were again in close. The Zero's engine quickly smoked and, just as quickly, the Zero pilot pulled back on his stick, trying to ram Joe's plane. Joe's twenty-year-old eyes and instincts were on it. "I pulled my stick back and the Zero went by, just feet under me."

Joe slammed his plane into another tight turn. "I thought 'He's smoking. He's dangerous. I've got to kill him before he kills me.'" Joe expected his opponent to be level, but the Zero pilot, newly respectful of his opponent, this time flipped over on his back and dove.

"The Zero was getting away. I pulled the Wildcat's nose up and tried to get a lead on him—like aiming out ahead of a flock of quail—to squeeze off a long-range burst. But then I saw two other Zeros cutting in on the dance to protect their leader." Joe now switched tactics, lining up the Zero coming in from the left. "I gave him some lead and fired a burst. The burst sieved his tail but nothing more." Alone and outnumbered, Joe decided it was time to get out. "The two Zeros followed, firing their cannons, but the Wildcat could dive as fast as a greased safe. There was no way they'd catch me."

Finally, Joe saw the Zeros break off, return to their crippled leader, and pop back into the cloud deck. "I looked around to see if there were anymore fat Vals hanging around. I found two heading back into the clouds. I banked their way, gunned the engine, and chased them for a few minutes. I couldn't catch them, so I raised the Wildcat's nose, lobbed a few rounds as they disappeared into the clouds, and turned back."

When Joe looked around, there wasn't an airplane in the sky. "It was a strange feeling. One second the sky was full of airplanes and all these things were happening. The next I was in the sky all by myself. No friends, no enemies. I felt like the loneliest guy in the world." It took a moment to shake the feeling off, then Joe headed down in search of his wingman, the division leader's wingman, and the division leader himself—now probably waiting for rescue somewhere on the water below.

⚓

Dick Roby finally managed to get his Wildcat launched from Tacloban. "I found a couple of Air Corps mechanics who figured out the Army light tanks used the same spark plugs as the Wildcats. So we changed all eighteen plugs and I was ready to go." As the afternoon waned, nine VC-10 pilots, including Dick, Jim Lischer, and Gene Seitz, flew one final CAP. When they retuned to Tacloban, the pilots found no place to eat or sleep. "I finally commandeered two carry-alls and we drove down south to an army base," Dick recalled. "We got there at ten P.M. and they fed us fried eggs and Canadian bacon, the first food we had in a day." The pilots bunked down in Army tents, but there wasn't much sleep to be had. Jim Lischer remembered waking up in a panic, surrounded by a cascade of explosions. "They had us billeted right next to an artillery unit, and they fired nonstop all night."

Further south at Dulag Tom Van Brunt also took Army accommodations—bunks in a Army Air Corps tent. "We were dead tired that night. There were thirteen of us from *St. Lo.* We couldn't believe it was over—and so bad: the ship gone and who knew how many friends gone with it. I was sacked out on a cot when one of the Army sergeants woke me up. The Japanese were counterattacking and we were on the perimeter. He asked me what kind of arms we had, and I told him just side arms, thirty-eights. He said, 'Get your men up and I'll take you to the armory. You can draw rifles.'"

The sergeant doused his flashlight and led them through the jungle. "Everyone was trying to keep real quiet. We got to what they called the armory tent. It was just a big tarp on one pole and to get in you had to crawl under the edges of it. There was another sergeant there with a flashlight. He showed us an M-1 rifle—first time any of us had ever seen one. He started checking us out on it but he obviously didn't think his checkout was going to be effective. He said 'Just a minute fellas.' He left for about five minutes, and when he came back he said 'The CO's changed his orders. No rifles. Go to the next tent and draw shovels. We'll show you where to dig holes. Get in them and don't move.'"

They dug deep two-man holes. Tom shared his with a VC-65 fighter pilot. "We sat there back-to-back all night long, tensed up, with our thirty-eights loaded and cocked, waiting for a Jap head to come over the edge. At about two-thirty A.M. we heard a plane; it was way up, we could just hear the drone of the motor. We assumed it was Japanese, but we didn't know. Then we heard a bomb start coming down, screaming, screaming. When it hit the ground all hell broke loose. The bomb had hit a back-up supply of gasoline and ammunition. We must have been two miles or so from it, but it was frightening to see and hear. There was no sleep that night."

RESCUE

Off Samar, Evening, October 26, through Evening, October 27

The survivors had not been in the water that long—not by the measure of other sailors and airmen adrift for many days and sometimes weeks in empty stretches of the Pacific. For the men from *Gambier Bay, Hoel, Johnston,* and *Roberts,* it had been the day of the sinking, a night, another day, and most of another night. Nevertheless, the ordeal—wounds, hunger and thirst, heat, and menacing sharks—was taking its toll. For many, survival toppled into delirium and desperation.

As the hours accumulated, men lost interest in anything but water and food. They grew lethargic and irritable. Dehydration drained strength from their muscles. Tongues swelled in their mouths; saliva became thick and evil-tasting; throats stiffened into raspy tubes. The men hallucinated; their minds wove vivid fantasies of impossible meals. With seawater all around, fixation overcame logic: if the water was wet, how could it hurt you?

Larry Epping clung to a raft with ten other *Gambier Bay* survivors. With every hour, it seemed less likely they would ever be found. Some people became frantic and some began drinking seawater. "One officer went suddenly crazy and began swimming away," recalled Larry. "I grabbed him by the hair, knocked him out with several punches, and heaved him into the raft." The raft drifted in the southwest current and eventually the men could begin to see a mass of land off on the horizon. A few decided to set off for shore. To Larry, trying to swim there seemed like no prospect at all.

⚓

The second night in the water, *Johnston* survivor Bob Hollenbaugh locked his arms as tightly as he could into the webbing of the floater net. "I fell asleep. By the time I woke up, I'd let go of the net and I was all by myself—not a soul around. It was just breaking light. I called out: 'Is there anybody around?' I hollered a couple more times. I finally heard a faint call and I headed for it. It was a couple of guys on a four-by-four, a piece of damage control shoring. One of them was a fireman from engineering and the other was one of the cooks. The three of us ended up hugging for life to that piece of shoring."

⚓

In another group of *Johnston* survivors, Bill Mercer had worked out a sleeping arrangement with J. B. Strickland. "I told Strick I would hold him up while he slept if he'd do the same for me. In about two seconds he was sound asleep. When I felt I had held him up for a couple of hours (it was probably more like five minutes), I woke him up and told him it was my turn. But by the time I'd leaned my head on Strick's shoulder, he'd already gone back to sleep."

As daylight neared, Bill's group could see that it was once again close to shore. "Seven of us decided to leave the raft and swim to the island. Strickland said he couldn't make it but encouraged the rest of us to try. We decided that if we couldn't all go, none of us would."

⚓

During the second night, *Roberts'* survivor Dick Rohde remembered being grabbed by shipmate Charlie Cronin.[8] "I tried to swim away from the net. I was going to look for my brother in India. He was in the Air Corps." Finally, Cronin was able to tie Dick to the net so that he couldn't swim away. "Once I was tied down, the delusions actually kept my hopes up. I kept imagining a hole leading down to a scuttlebutt with ice-cold water; or a bottomless jug of lemonade."

At dusk on the second day, the other group of *Roberts* survivors spotted land. "We got close enough to Samar to see palm trees silhouetted against the sun," recalled Dudley Moylan. The group briefly organized itself to try for the beach. "The good swimmers moved to the inshore side of the floater net and started swimming. Two guys on the raft paddled while everyone in the water on the offshore side kicked." They couldn't make it. As night approached, tide and current took over, pulling them out. During the night, some saw or imagined lights in the distance. Some heard or imagined voices. When morning came they could no longer see the island.

By dawn on the third day, order turned to near anarchy. During the first day and night, *Roberts'* CO Bob Copeland had clearly been in charge of the group, but exhaustion finally took its toll on him. Tom Stevenson watched the process. "At first he became quiet and his control seeped away. Then he was out of it, delusional."

Still, other survivors like Mel Harden never let go of the simple certainty of rescue. "I was clinging to the floater net, just determined to take things as they came."

⚓

A search flotilla comprised of two PCs and five LCIs left San Pedro Bay before sunset on October 25, headed for a spot where aircraft had reported several hundred survivors in the water. It was the morning of the 26th before the craft reached the location and began a systematic search. Fanning out abreast, separated at first by one-thousand-yard and then two-thousand-yard intervals, the craft trawled north to south in twenty-five-mile long swaths, combing empty ocean interrupted occasionally by oil slicks and patches of debris. It turned out they had been sent to wrong spot— some thirty miles south of any of the survivors. By mid-afternoon the searchers had found and retrieved only one survivor—a downed Japanese aviator sitting atop a drifting crate.

Following the logic of wind and currents, the search edged westward, closer to Samar. As darkness fell, boat crews encountered more debris and spotted flares in the western sky. Finally, near midnight, the craft began picking up American survivors—the first of them from *Gambier Bay*.

The *Gambier Bay* survivors had spotted ships' silhouettes coming in from the northwest. They had no way of knowing if they were American or Japanese. As one ship got closer, one of Larry Epping's raft mates shouted out. A response came back in a broad Southern drawl: "How y'all doing down there?"

The ships moved among the clusters of nets and rafts, first hauling in the seriously wounded before retrieving the others. "The boat crews said they couldn't pull us in fast enough," recalled Charlie Heinl. "The sharks were all around and nearly following us right in." Once aboard, Larry Epping was able to stand but he felt woozy. "I'd been awake for three straight days." By sunrise, seven hundred *Gambier Bay* survivors had been retrieved, all of them in waters only a few miles east of Samar. While one PC returned to San Pedro loaded with wounded, the other six craft resumed the search.

At 7:45 A.M., off to the northeast, rafts and nets carrying *Hoel* survivors were spotted and, a few minutes later, rafts, nets, and oil-soaked survivors from *Roberts*. *Hoel* survivor Sam Lucas remembered his group's uncertain efforts to hail the rescuers. "We had a yellow flag from the emergency kit; it was maybe three or four feet square. There was a little guy in our group named Bill Murray. We had Bill hold the flag and we hoisted him up between the rafts. We worried for a moment the ship was Japanese, so we pulled him back down." As the LCI approached the *Roberts* survivors, its crew seemed wary of the spectral black forms bobbing in the water. "They had guys standing by machine guns," recalled Mel Harden. "They hollered out all kinds of questions before they came close to pull us in."

Just before 9:00 A.M., the searchers encountered *Johnston* survivors. "At first, all of us except Strickland thought they were Japanese ships," Bill Mercer recalled. "But as they came closer and one of the boats drifted broadside to us we could see the beautiful American flag. We knew then that we had made it." According to flotilla logs, the last survivors had been picked up at 9:30 A.M.; the search ended at 10:00 A.M. The small flotilla, its crew spaces and decks crowded with 1,150 survivors, many of them wounded, all of them suffering from exposure, began the long, slow journey back to San Pedro Bay. En route, the ordeal was to claim several more victims—one of them was *Roberts'* Tony Serafini.

The men remembered climbing up nets, reaching deck, thinking they could stand, most finding they couldn't. "We all collapsed like sardines," Sam Lucas remembered. *Roberts* survivor Vince Goodrich thought he felt strong. "But when my body weight came out of the water my legs just folded up." Lou Gould was helped below and pointed to a bunk. "I held back at first, knowing how covered in oil I was, but then I just collapsed in the bunk and fell asleep." Mel Harden fell into a deep sleep on the LCI's fantail. "The next thing I knew I was in a basket and being taken to a bunk below decks. Dudley Moylan, for one, didn't want to go below. "I fought going down to a lower deck, I was just so afraid."

Some men, including *Johnston*'s Bob Hollenbaugh, remembered the first taste of survival. "They got me aboard and helped me down to the crew compartment. Someone sat me on the edge of a bunk and shoved a can of tomato juice in my hand. I drank it, rolled over, and don't remember a thing until I was in a bunk on an LST." On the LCI that picked up the *Hoel* survivors, Larry Morris remembered pea soup—"something I normally hated but which tasted pretty good." For *Gambier Bay* survivor Bill McClendon, it was figs. "They put us in the bunks. I had some water and fell asleep. But the next morning I was sitting on deck leaning against the pilot house when a guy came by and gave me a can of kadota figs. I ate one and then I ate the whole damn can. The figs had a lot of liquid and you didn't have to chew them—they just slid down. I've loved them ever since."

REQUIEM

Tacloban, October 27

On October 27, Ed Pfeifer, Emmett Crump, and Ralph Natali formed part of a contingent that went ashore to transfer *Grant's* dead to the custody of an Army burial unit. The detail, headed by *Grant's* CO T. A. Nisewaner, helped transfer a cargo of thirty-four corpses, each wrapped in a white mattress cover, from *Grant's* decks to the well of an LCVP that had come out from Leyte. Three of the dead were from Ed Pfeiffer's torpedo gang: Ed Carlson was one. The second was a torpedoman who'd been with Ed on the bridge—he had survived the night only to die the next morning. The third was a crewman from the forward torpedo mount; he'd inhaled scalding steam rushing from the forward stack and died instantly.

No one had fully shaken off the terror of the night. "It had all happened so fast," Emmett Crump remembered. "We had no idea what hit us." Once the shooting stopped, *Grant* didn't lack for help. *Newcomb* was the first alongside, and when she pulled away just after daylight, *Leary* replaced her. It was clear to *Leary* quartermaster Bob Durand that *Grant* was in trouble. "She looked all shot to hell. We pulled up portside to and tied up. I went over because I had a signalman buddy on the *Grant*. He showed me what happened. One incoming round blasted the whaleboat, the ship's doctor, and a repair party into dust. My buddy put himself between the pilothouse and the mast. The walkway across the pilothouse was Swiss cheese except for the area where he was standing. It was a hellish mess—steel parts, body parts. She was down in the water with her freeboard almost gone."

Leary's Leon Wolper also went onboard as part of a small repair party. It was hard to comprehend the damage to a ship he'd worked with his own hands to construct back in Charleston, barely a year before. "*Grant* was in sinking condition. I remember vividly that the water was up to the hawser pipe. A carpenter's mate and I went up forward. There was a lot of damage there. We stuffed mattresses into some of the biggest holes and then shored them with four-by-fours. Then we went back aft to the crew quarters. There was nobody there, but there were some letters on the mattresses—last letters to loved ones I guess. We gave them to the ship's officers."

⚓

Grant's burial cortege rode the LCVP toward Tacloban. Tacloban had been secured during the first days of invasion. By the morning of the 27th, Army engineers had completed clearing the debris left by Taffy 3's homeless aircraft, and installed the final sheets of Marston matting; thirty-three Army Fifth Air Force fighters landed to begin providing air support for the invading troops. These troops, pushing inland, had fought their way across a coastal plain to Leyte's foothills where they were meeting stiff Japanese resistance for the first time.

It would be tough going from here. But in the seas to the north, east, and south, there would, at least, be nothing to fear from Japanese ships or Japanese naval aircraft. There would be no further threat to supplies or the ongoing landings of more men and equipment. To the coffin nails that marked the destruction of Admiral Nishimura's attack force and the retreats of Admirals Shima's and Kurita's attack forces, a fourth had been added: On the 25th and 26th, Halsey's fleet aircraft had tracked down and destroyed most of the carriers and aircraft of Ozawa's decoy force. The United States and her allies would rule the Pacific unchallenged until war's end.

The LCVP ran aground before it could lower its ramp on dry land. In a scene reminiscent of MacArthur's walk ashore a week before, the *Grant* detail carried their dead shipmates through knee-deep water. Once ashore, they began loading the bodies into the backs of waiting trucks to be transported to a newly cleared temporary cemetery for burial. As the loading continued, a lone Japanese aircraft suddenly appeared over the harbor and swooped down twice to attack and strafe. Guns in the dock area and on ships in the harbor opened up on the intruder with a deafening barrage. Twice the detail had to dive for shelter under the trucks. Once the plane was splashed and the loading completed, the men said goodbyes—as much with thoughts as words—and made their way back to the beach.

EPILOGUE

They are almost all gone now,
And with them they are taking the flak
And firestorms, the names of old bombing runs.
Each day a little more of their memory goes out,
Darkens the way a house darkens,
Its rooms quietly filling with evening...

—from "The Old Liberators" by Robert Hedin[1]

LURLINE III

Before the war, *Lurline III*, a stately, 632-foot, 18,000-ton ocean liner, had
plied the waters from San Francisco and Los Angeles to Hawaii, carrying
passengers on cruises promising "golden hours under the sparkling Pacific
sun bring(ing) a new sense of peace." When peace became war, *Lurline* and
three other Matson Navigation Company liners became troop transports.
Her alabaster hull, stacks, and superstructure were repainted in dazzle
camouflage, and, for the next three years, as *Lurline* sailed west into the
sparkling Pacific sun, her spaces were crammed with untested troops
ticketed for the embattled island beaches of the Solomons, Gilberts, Carolines, Marianas, Marshalls, and Philippines. But in early November 1944
(the war not yet won, but its outcome certain), as *Lurline* stood dockside at
Hollandia, New Guinea, she was getting ready to sail east, her manifest
swelled with homeward-bound veterans. Dotting the green-uniformed
crowds of returning GIs and Marines were the surviving sailors and airmen
of *Gambier Bay*, *Hoel*, *Johnston*, and *Roberts*, most still wearing the salt-
and oil-caked clothes they'd worn when hauled from the sea.
    The first leg of the survivors' journey home had taken them south from
Leyte to Hollandia. The seriously wounded and injured, including Dick

Rohde (whose leg injury would confine him to a succession of hospitals for more than a year) and Dudley Moylan (who'd lost much of his hearing to shell concussions) from the *Roberts*, made the journey aboard the newly commissioned hospital ship USS *Comfort*. Larry Epping, Fred Mallgrave, and a handful of other *Gambier Bay* survivors rode to Hollandia on the aging destroyer *Shaw*, a survivor of the Japanese attack on Pearl Harbor.

Many more made the passage aboard a converted LST, sleeping (or trying to) on cots in the ship's hold. It was at the height of the monsoon season, and the fragile LST lumbered into the grip of a full storm, her blunt prow battered by towering waves and vicious gale-force winds. In *Johnston* survivor Bob Hollenbaugh's memory, "It was the damnedest ride I ever had in my life. It took a week to get to Hollandia, or at least it seemed like it did. One night I woke up hearing this rumbling. I looked down the aisle of cots and the deck was rolling like an ocean wave and everybody was tear assing up through a hatch to go topside. None of us spent much time below after that."

In New Guinea, some survivors were transferred to a base hospital to rest and repair for the Pacific crossing. "I was about three days in an Army hospital in New Guinea with nothing much wrong with me—exhaustion and some salt water sores," recalled *Gambier Bay* LSO Bill McClendon. "They kept serving us mutton—not very appetizing. When I heard the *Lurline* was in port and the *Gambier Bay* survivors were going to go on it, I got up, put my clothes on, left the hospital, flagged a jeep, went down to the dock. For all the Army knew, I was still in that hospital."

The scene at dockside was crowded and fractious. *Lurline* was filled to overflowing and eager passengers were being turned away. Lou Rice remembered lining up with other *Gambier Bay* survivors, their fates suspended in the balance between getting aboard and staying behind. "Our skipper was arguing with the captain of the *Lurline*. The *Lurline*'s skipper kept insisting he had a full ship with no place for anyone else. But it turned out our skipper had more seniority than the *Lurline*'s skipper—so we got on."

Among others shoehorned into *Lurline*'s spaces when she finally set sail were Bill Brown, Ted Gurzynski, Albert Brunelle, Dick Hamilton, and other survivors from PT 493. Although he did not know it and would not learn until he reached stateside, Ted Gurzynski was a new father: Ted Jr. was born on October 13, 1944, the same day the 493 Boat left Mios Woendi, New Guinea, bound for the Philippines.

For more than a week after their rescue from Panaon Island, the crewmen of the sunken 493 were stuck in Tacloban, awaiting an outbound ship. Farmed out to other squadron boats, they endured the furious kamikaze siege. Ted wondered whether he would ever escape the Philippines. "I had thirty days' survivor leave coming, but the kamikazes were aiming for us every day. I thought these sons of bitches were going to kill me before I had a chance to get out."

After a stop in Brisbane, *Lurline* headed directly for San Francisco. She steamed fast and straight through open sea, and the wary passengers quickly realized *Lurline* was traveling alone. "We never had an escort of any kind," Larry Epping recalled. "They said she could go so fast that we didn't need to worry about Japanese submarines." Of course, after months of being on constant alert for submarines—not to mention agonizing days of clinging to life in the company of sharks—most survivors did worry, and the worry faded only grudgingly as *Lurline* drew closer to home waters.

For those who managed to put aside their fear of Japanese torpedoes, the passage became a blank, somnolent division between the horrors behind them and the expectations of homecoming ahead. Lou Rice and his buddies "slept on the deck, any place we could find an open spot." Bob Hollenbaugh remembered the same routine, although in better accommodations: "They gave us cabins by rate. I was with two other first class petty officers in an inboard cabin. We had it pretty nice and I slept all but a few hours on the way back." Dudley Moylan, who recalled bunking with pilots from VC-10 (those who had still been aboard when *Gambier Bay* sank), remembered mostly sitting on deck and looking out—releasing his troubled thoughts into sea and sky. "Mentally I needed that."

During the trip, one moment of ordinary splendor became forever locked in Lou Rice's memory: "We had a nurse onboard who played the piano. She was playing one night for the guys when she got called on duty and had to leave. And this Marine says, 'Do you mind if I play a little bit?' And she said, 'Well, sure, if you play, go ahead.' And he did. The song he played that night still stays in my mind to this day: 'I'll Be Seeing You.' God, could he play a piano, he was a maestro! But I've got no idea who he was."

The journey aboard *Lurline* brought a renewed sense—peace, or at least of the possibility of peace.

⚓

Lurline passed under the Golden Gate Bridge on December 1 at nine o'clock in the morning. "Everybody crowded against the rail to get a glimpse of the city," *Gambier Bay*'s Fred Mallgrave remembered. "The *Lurline* crew kept telling us to get back—we were tipping the ship—or we'd all end up in the Bay."

Many survivors returned like Robinson Crusoe. Lou Rice debarked into the fog-shrouded San Francisco morning barefoot, wearing a "pair of dungarees from a guy on the LST." Ted Gurzynski wore dungarees cut off at the knees. "I got a sweater from a chaplain on the *Lurline*, but had to return it before I got off."

At least, Ted recalled, the greeting was warm. "When we hit dockside we got a big hero's welcome. There was a Navy band playing the Beer

Barrel Polka. They marched us to the mess hall and waited on us hand and foot. They got our grub. There were cigarettes and cigars and candy bars by each place setting. After two days we got a new issue of blues."

The survivors also got psychiatric screenings. *Gambier Bay*'s Tony Potochniak: "We went over to Treasure Island. We all had to go past the psychiatrists to see if we were fit to go on leave." For most—buoyed by the high spirits of being safely home—the screenings seemed a simple formality. For a few, however, the screenings were a tripwire, the first signal of torments scarcely understood. Ted Gurzynski was among these: "They gave me a questionnaire to fill out and I did—truthfully. One of the questions was 'What do you think of the U.S. Navy?' And I told them. About five days later everybody got their leave papers but me. They sent me to a doctor who told me bluntly: 'You're not fit to be out in society.' He was right. I was mean, bitter at the world—combat fatigue. They wanted to send me to a rest camp on the West Coast. I ended up crying, begging to go home because I had a new baby boy and hadn't seen him. Finally, they let me go with the promise I'd go into the VA hospital once I got back to Milwaukee."

The feelings roiling about Ted plagued him for years after. "I was really shaky. I couldn't stand noise or crowds. When I went back to Rhode Island following leave, I ended up in Newport Naval Hospital and then got discharged on disability. I was a basket case for years. Things were difficult at work—any noise would set me off. I was really angry and ready to swing at the world." While few others would be haunted as agonizingly and persistently as Ted Gurzynski, many, like the *Hoel*'s Sam Lucas, would find themselves pursued by anguished memories long after the war. "We were really shell-shocked, but in those days we didn't know how stressed we were, there wasn't a name for it. Even years later, I found myself dreaming the whole thing over and over."

⚓

Three days before *Lurline*'s arrival in San Francisco, the carrier USS *Franklin* docked in Seattle. *Franklin* had been the victim of two kamikaze strikes; one Japanese plane had slammed *Franklin*'s starboard side, while a second had plunged through her flight deck all the way to the gallery level. Fifty-six *Franklin* sailors had been killed, another sixty wounded; *Franklin* limped to Pearl Harbor for temporary repairs. From Pearl, *Franklin* set sail for Seattle; after dropping off passengers, she crawled to the nearby Bremerton shipyard for repairs. *St. Lo's* survivors hitched a ride, sleeping on the hangar level under a vast, flapping tarpaulin covering the gash in *Franklin*'s flight deck. Recalled survivor Larry Collins: "After Leyte we were taken first into Peleliu Harbor and put onto hospital ships. It was three days to Pearl Harbor. We were ashore a few days there, still wearing the clothes from when we'd jumped ship. Then we were put aboard the *Franklin* for the trip to Seattle."

The remnants of VC-10 and VC-65—pilots like Burt Bassett, Jim Lischer, Joe McGraw, Dick Roby, Gene Seitz, and Ton Van Brunt, who had flown and fought above the action off Samar—trickled home in the next days, weeks, and months. Billeted on *Fanshaw Bay* for the ride to Pearl Harbor, the pilots and crews scattered to other ships for the stateside leg. Dick Roby went aboard *Belleau Wood*, another aircraft carrier limping home after being damaged by kamikaze attack. Jim Lischer hopped aboard a destroyer in hopes of a speedy trip; as it was, the ship headed north instead of east in what proved to be a long and frigid voyage up near the Aleutians. Jim finally shifted to a slow troop transport that dragged into Seattle with its cold, bedraggled passengers bordering on mutiny.

BURNING BOATS

Five months after the *Lurline*'s arrival in San Francisco and the *Franklin*'s in Seattle, the *Admiral E. W. Eberle*, a new twenty-two-thousand-ton Coast Guard-manned troop ship, departed the Philippines bound for Los Angles. In addition to homebound GIs and civilian refugees from the battle for Manila, the *Eberle* carried veteran PT boat crews being rotated back to the States. Among these contingents were Don Bujold, Jake Hanley, Tom Tenner, and the rest of the crew of PT 127, the boat that had first signaled the Japanese approach into Surigao Strait.

The late October action in the Strait had been just the opening round for the PT squadrons in the Philippines. In the days following their work as skirmishers in Surigao Strait, many of the PTs battled the body crashers. The 524 Boat's Walter Kundis recalled: "We were under kamikaze attacks for most of the next couple weeks and we ended up shooting down three Japanese planes. One plane came in so close that the guy who was my loader on the forty-millimeter left the gun and jumped over the side. I was trying to shoot but there were no rounds in the chamber. The damn plane crashed just astern."

The boats had also probed and patrolled ever further along Leyte's enemy-infested coast. In late November, PT 127 had joined a strike into Ormoc Bay, a heavily fortified Japanese bastion on Leyte's southern midriff. One night near midnight, going in under the naked glare of spotlights and a hail of Japanese naval and shore battery gunfire, the 127 Boat successfully torpedoed a Japanese frigate. Tom Tenner recalled the 127's frantic, zigzag escape: "Everybody was firing at us, but our silhouette must have made us look like a bigger ship. They always shot over our heads." Later, when Ormoc was secured and divers began exploring the wrecks that littered the bay, the sunken Japanese frigate was found, a mortal thirty-foot rip in her hull.

⚓

To Tom Tenner and the other returning PT crewmen, the *Eberle*'s spaciousness was an amazing contrast to the cramped, sweaty confines of the Elcos. "The ship was huge. It even had an orchestra and there were dances on the way back." The *Eberle* arrived in Los Angeles on May 2, and four days later Tom boarded a cross-country train bound for Pittsburgh. "The train stopped in Dodge City, Kansas, on VE Day. We got the word somehow that the war was over in Europe and the Germans had surrendered. The train was going to stop in Dodge City for about and hour and a half. Everybody tore off that train and stampeded up to Dodge City intending to buy beer and booze and raise hell." Unfortunately, Dodge City turned out to be a dry town in a dry state.

Half a continent to the west, PT 491's Terry Chambers' VE Day celebration was anything but dry. Terry's dad was a California orange rancher and, like many farmers and ranchers during the war, employed German POWs to pick oranges. "They were housed at Santa Anita racetrack and Army guards brought crews out to pick oranges. I was home on leave when Germany surrendered. The German orange pickers were on the ranch that day along with their two Army guards. The ranch house had a swimming pool and a refrigerator filled with beer. So I pulled rank on the guards: I got the POWs—I don't think any of them spoke English—and the guards to come back to the house for beer and a pool party. For years, other orange ranches would get letters from the former POWs asking what had become of 'the crazy navy lieutenant.'"

⚓

By the time Germany surrendered, most of the crews from Ron 7, 12, 33, and 36 had been replaced and returned home, but their PTs never followed. As the battle to retake the Philippines wound down and the war moved north toward the Japanese home islands, the mahogany craft that had been the PT crewmen's cramped homes and lethal arsenals were slated for destruction.

Sam Goddess, a radioman who jointed Ron 12's 194 Boat after the action in Surigao, remembered the tedious, bittersweet process of destroying the 194 and other Ron 12 boats. "By then the 194 had sustained a lot of hull damage. We had to take off equipment and electronics, guns, torpedoes, pretty much anything of value that could be used someplace else. Then the boats were towed out to the shallows. They torched the boats using gasoline and they burned to the waterline while we watched—a sad day." On another day, PT 524's Walter Kundis watched the same fate befall the Ron 36 boats: "They started burning the boats. Most of them were in bad shape. They just lined them up on the beach and torched them." Ron 12's Andy Gavel, another 194 Boat veteran who did not return to the States until October 1945, perhaps saw the last of the fires. "They had sent new boats over toward the end of the war, and we were even blowing them up, sinking them in the bay."

NORTH TOWARD HOME

"I saw the *Abner Read*, a destroyer, go down stern first," recalled the *Leary*'s Leon Wolper. "We were on our way to relieve them for radar picket duty." It was November 1 when the *Abner Read* became the first destroyer sunk deliberately by a kamikaze attack. Explosions on the *Read* ignited a thick skim of fuel oil; *Leary* sailed through a towering plume of black smoke to pull seventy *Read* crewmen to safety.

Only a handful of the men who'd had ships shot out under them returned to the war, though some came close and many tried.[2] Meanwhile, the reward for Third and Seventh Fleet ships that survived the actions in Surigao Strait and off Samar was a quick and unceremonious return to business as usual. The Japanese Navy was spent; there would be few remaining engagements with Japanese ships, either surface or submarine. The roads home for ships and sailors pointed north, where the invasion of Japan's home islands promised to be the end game. On the journey toward this showdown, with stops for bloody invasions of fortresses like Iwo Jima and Okinawa, men on *Leary, McDermut, Melvin, Monssen*, and (following extensive dry-dock repairs) *Grant* renewed the grim business of shore bombardment, while taking up the new, desperate business of downing or deflecting kamikaze aircraft.

In the next months, kamikazes were in the haunted dreams of nearly every Western Pacific sailor. The concept was new, perplexing, and terrifying (indeed, it was not until the very end of the war, that the U.S. government revealed the phenomenon to the people at home). The kamikazes' prime targets were the big ships, especially the carriers. To better prepare for the incoming body crashers, U.S. fleet commanders sent destroyers (and their aerial radar detection capabilities) well out ahead to serve as early warning pickets. Stationed in isolation, the pickets became tempting targets of opportunity. The kamikazes became wild cards in each man's tally of his odds of making it through. Each sunrise dealt a new and perhaps fatal hand. Nearly every man who lived it had a story.

On January 15, in the Philippines' Lingayen Gulf, Clay Ulen, a gunner's mate aboard *Melvin* wrote this account: "Today I got my first look at the suicide job. One plane came over our bow, circled, and headed for us. We opened up with all our guns. He turned and dove straight into the *Belknap*. The explosion killed sixteen men. They are hard to hit. Tokyo Rose says we will be wiped out."

Ray Dupler, also on the *Melvin*, remembered another spectral brush: "We were on picket duty when a Japanese Betty came in at about masthead height. We only got a few pot shots off and it kept going. It was just about at dusk and I stood out on the bridge, praying we'd be spared until darkness came."

The *Monssen*'s Virgil Melvin also had a memory from Lingayen Gulf. "We'd been attacked a few times and we were all pretty spooked. Our new gun boss, Lieutenant Mike Clemens, got all the crews together trying to cheer us up. 'Listen guys, this couldn't be better. We got the bastards just where we want them. Hell, they're going to be flying straight into our sights.'"

An account from the *Leary*'s Leon Wolper, perhaps in Lingayen or perhaps later, off Okinawa: "We had a close call, a kamikaze coming out of the sun. I was on the stern, near the number five gun, looking at the durn thing coming closer and closer. I dove under the mount. It crashed in the water, seemed no more than ten feet off to port. There was a big ball of fire. I could feel the heat. Metal flew around and a piece lodged in the heel of my shoe."

Also off Okinawa in mid-April, an account from Dick Ralstin on the *McDermut*: "We approached to fuel alongside the *Missouri*'s starboard side. A kamikaze attacked *Missouri* and both ships broke off fueling to maneuver and evade. The plane was coming in at wave-top level and the *Missouri* lowered its starboard five-inch mounts to fire. The *Missouri*'s barrage missed the Japanese plane, but got *McDermut* squarely in the port side, killing five men."

On April 30, again off Okinawa, an account from the *Melvin*'s Bill Campbell, part of a salvage team boarding the USS *Hazelwood* after it received two kamikaze hits: "During the night the only way to go forward was by crawling on a narrow strip of deck on the starboard side. The port side was blocked by debris. On one of my trips I encountered something strange and unidentifiable—daybreak revealed it was a body part. On some bulkheads you could see the outlines where explosions had hurled the bodies."

⚓

The *Richard P. Leary*'s Leon Wolper kept a little book of dates and places marking the stations of the homeward pilgrimage for him, Robert Durand, Robert Read, and the rest of the *Leary*'s crew—an approximation of the pilgrimages of many other Pacific ships and sailors: "November 21st, went back to Manus... December 15th we left Manus... Arrived in Palau on December 18th... Left January 1st, 1945... Arrived Linguyan Gulf, Luzon January the 6th... The 9th day was D-Day on Linguyan Gulf... A lot of kamikazes flying around there... Left on the 22nd of January and arrived in Ulithe in the Carolines on January 22nd... Left February the 10th... Arrived in Saipan on February the 12th, and left on the 14th... Arrived off

Iwo Jima on the 16th...D-Day was on the 19th...Left Iwo Jima on March the 1st...Arrived back in Ulithe on March the 4th...Left Ulithe on the 21st of March. Arrived in Okinawa on the 25th of March...D-Day was April the 1st...We could see the landing craft passing us with Army people on them. I feel sorry for them because we have a place to sleep, even if it is on deck with kapok for a pillow...We left Okinawa on the 28th...Arrived in Leyte on May the 31st...Left on June the 28th...Back to Okinawa on July 1st...Left Okinawa on July 28th...Back to Leyte on July 31st...Left Leyte on August the 2nd...Arrived in Saipan on August the 5th and left on the 8th...We're going to help the Russians make a landing on the Kurile Islands...The war ends...We go straight to Adak, Alaska and then Attu...Left Attu on the 31st and arrived on the coast of Honshu on September 7th...Left on September the 25th and arrived in Tokyo Bay on September 27th...Left on the 30th...Arrived in Guam on October 4th...Left Guam on the 5th...Arrived in Pearl Harbor on October the 14th...Left on the 16th and arrived in San Diego on the 22nd...Home."

In November 1945, more than two months after the war's end, the *McDermut* and *Melvin* reached San Francisco. Setting out from Hawaii five days before, her decks and spaces crammed with extra passengers, *Melvin* had transited the channel between Oahu and Molokai, a natural funnel where trade winds create mounting seas. *Melvin*'s doctor Ed Hawk described the result. "Our crew was hardened, but almost all the passengers got sick. Miserable men would turn their heads seaward to throw up—and then turn them back. The ship was a mess.

"The next day dawned bright and clear with a calm sea. We broke out hoses to flush the decks with salt water. Within an hour the whole picture changed. The passengers cleaned up and got into fresh clothes. We were going home."

By the time of *McDermut*'s return, Dick Ralstin had advanced to first class motor machinist mate and had been more or less continuously at sea for two years. As the two DDs passed San Francisco Lightship and glided between the Presidio and the Marin headland toward San Francisco Bay, Dick recalled seeing only one greeter—a woman perched against the seaward railing of the Golden Gate Bridge, her arm waving. Spotting the same lone greeter, many sailors aboard the *McDermut* tossed their white hats up into the air. The hats drifted away in the morning breeze and settled into the bay.

ROOMS FILLING WITH EVENING

When Don Bujold returned from the Philippines in May 1945, he returned to Saginaw, Michigan, on leave. "I found out my cousin Stan Topham had been on the *Hoel* and was listed as missing. Stan and I grew up together in Saginaw. Stan had joined the Navy before I did and became a Radarman. My uncle said that Stan's dad wanted to talk with me and asked me to go over. When I got to Stan's house, his dad had a map of the Philippine Islands—a map he'd cut out of an atlas, I guess. My uncle wanted to know if it was possible that Stan had gotten ashore somewhere, and was being held or possibly being cared for by natives. I was fresh from the Pacific, and this was over six months after the battle. I tried to tell him the best way that I could that I doubted it very seriously. Here's a man fifty or sixty years old and naturally he's in tough shape, he's lost a son. I could appreciate that. He wanted to know if there was any possibility that he'd survived. They declared Stan dead soon after that."

⚓

Because of Dudley Moylan's hearing loss, caused by the explosions that rocked *Roberts*' bridge, he was restricted to shore duty. "I finished the war assigned to the receiving station in Miami. My father was in the Navy, too—he'd been an ensign in World War I. He'd gone back in and was stationed at Seventh Naval District Headquarters, where I got assigned. On one afternoon while I had watch in the receiving station he had watch at the senior headquarters. I remember saying to myself: 'My God, let's hope nothing happens.'"

⚓

During the early stages of his hospitalization, Dick Rohde risked losing his leg. Dick passed through a succession of military hospitals until he was discharged—able to walk unaided—from the Navy in November 1945. After graduating from Cornell University's School of Hospitality Management, Dick began a career managing university faculty clubs and private country clubs. Through life, Dick's experience on *Roberts* kept coming back, often in unexpected places. Once, during a *Roberts* reunion, when Dick and other survivors toured the Baseball Hall of Fame in Cooperstown, New York, museum staff surprised them with a conference call from Hall of Fame pitcher Bob Feller. Feller, stationed on the USS *Alabama*, part of the Third Fleet, during the Battle of Leyte Gulf, recalled the day when Halsey had gone chasing north while, behind him, Taffy 3 and the men of the *Roberts* had stood their ground.

⚓

After the war, Tom Stevenson returned to run his family's cargo ship business. For years, the business thrived, but eventually fell victim to high costs and foreign competition. Among the death blows were a series of law suits by former crewmen alleging respiratory damage from exposure to shipboard asbestos. Tom reviewed many of the claims and found them spurious. By then, he had his own perspective. He'd been diagnosed with emphysema, the result of this own exposure to asbestos powder when the *Roberts* had been rocked by Japanese gunfire.

⚓

For many years, Holly Crawforth knew nothing of the fate of Harry Tobin, the *St. Lo* crewman whose life jacket had kept Holly afloat. It wasn't until 1984, when the *Midway/St. Lo* survivors' association staged its first reunion, that Holly learned Harry Tobin been one of the *St. Lo*'s mess cooks. One survivor recalled Harry losing his life jacket as he went down the lifeline. Harry had drowned. A little more digging revealed that Harry Tobin had been raised during the Depression in an orphanage near Portland, Oregon. "A friend of his called me and I said I'd donate the jacket to the orphanage. They have a little museum and the life jacket is up there."

CITATIONS

Medals and commendations seem little to show for the dangers, efforts, and sacrifices that aircrews, sailors, and soldiers display in battle. Many of the words that accompany them are scripted, and none of the words can fully convey the surrounding horror and confusion. Nevertheless, they are often haunting and understated tributes to the actions of sacrifices of men and women in war.

⚓

Barry K. Atkins's Navy Cross citation, awarded for his actions in the *Melvin*'s sinking of Japanese battleship Fuso in Surigao Strait, reads in part: "For extraordinary heroism . . . in action against major units of the enemy Japanese Fleet . . . which contributed materially to the decisive defeat of enemy forces."

⚓

Bill Brown's Bronze Star citation reads in part: "Although wounded by shrapnel . . . Lieutenant Brown directed the heavy machine-gun fire of his boat against the searchlights and bridges of the Japanese vessels. Under continuing close-range heavy fire when serious flooding started during the action, he ordered the executive officer of the boat to head for the shore and, disregarding his own wounded condition, went below to the engine room to supervise damage control, keeping the craft afloat to reach shore on her own power. Successful in reaching shore as the last engine was put out of action by flooding, Lieutenant Brown was instrumental in getting all hands off before the boat sank and in keeping them together until picked up by another PT Boat."

⚓

Albert Brunelle's Navy Cross citation reads in part: "For distinguishing himself by extraordinary heroism . . . as a member of the Crew of PT 493. . . . Brunelle was on watch in the engine room when Japanese 4.7" shells twice passed through his compartment. . . . [A] large hole was blown in the side of his ship below the water line. In utter disregard for his own personal safety, he took off his own life jacket and stuffed it into the hole in an attempt to stem the inrushing water. He made emergency repairs . . . which enabled the boat . . . to maintain its course and escape from the enemy. His magnificent efforts, under the severest of conditions undoubtedly saved the lives of those on board who survived the enemy shelling."

⚓

Richard Hamilton's Silver Star citation reads in part: "For conspicuous gallantry and intrepidity as Third Officer of PT 493 when that vessel was holed and in sinking condition. . . . With his boat temporarily lodged on a rock ledge, . . . Hamilton although suffering a facial wound caused by an enemy shell splinter, courageously returned to the abandoned boat and destroyed confidential equipment, thereby preventing its capture by the enemy."

⚓

Joe McGraw's Navy Cross citation reads in part: "Ensign McGraw intercepted a flight of approximately twenty-one enemy twin-engine bombers and eight fighters about to attack our troop laden transports and, pressing home aggressive attacks, succeeded in shooting down two bombers and damaging a third. . . . Launched from another carrier . . . and, serving as section leader of the local Combat Air Patrol later in the afternoon, [he] led his division in intercepting and dispersing a numerically superior force, personally shooting down several hostile aircraft." (All of VC-10's pilot records and gun films were lost with the sinking of *Gambier Bay*. However, postwar interviews with VC-10 pilots, including squadron CO Ed Huxtable, determined that

Joe had made five air combat "kills"—establishing him as VC-10's only air combat ace and only one of five air combat aces among all composite squadron pilots.)

⚓

Gene Seitz' Distinguished Flying Cross citation reads in part: "Lieutenant Seitz was launched . . . in the midst of a torpedo attack. . . . Seeing an enemy torpedo plane crossing ahead of the carrier at low altitude, he coolly and deliberately charged his machine guns . . . sharply banked his plane and with a burst of fire, shot down the enemy torpedo plane with an expertly placed deflection shot. . . . He performed . . . with fearless determination in the face of grave danger."

⚓

Harley Thronson's Bronze Star citation reads in part: " . . . while searching for another PT reported missing, contacted an enemy cruiser which opened up with large caliber guns. . . . He fired his remaining two torpedoes, laid a smoke screen to effect a successful withdrawal . . . , found the missing PT and took aboard all survivors."

⚓

Tom Van Brunt's Navy Cross citation reads in part: "Flying without assistance from other aircraft, Lieutenant Van Brunt pressed home two daring attacks against an enemy Task Group, dropping three depth bombs alongside a heavy cruiser and scoring a direct hit on a hostile battleship."

⚓

The Navy Unit Commendation for the *Albert W. Grant* reads in part: "Conducting a determined torpedo attack against a Japanese task force in Surigao Strait on the night of October 24, the *Albert W. Grant* closed range to fire her first half salvo of torpedoes and succeeded in scoring hits on a Japanese battleship. Although severely damaged when heavy enemy guns opened fire as she turned to retire, she remained in the battle area and successfully launched her five remaining torpedoes, scoring hits on other enemy units. With all power gone, fires raging, compartments rapidly flooding and over one hundred casualties to care for, she fought throughout the night to remain afloat." Those eligible to wear the award include Emmett R. Crump, Ralph E. Natali, and Edward Pfeifer.

⚓

The Presidential Unit Citation for Task Unit 77.4.3, including the crews and air groups for USS *Fanshaw Bay* (VC-68); USS *Gambier Bay* (VC-l0); USS *Kalinin Bay* (VC-3); USS *Kitkun Bay* (VC-5); USS *St. Lo* (VC-65); USS *White Plains* (VC-4); USS *Hoel*, USS *Johnston*, USS *Heermann*, USS *Samuel B. Roberts*, USS *Raymond*, USS *Dennis*, and USS *John C. Butler* reads in part: "For extraordinary heroism in action against powerful units of the Japanese Fleet during the Battle off Samar, Philippines, October 25, 1944. Task Unit 77.4.3 was suddenly taken under attack by hostile cruisers on its port hand, destroyers on the starboard and battleships from the rear. Quickly laying down a heavy smoke screen, the gallant ships of the Task Unit waged battle fiercely against the superior speed and fire power of the advancing enemy, swiftly launching and rearming aircraft and violently zigzagging in protection of vessels stricken by hostile armor-piercing shells, anti-personnel projectiles and suicide bombers. With one carrier of the group sunk, others badly damaged and squadron aircraft courageously coordinating in the attacks by making dry runs over the enemy Fleet as the Japanese relentlessly closed in for the kill, two of the Unit's valiant destroyers and one destroyer escort charged the battleships point-blank and, expending their last torpedoes in desperate defense of the entire group, went down under the enemy's heavy shells as a climax to two and one half hours of sustained and furious combat. The courageous determination and the superb teamwork of the officers and men who fought the embarked planes and who manned the ships of Task Unit 77.4.3 were instrumental in effecting the retirement of a hostile force threatening our Leyte invasion operations."

Those eligible to wear the award include Burt Bassett, George Carbon, Verner Carlsen, Robert Chastain, Larry Collins, Holly Crawforth, Larry Epping, Vince Goodrich, Lou Gould, Mel Harden, Charles Heinl, Bob Hollenbaugh, Jim Lischer, Fred Mallgrave, Bill McClendon, Joe McGraw, William Mercer, Larry Morris, Dudley Moylan, Glenn Parkin, Tony Potochniak, Dick Roby, Dick Rohde, Gene Seitz, Tom Stevenson, Bill Wilson, and Tom Van Brunt.

NOTES

CHAPTER 1

1. *Lexington* was sunk by Japanese torpedo bombers during the 1942 Battle of the Coral Sea.

2. Now part of Oklahoma State University.

3. The arm insignia for the acting recruit chief resembled the insignia for a Navy chief petty officer, except that in the insignia's center a picture of a granny knot (the simple knot often used to tie laced shoes) replaced the symbol for a particular rating.

4. The United States came late to the concept. Several European countries, including Germany and Italy, started similar programs in the mid-1930s. The name CPTP was chosen to suggest that all the flight training for young men had a peaceful intent.

5. The Grasshopper's official name was the Aeronca Model 65 Defender.

6. *Hornet* was the aircraft carrier that launched the Doolittle air raid on Tokyo in early 1942.

7. During this October 26–27, 1942, battle the Japanese scored a tactical victory, sinking *Hornet* while losing none of their ships. Strategically, however, the American task force (of which *Enterprise* was a wounded part) had succeeding in blocking enemy plans to retake Henderson Field, the vital airstrip on Guadalcanal. The Americans bought time to strengthen their hold on Guadalcanal—a hold they never relinquished.

8. Until well after the war, Navy petty officers in deck or seaman categories (e.g., boatswain mate, signalman, gunner's mate, fire controlman, quartermaster, and torpedoman's mate) wore insignia on the right sleeve of the their uniforms (right arm rates); petty officers in artificer and engine room categories (e.g., radioman, sonar man, machinist mate, and shipfitter) wore insignia on the left sleeve (left arm rates).

9. *Yorktown* was sunk at the Battle of Midway.

10. Yellow Peril also stood for the risks the SNJ held for its novice students and their instructors as well as the hurt its students planned to rain down on an Asian enemy.

11. Consolidated Aircraft Corporation Patrol Bomber. Tom Van Brunt had gotten his wings flying PBYs, but after June 1942 he never flew one again.

12. The ships were preserved using lead-based reddish paint.

13. Lend-Lease was a program conceived prior to America's entry into the war as a means of sending older combat vessels to countries such as Great Britain in exchange for American access to bases and ports in those countries.

CHAPTER 2

1. USS *Fletcher* (DD-445) was named for the nineteenth-century Medal of Honor winner and Atlantic Fleet commander Admiral Frank Fletcher. During World War II, his son, Vice Admiral Frank Fletcher, served as a carrier group commander in the Southwest Pacific.

2. Invented by the nineteenth-century British engineer Thomas Whitehead, the self-propelled torpedo took its name from a type of electric eel that mortally stings its victim. In earlier wars and into World War I, torpedo was a term that applied to a wide range of explosive weapons (including the land mine) that killed by stealth and surprise. Whitehead's first torpedo was powered by compressed air and carried eighteen pounds of dynamite. Crucial to its effectiveness was the performance of a self-regulating gyroscope mechanism used to keep the torpedo traveling at a constant preset depth. The existence of the ship-to-ship free riding torpedo added a new dynamic to battle at sea. It could be delivered from a distance; gyroscope and propulsion noise permitting, it could often approach unheard and unseen; it could hit a ship below the waterline, where it was often least armored and most vulnerable.

3. The 5-in. 38-caliber designation is for a gun barrel bore five inches in diameter (gun barrel diameters are also the measures for the 40- and 20-mm guns) and a gun barrel length of 190 inches (5×38). The 5-in. 38 design was chosen by the Navy as early as 1930 during planning of new destroyer construction. The 5-in. 38 was a halfway compromise between two 5-in. models under consideration. The barrel length of a 5-in. 51 gun design was shortened. The new barrel was exactly halfway between the competing 51-caliber and 25-caliber designs.

4. Some ships crewmen simply designated the 5-in. 38 mounts as mounts 1 through 5.

5. An electrical device called a selsyn (combined of "self" and "synchronization" and later known as a synchro) made remote shipboard fire control possible. The selsyn consisted of a generator connected remotely and electronically to a motor. Angular rotation in the generator could be reproduced simultaneously in the motor. The motor only needed to have enough power to move a dial or a cam. But the cam could then move electrical contacts to control very large motors powering very big things such as guns.

6. *Butler* was the lead ship of a class of destroyer escorts. The ship was named for Navy aviator John C. Butler, a member of Bombing Squadron 3 aboard the fleet carrier *Yorktown*. Butler was killed during the Battle of Midway and was a posthumous recipient of the Navy Cross. Eighty-three Butler class DEs were built during the war.

7. An alternative name for the PT was Motor Torpedo Boat or MTB.

8. Two hundred of a slightly shorter, slower, wetter, but tighter-turning PT model were produced by Higgins in New Orleans. These became known as Higgins boats.

9. The CVE's first designation was AVG (for auxiliary aircraft escort vessel) and then ACV (for auxiliary aircraft carrier). The biggest fleet carriers were designated CVAs (for attack), the smaller fleet carriers CVLs.

10. *Essex* had an 872-foot flight deck.

11. The Cubist painting-like dazzle design didn't obscure a ship by blending it into the background. Instead, the jumble of geometric designs made it difficult for observers on opposing ships to judge the ship's course and angle of approach.

12. Neither Stewart nor Bell survived the Battle of Leyte Gulf.

CHAPTER 3

1. Lieutenant (junior grade) C. A. Dugan, USNR.

2. Lieutenant (junior grade) Dean Gilliatt, USNR.

3. Many suspected Amelia Earhart crashed near Saipan during her 1937 around-the-world flight, and that she and her navigator were captured by the Japanese and eventually shot as spies.

4. Following the war, *Melvin* was credited with the sinking of Japanese submarine RO-36.

5. Lieutenant C. A. Mathieu, Medical Corps, USNR.

6. For identification purposes, Japanese bomber aircraft were usually given female first names, whereas fighter aircraft were given male first names. The Betty and the Fran were both twin-engine bombers.

7. Lieutenant R. C. Hagan.

8. Engine magnetos are magnet with coils of wire revolving between their poles to generate current; the current generated ignites the engine.

9. Lieutenant Commander Ralph M. Jones.

10. Ensign William Brooks, USNR.

11. Lieutenant Commander F. D. Tappaan, USNR.

12. Lieutenant (jg) John A Cady, USNR.

13. The exploit won Lieutenant Preston the Congressional Medal of Honor, one of only two awarded to PT sailors. His citation reads, in part: "For conspicuous gallantry and intrepidity...while effecting the rescue of a Navy pilot shot down in Wasile Bay, Halmahera Island, less than 200 yards from a strongly defended Japanese dock and supply area, 16 September 1944. Volunteering for a perilous mission unsuccessfully attempted by the pilot's squadron mates and a PBY plane, Lt. Comdr. [then Lieutenant] Preston led PT-489 and PT-363 through 60 miles of restricted, heavily mined waters. Twice turned back while running the gauntlet of fire from powerful coastal defense guns guarding the 11-mile strait at the entrance to the bay, he was again turned back by furious fire in the immediate area of the downed airman. Aided by an aircraft smokescreen, he finally succeeded in reaching his objective and, under vicious fire delivered at 150-yard range, took the pilot aboard and cleared the area, sinking a small hostile cargo vessel with 40-mm. fire during retirement. Increasingly vulnerable when covering aircraft were forced to leave because of insufficient fuel, Lt. Comdr. Preston raced PT boats 489 and 363 at high speed for 20 minutes through shell-splashed water and across minefields to safety. Under continuous fire for 2½ hours, Lt. Comdr. Preston successfully achieved a mission considered suicidal in its tremendous hazards, and brought his boats through without personnel casualties and with but superficial damage from shrapnel."

CHAPTER 4

1. Command of the Central Pacific Fleet alternated between Admirals Spruance and Halsey. When the fleet was under Spruance's command, as it had been during the Battle of the Philippine Sea, it was named Fifth Fleet. When the fleet was under Halsey's command, as it would be for the Philippine invasion, it was named Third Fleet.

2. *Midway* had actually begun construction January 23, 1943, as *Chopin Bay* and was renamed *Midway* two months later.

3. Lieutenant Lloyd Gurnett, USNR.

4. Lieutenant J. H. Moran II, USNR.

5. Lieutenant (junior grade) J. M. McElfresh, USNR.

6. USS *Henderson*, built in 1916, had been designed as an advance floating Marine base, designated "Naval Transport Number One." *Henderson* was decommissioned in 1943, renamed the USS *Bountiful*, and served out the rest of the war as a hospital ship.

CHAPTER 5

1. As early as 1943, Japanese warships were using radar detection technology that enabled them to receive and plot electric impulses from radar. With this

technology, the Japanese were sometimes able to detect the presence of American warships well before visibly sighting them.

2. Hospital Corpsman Third Class William A. Gaffney, USNR.

3. Lieutenant (junior grade) Ian D. Malcolm, USNR.

4. Lieutenant (junior grade) Nicholas Carter, USNR.

5. Commissaryman First Class Anthony P. Tatarek, USNR.

6. Radioman Second Class William Sekerak, USNR.

7. Commander C. K. Bergin, USN.

8. Lieutenant (junior grade) James H. Woods Jr., USNR.

9. A postwar analysis conducted by the U.S. Naval War College in 1958 formally established which U.S. ships had fired the torpedoes that damaged and sank Japanese warships during the Surigao Strait action.

CHAPTER 6

1. Talk Between Ships is a system that linked telephone handsets on the bridge of each ship to loudspeakers on the bridge of other ships. Although TBS had restricted transmission and reception range, atmospheric conditions often permitted TBS traffic to be picked up at considerable distances.

2. Ensign P. P. Zeola, USNR, survived the battle.

3. Lieutenant (junior grade) H. A. Pyzdrowski, USNR, survived the battle.

4. Air Motor Machinist Mate Second Class John E. South.

5. Air Radioman Third Class Lester U. Frederickson.

6. Ensign P. A. Bennett, USNR, survived the battle.

7. Samuel Moody survived the battle.

8. Walter O. Howard survived the battle.

9. J. B. Strickland survived the battle.

10. Seaman First Class Glenn E. Heriford was killed during the battle.

11. DEs *Raymond* and *Dennis* made independent unsuccessful torpedo runs, *Raymond* against cruiser *Haguro*, *Dennis* at either cruiser *Chokai* or cruiser *Tone*.

12. Seaman First Class William Ingram Jr. was killed during the battle.

13. Gunner's Mate Third Class Krupp was killed during the battle.

14. Seaman First Class Phillip A. Akerman was killed during the battle.

15. Seaman First Class Sam Blue survived the battle.

16. Chief Electricians Mate Charles Staubach was killed during the battle.

17. Ensign B. F. Dillard, USNR.

18. Marston matting, also called PSP (Pierced Steel Planking), consisted of planks of perforated steel used for runway construction in the tropics.

CHAPTER 7

1. Raymond Lamont-Brown, *Kamikaze: Japan's Suicide Samurai*, p. 30.

2. Seaman First Class William M. Murray.

3. Shipfitter First Class Donald J. Hienritz.

4. Water Tender Second Class Charles C. Sampson.

5. Seaman First Class Erling W. Husvik.

6. Commander Fred "Buzz" Borries, USN. Borries was *Gambier Bay*'s "Air Boss" in charge of flight operations.

7. A pistol used for firing colored signal flares.

8. Yeoman Second Class Charles H. Cronin Jr.

EPILOGUE

1. Robert Hedin, *The Old Liberators: New and Selected Poems and Translations* (Holy Cow! Press, Duluth, MN, 1998).

2. A few did. The *Roberts'* Vince Goodrich was assigned to the USS *Kane*, which took him back to the Pacific. One night in late July 1945, as Vince stood watch on *Kane*'s bridge while it cruised in the Philippine Sea, *Kane*'s CIC identified a surface radar contact. It turned out the cruiser *Indianapolis*, en route to Leyte Gulf from Tinian Island, where it had delivered the first atomic bomb. On July 30, the unescorted *Indianapolis* was sunk by two torpedoes from a Japanese submarine. Bill Brown and Richard Hamilton of PT 493 were assigned to Elco boats in the Mediterranean Sea before VE Day. "We got assigned to a squadron in Southern France. It was nuts. We didn't have to go back, and I had a new child. But we just had it in our mind to go after a little more." Richard Hamilton received France's Croix de Guerre.

BIBLIOGRAPHIC ESSAY

Four excellent and authoritative books underpin the factual framework of this book. Samuel Eliot Morison's *History of United States Naval Operations in World War II* is an essential resource, especially given Morison's cockpit view as the U.S. Navy's official historian for sea operations in both the European and Pacific Wars. Morison's *Volume XII: Leyte June 1944–January 1945* gives a full account of the Philippine engagements before, during, and after the events covered here and contains detailed battle maps and complete rosters of command relationships and participating vessels. (Other volumes in the series provided ongoing context and background information.)

Thomas J. Cutler's *The Battle of Leyte Gulf: 23–26 October 1944*, is a masterful account by another naval historian, researched and written to coincide with the fiftieth anniversary of the battle. Cutler's book makes extensive use of recordings and transcripts from the U.S. Naval Institute's Oral History Program.

The Japanese perspective of Leyte is represented in two of these four books. John Toland's *The Rising Sun: The Decline and Fall of the Japanese Empire, 1936–1945* is a compelling one-volume Pulitzer Prize–winning history of Japan's decade of conquest and downfall. Although Leyte Gulf is only one episode in Toland's sprawling cavalcade, he details Leyte's drama and meaning as the longed-for decisive sea battle on which Japan staked its empire's success. Toland's account of Leyte is based on direct interviews (via his Japanese-born wife) of Japanese political and military sources.

Japan's perspective is also represented in Edwin P. Hoyt's *The Battle of Leyte Gulf: The Death Knell of the Japanese Fleet*. A former soldier and later resident in Japan, Hoyt provides Japan's view in a number of other World War II histories. For his Leyte Gulf book, Hoyt also relied heavily on research into the Archives of the U.S. Naval History Division. These then-classified archives provide action accounts of both U.S. and Japanese air, land, and naval units.

ARTICLES

"A Roll in the Sky with a Navy SNJ," by Rob Guglielmetti, Aviation Publishing Group, August 31, 2003.

"Cornfields & Carriers," by Rob Newell, *Military Officer* (membership magazine of Military Officers Association of America), October, 2002, http://www.moaa.org/magazine/October2002/f_cornfields.asp

"Design and Development of the PTs," unidentified author; Internet site of Peter Tare, Inc. http://www.petertare.org/nav.htm

"Leyte Gulf Remembered," by John D. Ahlstrom, Naval Institute *Proceedings*, August 1984

"Lifeboat," by Elizabeth McCracken, *New York Times Magazine*, December 28, 2003, pp. 22–23.

"Lone PT Attacked Japanese Fleet," *New York Times*, November 14, 1944, p. 4.

"Sniper Ship," by John Bishop, *The Saturday Evening Post*, November 4 and November 11, 1944.

BOOKS

Busch, Noel F., *The Emperor's Sword: Japan vs. Russia in the Battle of Tsushima*, Funk & Wagnall, New York, 1969.

Cutler, Thomas J., *The Battle of Leyte Gulf: 23–26 October 1944*, Naval Institute Press, Annapolis, MD, 1994.

Davis, Martin, *Destroyer Escorts of World War II*, Pictorial Histories Publishing Company, Missoula, MT, 1987.

Friedman, Norman, *U.S. Destroyers, An Illustrated Design History*, United States Naval Institute, Annapolis, MD, 1982.

Hoyt, Edwin P., *The Battle of Leyte Gulf: The Death Knell of the Japanese Fleet*, Weybright and Talley, New York, 1972.

———, *Japan's War: the Great Pacific Conflict*, Cooper Square Press, New York, 2001.

Jones, Ken, *Destroyer Squadron 23: Combat Exploits of Arleigh Burke's Gallant Force*, Naval Institute Press, Annapolis, MD, 1997.

Joyner, Tim, *Magellan*, International Marine, Camden, ME, 1992.

Lamont-Brown, Raymond, *Kamikaze: Japan's Suicide Samurai*, Arms and Armour Press, London, 1997.

Manchester, William, *American Caesar, Douglas MacArthur 1880–1964*, Random House, New York, 1978.

Michener, James A., *Tales of the South Pacific*, Macmillan Publishing Company, New York, 1986.

Morison, Samuel Eliot, *History of United States Naval Operations in World War II, Volume III: The Rising Sun in the Pacific, 1931–April 1942*, Little Brown and Company, Boston, 1975.

———, *History of United States Naval Operations in World War II, Volume IV, Coral Sea, Midway and Submarine Actions, May 1942–August 1942*, Little Brown and Company, Boston, 1975.

————, *History of United States Naval Operations in World War II, Volume V, The Struggle for Guadalcanal, August 1942–February 1943*, Little Brown and Company, Boston, 1975.

————, *History of United States Naval Operations in World War II, Volume VI, Breaking the Bismarks Barrier, 22 July 1942–1 May 1944*, Little Brown and Company, Boston, 1975.

————, *History of United States Naval Operations in World War II, Volume VII, Aleutians, Gilberts and Marshalls, June 1942–April 1944*, Little Brown and Company, Boston, 1975.

————, *History of United States Naval Operations in World War II, Volume VIII, New Guinea and the Marianas, March 1944–August 1944*, Little Brown and Company, Boston, 1975.

————, *History of United States Naval Operations in World War II, Volume XII: Leyte June 1944–January 1945*, Little Brown and Company, Boston, 1975.

Parkin, Robert Sinclair, *Blood on the Sea: American Destroyers Lost in World War II*, Sarpedon, New York, 1996.

Parr, Charles McKew, *Ferdinand Magellan, Circumnavigator*, Thomas Y. Crowell Company, New York.

Prang, Gordon W., Donald M. Goldstein, and Katherine V. Dillon, *At Dawn We Slept: The Untold Story of Pearl Harbor*, Penguin Books, New York, 1982.

Spector, Ronald H., *Eagle Against the Sun: The American War with Japan*, Vintage Books, New York, 1985.

Stafford, Edward P., *Little Ship, Big War: The Saga of DE 343*, William Morrow and Company, Inc., New York, 1984.

Surrels, Ron, *DD522: Diary of a Destroyer*, Valley Graphics, Inc., Plymouth, NH, 1996.

Thompson, Robert Smith, *Empires on the Pacific: World War II and the Struggle for the Mastery of Asia*, Basic Books, New York, 2001.

Toland, John, *The Rising Sun: The Decline and Fall of the Japanese Empire, 1936–1945*, The Modern Library, New York, 1987.

Wouk, Herman, *War and Remembrance*, Little, Brown and Company, Boston, 1978.

Zimmermann, Warren, *First Great Triumph: How Five Americans Made Their Country a World Power*, Farrar, Straus and Giroux, New York, 2002.

UNPUBLISHED (OR PRIVATELY PUBLISHED) ACCOUNTS AND REMINISCENCES

Brown, R. William, *Saga of PT-493, "The Carole Baby."*

Chambers, Terry, *Date Line November 1944—Tacloban, Leyte, Philippine Islands*.

Chambers, Terry, *Fun in the Philippines*, autobiographical chapter.

Copeland, Robert W., *The Spirit of the "Sammy-B,"* USS SAMUEL B. ROBERTS (DE 413) Survivors Association.

Czarnecki, Joseph, *Performance of US Battleships at Surigao Strait*, http://www.warships1.com

Hawk, Edgar A., *This is Our Story 50 Years Later, U.S.S. Melvin DD680*. Published October 1944 and distributed to crewmembers attending the reunion to commemorate the fifty-year anniversary of the Ship's contribution to the Battle of Leyte Gulf.

Malcolm, Ian, *The Battle of Surigao Strait Revisited*.

Action Report, Commander Task Unit 77.4.32 (Commander Carrier Division 26) Serial 015, 18 November, 1944, Office of Naval Records and Library.

USS Gambier Bay, an Incident of Naval Warfare in World War Two, Morningbird Press, 1998.

The Battle for Leyte Gulf, Strategic and Tactical Analysis, Volume V, Battle of Surigao Strait, October 24–25, U.S. Naval War College, 1958.

Naval Ordnance and Gunnery, Volume 1, Naval Ordnance, Department of Ordnance and Gunnery, United States Naval Academy, 1957.

INDEX

Names of U.S. combatant ships are typeset in SMALL CAPITALS. Names of Japanese combatant ships are typeset in *ITALICIZED SMALL CAPITALS*. Names of Voices are typeset in **boldface** type.

ABOUT THE AUTHOR

DAVID SEARS is a business consultant. For this book he researched many battles for examples of military leadership applicable to business settings. He is the author of *Successful Talent Strategies* (2002) and *Best Sellers* (2004).